Child of Light
MARY SHELLEY

ALSO BY MURIEL SPARK

NOVELS

The Comforters
Robinson
Memento Mori
The Bachelors
The Ballad of Peckham Rye
The Prime of Miss Jean Brodie
The Girls of Slender Means
The Mandelbaum Gate
The Public Image
The Driver's Seat
Not to Disturb
The Hothouse by the East River
The Abbess of Crewe
The Takeover
Territorial Rights
Loitering with Intent
The Only Problem

DRAMA

Doctors of Philosophy

CRITICISM AND BIOGRAPHY

The Brontë Letters
John Masefield
Child of Light (1951)

POETRY

Collected Poems I
Going Up to Sotheby's
    and Other Poems

STORIES

Collected Stories I
The Go-Away Bird
Voices at Play
Bang-bang You're Dead
    and Other Stories
The Stories of Muriel Spark

FOR CHILDREN

The Very Fine Clock

MURIEL SPARK

Child of Light
MARY SHELLEY

 WELCOME RAIN
New York

CHILD OF LIGHT: MARY SHELLEY
By Muriel Spark
All rights reserved.

© Muriel Spark 1951
© Copyright Administration Ltd. 1987

First published in the United States in 1987
by E.P. Dutton, New York, NY.

Direct any inquiries to
Welcome Rain Publishers LLC
23 West 26th Street
New York, NY 10010.

Library of Congress CIP data available from the publisher.

ISBN 1-56649-236-X
Printed in the United States of America
by VERSA PRESS

First Welcome Rain edition: March 2002

1 3 5 7 9 10 8 6 4 2

Contents

Eight pages of illustrations follow page 146.

[vii]

Preface

Mary Shelley was born in 1797 and died in 1851. The main facts of her life, the focus of all interest in her, are as follows:

She was the daughter of two equally progressive thinkers, William Godwin and Mary Wollstonecraft, which set the cast of her persevering intellect and her advanced education. She was the consort and then second wife of the poet Percy Bysshe Shelley, a union which lasted eight years till his death in 1822, in the course of which she was frequently pregnant, and which left her with vivid memories of an exciting youth and one surviving child, a son. She was the author of novels and stories, two of them outstanding: the famous work of science fiction, *Frankenstein,* and the futuristic novel *The Last Man.* She was the editor of Shelley's works, contributing greatly both to the understanding of Shelley's writings and to the history of biographical-literary criticism, which she pioneered.

This was the framework in which she lived out the wear and tear of everyday life in the first half of the nineteenth century, and however variously the whole story is interpreted, no-one can take these facts away.

In 1951, the centenary year of Mary Wollstonecraft Shelley's death, I published *Child of Light: A Reassessment of Mary Shelley.* It appeared in a small edition in the United Kingdom. In those days I was much occupied with nineteenth-century writers: Wordsworth, the Brontës, John Henry Newman were those I wrote about besides Mary Shelley.

Child of Light was never published in the United States of America but some years ago it was offered for sale there, without my permission or participation, in a "pirated" edition—simply a photo-copy of the original British edition, with a perfunctory binding, the price being so high as fortunately to render its circulation very limited indeed. This is one of the reasons why I decided to publish the book with substantial revisions, and with all my best care.

Since the years when I wrote *Child of Light* a great deal has happened to the Mary Shelley scholarship on which this book leans, and a great deal has happened to me. Thirty-six or more years ago the last thing I would have thought of was that I should write a novel, and now I do practically nothing else but write novels.

In the introduction to my 1951 edition I wrote: "It is more than time Mary Shelley was reconsidered, especially in her remarkably neglected capacity as a novelist." She is no longer remarkably neglected. *Frankenstein* is widely read, discussed, filmed and televised. In 1951 *The Last Man* was available only as a bibliophile's item—it had not been reprinted since 1826. I appended an abridged version of *The Last Man* to my book in order to discuss it. This is no longer necessary; *The Last Man* is available in paperback editions in Britain and the United States.

In my first assessment of Mary Shelley's life story I held the then widely-diffused view that after the death of Shelley she gradually craved more and more for bourgeois respectability. I now think this is an over-simplification. It has been the view of others, starting with her contemporary, Shelley's friend Trelawny. I now know that when we look at her change of attitudes and aspirations we are not talking so much about Mary Shelley as about human nature and its courage.

Any novelist or writer wants and needs to enter into the fullness of social life in all its various stratifications. Mary Shelley had spent the best part of her married life struggling from place to place in Italy, with her husband, her step-sister, her babies, her books and her friends, and all their endless financial problems. When she became a widow with a son to support, she naturally had to concentrate on her professional work, and for her son's education, appease Shelley's father, Sir Timothy. She managed to achieve this, without dropping her former friends and at the same time acquiring new ones.

Her greatest difficulties were the conventional pressures of the age she lived in, and a tendency to depression. In her widowhood she was blackmailed over some sentimental or love letters she had written to an unmarried man. That she could be blackmailed on such trivial grounds reflects an absurdity of history, and not, as she felt, of herself. Her journals, more than her letters, record her depressive feelings, her loneliness, her grief for the loss of Shelley and the desertion of people on whom she had mistakenly fixed her hopes. Very often the *Journals* have a touch of the analyst's couch, and perhaps this mode of relieving her most melancholy feelings was efficacious.

When I came to revise *Child of Light* I was extremely fortunate in obtaining the generous and invaluable comments of Betty T. Bennett, editor of the definitive *Letters of Mary Wollstonecraft Shelley*, and a foremost Mary Shelley scholar. Thanks to Professor Bennett's ample indications of the vast amount of work done and new discoveries, made on the subject of Mary Shelley since my first book appeared, I have been able to bring this book up to date; it is not intended to be definitive and detailed; it is a survey with a minimum of footnotes. I have also had the great advantage of the courtesy of the Oxford University Press in permitting me to consult the new and exhaustive edition of *The Journals of Mary Shelley* so admirably and finely edited by Paula R. Feldman and Diana Scott-Kilvert.

In this way I have been able to incorporate into Mary Shelley's life story many new elements, and have been persuaded by new facts to give more weight to factors that were previously unknown or that I had overlooked. These include Mary Shelley's ambiguous friendship with Isabel Robinson and her transvestite "husband," Walter Sholto Douglas (a brilliant piece of detective-scholarship on Betty T. Bennett's part); the hitherto unsuspected extent of Mary Shelley's attachment to Aubrey Beauclerk; and the fuller identity of the blackmailer-forger, "G. Byron."

On first reading through my work after so many years, I was amused to perceive that my prose style had taken on a touch of Mary Shelley's. Through my experience as a writer of fiction I know now that I have a "writing ear," that it is the act of imaginatively getting under the skin of a character that produces the individual character's diction. But I recall when I first wrote the book that I was very careful not to make it novelistic. I have always disliked the sort of biography which states "X lay on the bed and watched the candle flickering on the roof beams," when there is no evidence that X did so.

M.S.

I would like to emphasise, again, my indebtedness to Betty T. Bennett and her *The Letters of Mary Wollstonecraft Shelley* (The Johns Hopkins University Press), and to the editors, Paula R. Feldman and Diana Scott-Kilvert, of *The Journals of Mary Shelley* (Oxford at The Clarendon Press); and to express my gratitude for the kind and practical assistance in many ways of: Sir Joseph Cheyne, Curator of the Keats-Shelley Memorial Association, Rome; Miss Penelope Jardine; the Hon. G. R. Strutt; Mr. Euan Cameron; and the editors of E. P. Dutton, New York.

M.S.

The first version of this book (*Child of Light,* 1951) carried the following notice:

My acknowledgements are due to The University of Oklahoma Press for permission to quote from *The Letters of Mary Shelley* (1944), collected and edited by Frederick L. Jones, whose work here, and in his edition of *Mary Shelley's Journal* (University of Oklahoma Press, 1947), has proved of exceptional service to me, as it must to all Shelley students. I am further indebted to the Oxford University Press as representatives of The University of Oklahoma Press, for the valuable time they have spent on my behalf; and to Messrs. John Lane The Bodley Head Limited for permission to quote from *New Shelley Letters* (1948), edited by W. S. Scott.

I should also like to record my gratitude to the Rev. W. S. Scott; to Mr. G. A. Stolar; and to the late Mr. H. K. Grant (Hon. Librarian of the Poetry Society), for their encouraging assistance in obtaining material for reference. And to the librarians of the British Museum and the North Library, I have a deep sense of obligation for their unfailing and courteous services.

M.S.

Textual Note

Where parts of quotations have been left out by me, I have indicated the omission thus: (. . .), except at the beginning or end of substantial extracts.

Where the sign . . . is shown without parenthesis, it indicates the original text so far as is known.

In the interests of fluent readability much of the erratic spelling and punctuation of Mary Shelley and others are not reproduced.

Mary Shelley's step-sister's name presents another problem: soon after 1814 she changed her name from "Jane" to "Claire" Clairmont, and this was sometimes spelt "Clare." The spelling "Claire" is adhered to throughout.

M.S.

PART I

Biographical

Chapter I

. . . ere my fame become
A star among the stars of mortal night,
If it indeed may cleave its natal gloom,
Its doubtful promise thus I would unite
With thy beloved name, thou Child of love and light.
        SHELLEY, *The Revolt of Islam*
        (dedication to Mary Shelley)

We are hardly impressed with a sense of love and light when we look back now on that period of transition between the eighteenth and nineteenth centuries—the period of revolution and reaction which gave effect to the fame of Mary Shelley's parents, William Godwin and Mary Wollstonecraft.

Reason had not yet given way to feeling as the cult of the elect; and if we think now of the rationalist tracts, the elaborate arguments to prove man's perfectibility, the manifestos on the Rights of Man and the vindications of the Rights of Woman which drained their most vehement passions, love, we feel, had little place there. As for light, we are more likely to note its absence than otherwise, if at all we trouble to picture the atmospheric environment in which the progressives of the day progressed. In retrospect, Godwin as a man seems arrested always in a gloomy monochrome of thought, while Mary Wollstonecraft, warmer and more reckless, flounders through a monotonous series of misfortunes. But the importance of

[3]

both William Godwin and Mary Wollstonecraft is enormous. They both wrote effective propaganda. It is a promotional genre which acts on its own time, and may or may not pioneer whole future ways of life. Reason and justice were their literary themes. When they attempted to put their theories into practise they often had to modify their theories. Thoughts had to be expressed in the light of what ought to be; life had to be lived in the untidy actuality that it is.

To visualise Mary Shelley's parents in the actual setting they occupied, we find them, as they were, celebrated figures in the cause of enlightenment, conscious of no gloom but that of the ignorance surrounding them, and confirmed in the belief that they bore a light to emblazon history. And in fact, the light has in some manner sifted on to history, so that we no longer notice the original torch-bearers; reform has deprived the reformers of their justification. In the same way, we should be wrong to assume that the brief union between Mary Wollstonecraft and William Godwin, strangely dispassionate and calculated as it appears, is indescribable as love. The way of life they discovered together for a short time had a softening influence on both; they were devoted to the same cause, and two people who love the same thing find it easy to love each other.

When Mary Wollstonecraft became Godwin's mistress, she had already made her name as a pioneer feminist, with her book *A Vindication of the Rights of Woman;* it is now, more than ever, required reading for studies in women's rights. To the large public, this was a monstrously wanton piece of literature; while the intelligentsia considered it a daring thrust for the rational liberation cause.

Born in London in 1759, Mary Wollstonecraft belonged to that type of family whose social category was then becoming difficult to define. The Wollstonecrafts were impoverished to the point of want, yet their family connections bore that strain of gentility which banned them from giving their children an education and environment to suit them for work outside their home. Tied to household drudgery, the females of the family were yet neither of "the leisured class" nor of "the poor." Mary Wollstonecraft's father was a spendthrift and a drunkard, moving whenever failing fortunes compelled him, from one hopeless enterprise to the other. Her mother, a weak type of woman, submitted to his continual bullying, and Mary from an early age acted as protector to the family, meanwhile seizing what fragmentary opportunities of education came her way. For a time she sought independence by becoming a companion to a rich, querulous lady; and here again she found herself in a mid-way position, being neither quite a domestic nor the equal of her mistress. It was not until she became friendly with a publisher who encouraged her to study French and German, and gave her translating work, that she began to feel herself a member of society. The circle which she now entered drew its spirit from the French Revolution, and Mary eagerly took its cause to herself.

Edmund Burke's retort to the famous pro-revolutionary sermon by Dr. Price at the Old Jewry in 1789 evoked, that same year, a spirited answer from Mary in her *Letter to Edmund Burke.* Though this publication was overshadowed by Tom Paine's *Rights of Man*, it served to confirm Mary as one of the set. The question of everyone's rights was in the air, and it was a salutary time for the appearance, two years later, of Mary Wollstonecraft's *Rights of Woman.* In all her main writings she gave vent to much pent-up indignation by drawing on her own early experience of a tyrannous drunkard father: one might imagine, from reading her account, that all fathers of the day were tyrants, all men seducers, all women miserable victims of the system. Mary Wollstonecraft understood the uses of overstatement as well as Jane Austen knew those of understatement. But it is on the important question of the education of women that she is most balanced and interesting.

All this time, Mary Wollstonecraft was by no means financially secure, but she was warm-hearted, and continued to share her small earnings with her needy family. Her attachment to Fuseli, the Swiss painter, should be mentioned, since it shows an impulsive, even reckless side of her nature that was noticeably inherited by Mary Shelley. Mary Wollstonecraft pursued a friendship she had made with the talented, witty artist, in terms that left her emotional disinterestedness in some doubt. Fuseli was already married, and Mary Wollstonecraft was firmly discouraged; and when, many years later, she attempted to retrieve the over-ardent letters she had addressed to him, Fuseli did not comply, either through wilfulness or indifference. The letters were found among the painter's papers after his death.

Her next enterprise was a visit to Paris to report on the Revolution. Here Mary Wollstonecraft met Gilbert Imlay, an American who had fought in the War of Independence and with whom she fell deeply in love. The affection was mutual at first, and before long they were living together. She might well have wished to be married, but was not unduly concerned that no legal tie bound her to Imlay, taking pride no doubt in the personal triumph of their voluntary relationship. But her nature, in spite of her intellectual ability, was predominantly coloured by passion, and she abandoned herself, her thoughts, and all her actions to the furtherance of their union. Imlay, however, was not an enduring type of lover. Attracted by Mary Wollstonecraft's manner and appearance—and she is described as having many personal graces—he does not seem to have been able to tolerate her company for long periods. Mary Wollstonecraft gave birth to their child, Fanny, while Imlay's absences from Paris became longer, his promises of return vaguer. The distracted exponent of the rights of woman was driven to attempted suicide for the sake of her lover.

After her second mishandled suicidal attempt, she made a suggestion to Imlay which may find an echo in Mary Shelley's behaviour, long after her mother's death. This suggestion, made by Mary Wollstonecraft under feverish stress, was that she should share a home with Imlay and his new mistress. To pacify her, Imlay agreed, but withdrew his acquiescence shortly afterwards.

Mary Wollstonecraft's love letters to Imlay and her sociological work make as antithetical reading as ever came from any one pen. They represent, in fact, two facets of character that were never reconciled, although to some extent they were modified by the exhausting quality of her experiences; her passion, after she was deserted by Imlay, became chastened; her social indignation, after the *Rights of Woman,* abated. But a certain habit of depressiveness which persisted from her early formative years may have been perpetuated in her daughter Fanny Imlay. Her daughter by Godwin, the later Mary Shelley, also acquired from her mother a strong pessimistic strain, but in her Godwin's intellectual stoicism tempered the passionate pessimism which finally drove Fanny Imlay to suicide.

Mary Wollstonecraft had met William Godwin in her earlier days, when, though mainly occupied in writing and translating for a publisher, she had begun to acquire a reputation for talent. Godwin had not been greatly impressed by her, but upon their renewed acquaintance, shortly after Mary's spiritual defeat at Imlay's hands, Godwin wrote,

> The partiality we conceived for each other was in that mode which I have always considered as the purest and most refined kind of love. It grew with equal advances in the minds of each. . . . One sex did not take the priority which long established custom has awarded it. . . . When in the course of things the disclosure came there was nothing in the matter for either party to disclose to the other. There was no period of throes and resolute explanations attendant upon the tale. It was friendship melting into love.

It would be difficult to say how accurately Godwin expressed Mary Wollstonecraft's feelings in these sentences, which certainly bear the bleak authenticity of his own experience. Most probably he was not far wrong. Godwin knew of Mary's recent humiliations; and his non-moralising attitude must have soothed her. We dearly love to see our follies and weaknesses promoted to a theoretical rectitude; we feel warmly towards those who can offer a meaning for our suffering and ignominy. All this Godwin was in a position to do, and it is most likely that Mary Wollstonecraft, drained of passion and disillusioned about female emancipation, loved him because he reinstated her confidence and pride.

William Godwin was over forty years of age when he and Mary Wollstonecraft embarked on their union, setting up each in a separate house in Somers Town, in deference to their ideas of independence. She, with her child Fanny Imlay, lived but a few doors away from Godwin, and the couple formed the habit of sending notes to each other, some of which survive to show their arrangement working to all apparent satisfaction.

Godwin was brought up in a Nonconformist environment. His father was a dissenting minister and he himself was a practising "reverend" until the age of twenty-nine when he dropped the title. In his later emancipation which came to maturity in his *Enquiry Concerning Political Justice,* published in 1793, some writers have seen an emotional revolt against puritanical restraint, rather than a reasoned arrival at a rationalist philosophy. If this is so, it provides a temperamental parallel with Mary Wollstonecraft and her subjective approach; but in Godwin's case the subjective element is far more difficult to detect and is so strongly restrained in fact, that his remorseless logic hardly makes reasonable human reading. So far as his influence on Mary Shelley is to be sought in Godwin's early life, it is worth noting that he was remarkably addicted to study, pursuing knowledge of all varieties of literature from the classics to contemporaneous thought, with none but inner compulsion.

His friends were drawn from those who espoused the dangerous objectives of the Revolution, and Godwin showed no small personal courage in supporting them on many occasions and in publicly recording his opinions on human liberty, before *Political Justice* presented his comprehensive proposals for a reformed social system. This work immediately raised him from obscurity to the level of a modern sage. "No one," wrote Hazlitt some years later, "was more talked of, more looked up to, more sought after, and wherever liberty, truth, justice was the theme, his name was not far off. . . . No work in our time gave such a blow to the philosophical mind of the country as the celebrated *Enquiry Concerning Political Justice.*"

The principle that concerns us most here is that which bears on Godwin's attitude to property, since it is a prominent factor in his relationship with his daughter and the poet Shelley. Godwin envisaged a system whereby property should be distributed according to each man's reasonable needs. And the just administration of property, Godwin said, does not stop there. "Every man is entitled, so far as the general stock will suffice, not only to the means of being but of well-being."

Godwin did not hesitate to apply this doctrine to himself, and if we understand this we can encounter without shock the frequent money demands that Godwin made, as though by prerogative, on his daughter and Shelley, while refusing to condone their behaviour. Godwin was merely fulfilling one set of his principles: a courageous and original thinker, he had made certain valuable contributions to society, and he accepted the idea that Shelley, the son of a wealthy baronet, should provide him with the means of well-being. Shelley, who had approached the philosopher with the offer of means, and who held *Political Justice* as something sacred, was never really in doubt that Godwin was later entitled to the money he asked. Many of Shelley's biographers have not grasped the fact that Godwin and Shelley were putting into practice a law, which, while outside the Law, was respected by both of them. Of course, this arrangement did not allow for the very human circumstance that people prefer to be generous to people they like; Shelley lost his personal respect—though never his intellectual regard—for Godwin and was very short of money himself, and so Godwin's demands very often annoyed him. But in justice to Godwin we should not consider whether his view is an acceptable one to ourselves, but remember that he was himself generous to others, when he had the means, in accordance with his principles. In this, his daughter Mary resembled him. And to be sure, there are other aspects of Godwin's relationship with Shelley which merit such indignation that it is strange and perhaps significant that Shelley's supporters have chosen this material issue as a wholehearted theme of contempt for Godwin.

The reaction that followed the war with revolutionary France had set in by the time Godwin and Mary Wollstonecraft set up together in Somers Town. It was no longer possible to repudiate the law, to strike at the roots of government, to dangle before men's eyes the ideal of a perfected society liberated from coercive rule, without incurring more than a frown from authority. Public tolerance of Godwin swung to a general hostility. To his friends, among the left-wing thinkers of his time, and to many of the rising generation,

Godwin continued to occupy his lofty position, instructing, writing and studying with all his former industry. He first entered on an unconventional union with Mary Wollstonecraft, then married her conventionally at Old St. Pancras Church: a child was coming, and Godwin was moved to waive his disapproval of marriage for Mary Wollstonecraft's sake. He still stood by his principles, he told a friend, though "nothing but a regard for the happiness of the individual, which I have no right to injure, would have induced me to submit to an institution which I wish to see abolished."

It seems clear that Mary Wollstonecraft's distrust and fear of men, aggravated by Imlay's treatment of her, was still latent within her. She had known life as a discarded mistress, as the mother of an illegitimate child, and she ardently desired this marriage before her next child was born. None the less, this tends to support the view that Mary Wollstonecraft's character never achieved integration. She was attracted towards the unconventional mode of life and the type of mind that embraced it; but life had taught her that convention was a protector, and she was equally attracted towards the security it offered. It is to Godwin's credit as a human being, if not as a practitioner of his own faith, that he recognised her anxiety and alleviated it at the cost of abstract principles. Especially is this so when Godwin must have felt the criticism of his intellectual friends as keenly as he did the congratulations of others. "Your broken resolution in regard to matrimony encourages me to hope that you will ere long embrace the Gospel . . . ," wrote his mother, whose gentle words must have fairly tried the philosopher.

Meanwhile William Godwin and Mary Wollstonecraft became enveloped in a domestic intimacy whose delights seem to have surprised them both. The friendly, even flirtatious notes continued to pass between them. "I am better this morning," she wrote, "but it snows so incessantly that I do not know how I shall be able to keep my appointment this evening. What say you? But you have no petticoats to dangle in the snow. Poor women, how they are beset with plagues, within and without." While Godwin, during a few weeks' absence from London, informed Mary, "You cannot imagine how happy your letter made me. No creature expresses, because no creature feels, the tender affection as perfectly as you do, and after all one's philosophy it must be confessed that the knowledge that there is some one that takes an interest in one's happiness, something like that which each man feels for his own, is extremely gratifying. Tell Fanny we have chosen a mug for her. . . ."

The middle-aged scholar had come late to love, and when Mary Wollstonecraft was confined on 30th August 1797, he behaved with less calm than she did, sending him the message: "I have no doubt of seeing the animal today. . . . Pray send me the newspaper. . . ."

Mary Wollstonecraft's child, a girl, was born that night, and soon afterwards the mother showed signs of fever. Doctors were fetched and poisoning was diagnosed. For the next ten days medical men and nurses came and went, Godwin in the midst of all showing steady tenderness and devotion to the woman who had so humanised him. Racked by the agonies of poison, Mary took no heed of her newborn child, but lay confused and spent.

She died on 10th September, leaving Godwin the poorer for the only true grace he ever experienced in womanly affections, and the richer for two children—one aged two, Imlay's daughter Fanny Imlay, and the other his own child, Mary.

Chapter 2

When in later years Mary Shelley looked back on her childhood, the time she recalled with the fondest clarity was not her early home life, but the period she spent away from her family. In her introduction to a revised edition of *Frankenstein* she reminisced:

> I lived principally in the country as a girl, and passed a considerable time in Scotland. I made occasional visits to the more picturesque parts; but my habitual residence was on the blank and dreary northern shores of the Tay, near Dundee. Blank and dreary on retrospection I call them; they were not so to me then. They were the eyry of freedom.

Godwin's short and happy union with Mary Wollstonecraft had so enamoured him of matrimony that before long he was casting round for a second wife, finding reasons outside his own inclinations to support his desire for marriage. "The poor children!" was his cry, and to be sure, the two infant girls Mary Wollstonecraft left in his charge presented him with a duty he considered too serious to fulfil by leaving them to the care of servants.

After making unsuccessful proposals to two women of his acquaintance, Godwin married his next-door neighbour, Mrs. Clairmont, four years after his first wife's death. The second Mrs. Godwin, a middle-aged widow with two young children, was a strange choice for Godwin, being neither more nor less than a woman of average education, a business sense, some good domestic qualities, and an aptitude for malicious invention. "A sensible, amiable woman" one of Godwin's friends called her, but most of his circle deplored her commonplace vulgarity and were inclined to blame her for not being Mary Wollstonecraft. Godwin, of course, should have been more discriminating; this woman, who might have made a tolerable companion to the ordinary man, felt her inferiority and in her muddled way compensated by doing all the damage she could. She left her mark on Godwin, on his children, and on her own children.

Charles and Jane Clairmont—the latter a little younger than Mary Godwin—together with Fanny, who was given Godwin's surname, made up the family until a year later the new Mrs. Godwin gave birth to a son, William. By 1805, at his wife's suggestion, Godwin became a publisher whose main business was the production of books "for the use and amusement of children"; Mrs. Godwin, proving after all at least one departure from the commonplace, set about translating some children's books from the French, while Godwin self-consciously wrote stories for juveniles under the name of Baldwin. His firm also published the Lambs' *Tales from Shakespeare.* They flourished at first, and the family moved to Skinner Street, Holborn, next door to new office premises.

Godwin took a fair amount of interest in the children's education, and though Mrs. Godwin's concern over household trivialities caused both Mary and her own daughter, Jane, some resentment, they were compensated by the comings and goings of such rare personalities as Lamb and Coleridge to the house. One evening, we are told, Mary and Jane hid behind the sofa to hear Coleridge read his *Ancient Mariner,* and on being discovered would have been banished to bed had it not been for the poet's intercession.

When Mary was nearly fourteen years old, Mrs. Godwin took her and her own children to Ramsgate, while Fanny, now grown up, amenable, and to all appearances contented, was left at home to keep house. The family stayed with a Miss Petman who kept a girls' school in Ramsgate, and there Mary remained as a boarder for a few months after the others had returned to London. The sea air, it was hoped, would benefit Mary, who suffered from a weakness in one arm—a "weakness" which is not described in precise terms; and as no complaint of a weak or defective arm is made by Mary in later years we can assume this was a temporary ailment. She seems to have recovered during her absence from home, to have contracted the weakness again on her return to London, and to have recovered again after her next departure from the Godwin household, to stay in Scotland, and therefore it may not be immoderate to suggest—although we cannot of course be certain—that this ailment was in some measure aggravated by Mary's admitted dislike of Mrs. Godwin, whom she secretly compared with the illustrious mother she had never known except by hearsay.

By the time Mary had reached her teens, her personality had developed under Godwin's tutelage and her nature had become the more spirited for her resentment of her step-mother and classic idealization of her own mother. Feeling herself an exceptional being, she could not then, nor did she ever, dispose herself tolerantly towards Mrs. Godwin. In answer to an enquiry about the education of his children, Godwin's reply illuminates what little we know of Mary's girlhood:

> Your inquiries relate principally to the two daughters of Mary Wollstonecraft. They are neither of them brought up with an exclusive attention to the system and ideas of their mother. I lost her in 1797, and in 1801 I married a second time. One among the motives which led me to choose this was the feeling I had in myself of an incompetence for the education of daughters. The present Mrs. Godwin has great strength and activity in mind, but is not exclusively a follower of the notions of their mother. . . .

Of the two persons to whom your inquiries relate, my own daughter is considerably superior in capacity to the one her mother had before. Fanny, the eldest, is of a quiet, modest, unshowy disposition, somewhat given to indolence, which is her greatest fault, but sober, observing, peculiarly clear and distinct in the faculty of memory, and disposed to exercise her own thoughts and follow her own judgment. Mary, my daughter, is the reverse of her in many particulars. She is singularly bold, somewhat imperious and active of mind. Her desire of knowledge is great, and her perseverance in everything she undertakes almost invincible. My own daughter is, I believe, very pretty. Fanny is by no means handsome, but, in general, prepossessing.

It was Mary's second visit away from home about which she wrote in such nostalgic terms in her introduction to *Frankenstein*. An admirer of Godwin, Mr. William Baxter, invited Mary to spend a prolonged holiday at his home near Dundee with his own family, which included several girls near Mary's age. In June 1812, Mary left for Scotland, and once more it is from Godwin's correspondence that a fairly objective picture of Mary, and her father's concern for her, can be formed:

Skinner Street, London.
8th June 1812.

My dear Sir—I have shipped off to you by yesterday's packet, the *Osnaburgh*, Captain Wishart, my only daughter. I attended her, with her two sisters, to the wharf, and remained an hour on board, till the vessel got under way. I cannot help feeling a thousand anxieties in parting with her, for the first time, for so great a distance, and these anxieties were increased by the manner of sending her, on board a ship, with not a single face around her that she had ever seen till that morning. She is four months short of fifteen years of age. I, however, spoke to the captain, using your name; I beside gave her in charge to a lady, by name I believe Mrs. Nelson, of Great St. Helen's, London, who was going to your part of the island in attendance upon an invalid husband. She was surrounded by three daughters when I spoke to her, and she answered me very agreeably, "I shall have none of my own daughters with me, and shall therefore have the more leisure to attend to yours."

I daresay she will arrive more dead than alive, as she is extremely subject to sea-sickness, and the voyage will, not improbably, last nearly a week. Mr. Cline, the surgeon, however, decides that a sea-voyage would probably be of more service to her than anything.

I am quite confounded to think what trouble I am bringing on you and your family, and to what a degree I may be said to have taken you in when I took you at your word in your invitation upon so slight an acquaintance. The old proverb says, "He is a wise father who knows his own child," and I feel the justness of the apothegm on the present occasion.

There never can be a perfect equality between father and child, and if he has other objects and avocations to fill up the greater part of his time, the ordinary resource is for him to proclaim his wishes and commands in a way somewhat sententious and authoritative, and occasionally to utter his censures with seriousness and emphasis.

It can, therefore, seldom happen that he is the confidant of his child, or that the child does not feel some degree of awe or restraint in intercourse with him. I am not, therefore, a perfect judge of Mary's character. I believe she has nothing of what is commonly called vices, and that she has considerable talent. But I tremble for the trouble I may be bringing on you in this visit. In my last I desired that you would consider the first two or three weeks as a trial, how far you can ensure her, or, more fairly and impartially speaking, how far her habits and conceptions may be such as to put your family very unreasonably out of their way; and I expect from the frankness and ingenuousness of yours of the 29th inst. (which by the way was so ingenuous as to come without a seal) that you will not for a moment hesitate to inform me if such should be the case. When I say all this, I hope you will be aware that I do not desire that she should be treated with extraordinary attention, or that any one of your family should put themselves in the smallest degree out of their way on her account. I am anxious that she should be brought up (in this respect) like a philosopher, even like a cynic. It will add greatly to the strength and worth of her character. I should also observe that she has no love of dissipation, and will be perfectly satisfied with your woods and your mountains. I wish, too, that she should be *excited* to industry. She has occasionally great perseverance, but occasionally, too, she shows great need to be roused.

You are aware that she comes to the seaside for the purpose of bathing. I should wish that you would inquire now and then into the regularity of that. She will want also some treatment for her arm, but she has Mr. Cline's directions completely in all these points, and will probably not require a professional man to look after her while she is with you. In all other respects except her arm she has admirable health, has an excellent appetite, and is capable of enduring fatigue. . . . I am, my dear sir, with great regard, yours,

—William Godwin.

Mary throve in her new freedom. It was a release both from petty friction with her step-mother and from the distracting artifice of a London environment. There, in the stability of a congenial home life and expansive surroundings, she began to find within herself a corresponding "still centre" and spiritual breadth. "It was beneath the trees of the grounds belonging to our house," she wrote in her introduction to *Frankenstein,* "or on the bleak sides of the woodless mountains near, that my true compositions, the airy flights of my imagination, were born and fostered." Long periods of leisure invited forth the rich freight of her imagination; "airy flights" she called these fantasies in after years, but she was mistakenly identifying herself, then, with Shelley; for Mary's imagination, animated by those months among the Perthshire hills, was in no way ethereal. Her vision was not of the bright, revelatory order, nor yet did the experience of fantasy reach her, as it did Shelley, through a sort of nebulous lustre. As she developed, her mind seems to have derived its complexion from the substance of reality, with a tendency to reproduce, in fictional terms, massive and broad outlines as of the earth. Mary was right in looking back on her visit to Scotland as a period of creative gestation; early examples of her writing date from that time. The comparative vastness of the hills and wooded landscape evoked a latent response to actuality, as later the Swiss mountains were to stimulate her creative powers.

Mary's stay in Scotland was interrupted by her return to London with one of the Baxter girls, but after seven months Mary returned with her friend for a further ten months.

Meanwhile, Godwin's financial troubles, which were to pursue him almost to the margin of the grave, had become more involved. But he retained the admiration and friendship of such men as Hazlitt, Lamb and Coleridge who frequented his household. Early in 1812, before Mary had left for Scotland, Godwin had added the poet Shelley to his retinue. Shelley had written that Godwin would be surprised at hearing from a stranger but that the name of Godwin had always aroused in him feelings of reverence and admiration.

By the time Mary returned finally to London in May 1814, Shelley and his wife Harriet had become almost daily visitors at Skinner Street. The poet's reverence for Godwin's work flattered the philosopher, though it is apparent from Godwin's advice to Shelley on the latter's harebrained political mission to Ireland in 1812, that the older man was somewhat dismayed by the poet's fanatical interpretation of *Political Justice*. Shelley, however, had appeared at a time when Godwin's financial affairs were rapidly deteriorating. Shelley's own position was by no means stable, for since his expulsion from Oxford and his estrangement from the Shelley family, he could barely live on the allowance his father made him. As the heir to a wealthy baronetcy, however, he was able to raise money on the strength of expectancies; and Shelley procured considerable sums of money in this way, to place at Godwin's disposal, with promises of further endeavours. He was welcome, then, as a man of fortune who counted it a privilege to fortify a man of genius. But Godwin did not fail to appreciate, too, the fact of

Shelley's own intense intellectual curiosity, his originality of thought and his eloquence.

To Mary, now a girl approaching seventeen, the continual appearances of Shelley at Skinner Street provided an entirely new experience. She had always enjoyed the company of her father's friends, and had listened enrapt to their conversations. But they were mostly middle-aged or old men. Shelley, a fine-featured youth of twenty-one, had both physical and mental attractions for her. Added to his exceptional powers of dialectic, there was in him a characteristic audacity and flexibility of bearing which was lacking in her father's older friends; and Shelley's visits became a source of consolation to Mary, now once more under the distasteful domination of her step-mother.

Mary formed the habit of taking her books to her mother's grave in St. Pancras Churchyard, there to find some peace after her irksome household duties, and to pursue her studies in an atmosphere of communion with a mind greater than the second Mrs. Godwin's. And it was there, before long, that she was meeting Shelley in secret.

By October 1814, Shelley had separated from his wife. But it was not necessarily his newly-conceived love for Mary that precipitated this break. On 3rd October 1814 Shelley wrote to his friend Thomas Jefferson Hogg explaining his state of mind before he met Mary:

> . . . In the beginning of spring, I spent two months at Mrs. Boinville's [a friend of Shelley and Harriet] without my wife. If I except the succeeding period those two months were probably the happiest of my life: the calmest, the serenest, the most free from care. The contemplation of female excellence is the favourite food of my imagination. There was ample scope for admiration: novelty added a peculiar charm to the intrinsic merit of the objects: I had been unaccustomed to the mildness, the intelligence, the delicacy of a cultivated female. The presence of Mrs. Boinville and her daughter afforded a strange contrast to my former friendship and deplorable condition. I suddenly perceived that the entire devotion with which I had

resigned all prospects of utility or happiness to the single purpose of cultivating Harriet was a gross and despicable superstition. Perhaps every degree of affectionate intimacy with a female, however slight, partakes of the nature of love. Love makes men quick-sighted, and is only called blind by the [*illegible*] because he perceives the existence of relations invisible to grosser spirits. I saw the full extent of the calamity which my rash & heartless union with Harriet: a union over whose entrance might justly be inscribed

"Lasciate ogni speranza, voi ch'entrate!"

had produced. I felt as if a dead & living body had been linked together in loathsome and horrible communion. It was no longer possible to practise self deception: I believed that one revolting duty yet remained, to continue to deceive my wife. I wandered in the fields alone. The season was most beautiful. The evenings were so serene & mild. I never had before felt so intensely the subduing voluptuousness of the impulses of spring. Manifestations of my approaching change tinged my waking thoughts, & afforded inexhaustible subject for the visions of my sleep. I recollect that one day I undertook to walk from Bracknell to my father's (40 miles). A train of visionary events arranged themselves in my imagination until ideas almost acquired the intensity of sensations. Already I had met the female who was destined to be mine, already had she replied to my exulting recognition, already were the difficulties surmounted that opposed an entire union. I had even proceeded so far as to compose a letter to Harriet on the subject of my passion for another. Thus was my walk beguiled, at the conclusion of which I was hardly sensible of fatigue.

If Shelley's account is true, and indeed it is passionately convincing, we see the young poet's recognition, during that solitary forty-mile walk, of the fact that his marriage had failed. "A train of visionary events arranged themselves in my imagination until ideas almost acquired the intensity of sensations." Here was a type of poetic mind working at a fundamental tempo of amorality and timelessness. Already Shelley not only rejected his married life with Harriet, but accepted a new relationship. He had not Mary nor any other specific woman in mind when he conceived this new passion, but so carried away was he by his visionary ideal mate that, as he wrote, "I had even proceeded so far as to compose a letter to Harriet on the subject of my passion for another." Shelley was in this emotionally receptive state when he discovered that Mary matched the woman of his day-dream. He was, in fact, looking for her. And continuing his letter to Hogg he describes his discovery of Mary:

In the month of June I came to London to accomplish some business with Godwin that had been long depending. The circumstances of the case required an almost constant residence at his house. There I met his daughter Mary. The originality and loveliness of Mary's character was apparent to me from her very motions and tones of voice. The irresistible wildness and sublimity of her feelings showed itself in her gestures and her looks—Her smile, how persuasive it was, and how pathetic! She is gentle, to be convinced and tender; yet not incapable of ardent indignation and hatred. I do not think that there is an excellence at which human nature can arrive, that she does not indisputably possess, or of which her character does not afford manifest intimations. I speak thus of Mary now . . . and so intimately are our natures now united, that I feel whilst I describe her excellencies as if I were an egoist expiating upon his own perfections. *Then,* how deeply did I feel my inferiority, how willingly confess myself far surpassed in originality, in genuine elevation and magnificence of the intellectual nature until she consented to share her capabilities with me. I speedily conceived an ardent passion to possess this inestimable treasure. In my own mind this feeling assumed a variety of shapes, I disguised from myself the true nature of my affection. I endeavoured also to conceal it from Mary, but without success. I was vacillating and infirm of purpose: I shuddered to transgress a real duty, and could not in this instance perceive the boundaries by which virtue was separated from madness, *when* self devotion becomes the very prodigality of idiotism. Her understanding was made clear by a spirit that sees into the truth of things, my affections preserved pure and sacred from the corrupting contamination of vulgar superstitions. No expressions can convey the remotest conception of the *manner* in which she dispelled my delusions. The sublimer and rapturous moment when she confessed herself mine, who had so long been hers in secret, cannot be painted to mortal imaginations.—Let it suffice to you, who are my friend, to know and to rejoice that she is mine: that at length I possess the inalienable treasure, that I sought and I have found.

Despite all this talk about the nicer emotional interchanges, Shelley's wooing of Mary was swift and effective. Within a month of Mary's return from Scotland she was in love with him.[1] She had met Shelley the year before, with Harriet, but then she had been a schoolgirl; now her appearance and manners delighted the poet. She was never the type of woman who, in her time, was usually called "handsome." She was slim and extremely fair but it was her intelligent sidelong hazel eyes that distinguished her features from the round-eyed vacant prettiness of the very young and fair of her period.

Godwin was by no means blind to what was afoot between Shelley and Mary, and he disapproved profoundly. Many later critics have found in his attitude a symptom of hypocrisy and inconsistency with his own professed principles; and it has been assumed that Godwin opposed their relationship for conventional reasons while lacking the integrity to dismiss such a valuable source of income as Shelley from his doors. There is no evidence, however, to show that Godwin's disapproval did not arise from a conviction that Shelley, a married man whose wife had often been the Godwins' guest, was an unsuitable partner for his daughter.

1. I suggest that a significant date in this rapid love affair was 27th June. Shelley's journal entry for 4th August 1814 reads: "Mary told me that this was my birthday. I thought it had been the 27th of June." He did not, of course, forget his birthday, but probably referred to the day when he and Mary first spoke of their love.

The subsequent hardening of Godwin's intellectual arteries had not yet set in, and his mind was quite capable of separating two unrelated considerations: firstly, that of Shelley the poet and thinker in which capacity Shelley was also Godwin's benefactor; and secondly, Shelley the man. This is, after all, a feat which many of Shelley's critics have been only too ready to perform, and today we may note that in Shelley's personality there were a number of factors pointing to mental instability, including irresponsible behaviour ingeniously self-justified and a volatile moodiness, without in any way detracting from our appreciation of Shelley's work. It may even seem that the very inconsistencies of his outward life appear throughout his work in the consistency of poetic experience and thought. But it was not Shelley's poetry and thought that Godwin had under consideration in the matter between Shelley and Mary. The clear-sighted thinker was in a better position even than Shelley's posterity to judge the young man's character. Godwin knew the man, and feared for his sixteen-year-old daughter's happiness. In one sense he proved right, for Mary had many material trials ahead of her, and indeed, Shelley in his airy manner did not even make adequate provision for her maintenance during their first flight abroad. Godwin, however, did not perceive how imperative was the attraction between the lovers.[2] His remonstrances proved vain. "Her perseverance in everything she undertakes [is] almost invincible" Godwin himself had written of Mary, and neither she, dissatisfied with her home, nor Shelley, newly released from Harriet and her formidable sister Eliza, would forfeit the deep passion they felt for each other.

Mary's half-sister Fanny, outwardly subdued, domesticated and dutiful whatever her hidden feelings, seems not to have been invited to share in the secret when Shelley and Mary decided to run away; but in Jane Clairmont (who soon afterwards began to style herself "Claire," the name by which she was thereafter known)

2. A further important factor in Godwin's attitude to the elopement is revealed by David Fleisher in his *William Godwin* (1951). Mr. Fleisher points out that by 1814 Godwin had expressly amended his views on marriage. "It is clear," Mr. Fleisher writes, "that Shelley was acting, and that he knew he was acting, in opposition to views which Godwin had maintained for approximately fifteen years." But cf. pp. 9–10.

Mary found a more intriguing spirit. Claire, always "game" and avid for adventure, was taken into Mary's confidence. On 28th July 1814, Mary and Shelley eloped, accompanied by Claire. That day the lovers started a joint diary; Shelley makes the first entry:

28th July—The night preceding this morning, all being decided, I ordered a chaise to be ready by 4 o'clock. I watched until the lightning & the stars became pale. At length it was 4. I believed it not possible that we should succeed; still there appeared to lurk some danger even in certainty. I went; I saw her; she came to me. Yet one quarter of an hour remained. Still some arrangements must be made, & she left me for a short time. How dreadful did this time appear; it seemed that we trifled with life & hope; a few minutes passed, she was in my arms—we were safe; we were on our road to Dover.

Chapter 3

We are as clouds that veil the midnight moon;
How restlessly they speed, and gleam, and quiver,
Streaking the darkness radiantly!—yet soon
Night closes round, and they are lost for ever:
                            SHELLEY, *Mutability*

"To express it delicately," wrote Byron in 1820 to a friend, "I think Madame Claire is a damned bitch." This was one of Byron's occasional approaches to accuracy. But rattling along the road to Dover six years earlier, Mary seems to have had no afterthoughts about Claire's presence with the runaway party. Why Claire joined Shelley and Mary we cannot say, though many conflicting suggestions have been made; in all probability she went on the invitation of Shelley, who was always delighted to play the liberator to those who complained of oppression; and Claire was quite obviously eager to accompany them, while Mary, who had moved closer to Claire since her return from Scotland, may well have welcomed the opportunity of having someone familiar to her, as a companion on her new venture. Mary was ill, probably from excitement as well as from the journey, all the way to Dover, and again during their very rough crossing to Calais. The next day they spent in Calais, as Shelley's diary entry tells us:

29th July—I said, Mary, look, the sun rises over France. We walked over the sands to the inn; we were shown into an apartment that answered the purpose both of a sitting & sleeping room. (. . .) In the evening Captain Davison came and told us that a fat lady had arrived, who said that I had run away with her daughter; it was Mrs. Godwin.

Not Mary, but sixteen-year-old Claire it was whom Mrs. Godwin had pursued across the Channel. Mary and Shelley brought no pressure on Claire to remain with them; but after the girl had listened to Mrs. Godwin's arguments for a whole night, she told her mother she was remaining with Shelley. Mrs. Godwin "departed without answering a word."

The next day they started out on their three weeks' journey across France into Switzerland, in a spirit of general élan and carefree indifference to all the discomforts that beset them. Mary and Shelley continued their joint journal, written sometimes by one sometimes by the other, though later Mary was the more regular recorder. Briefly worded though it is, this journal offers the best evidence of the essential success of their enterprise; for though Mary was often unwell and they were frequently embarrassed through lack of funds, their love stood this very rigorous test.

By 2nd August they were in Paris:

Journal 2nd August— . . . Mary looked over with me the papers contained in her box. They consisted of her own writings, letters from her father & her friends, & my letters. She showed me one letter from Harriet which recommended her to write that to me which should calm me, & enable me to subdue my love for her.—She promised that I should be permitted to read & study those productions of her mind that preceded our intercourse. (. . .) In the evening we walked to the gardens of the Tuileries. (. . .) Mary was not well. (. . .) We returned, & were too happy to sleep.

Shelley was expecting a letter with some money but it did not arrive; so he sold his watch and chain and went to see a Frenchman about raising funds. But this did not worry them unduly for they were finding, every day, some new delight in each other's company.

Journal 3rd August— Mary read to me some passages from Lord Byron's poems. I was not before so clearly aware how much of the colouring of our own feelings throw upon the liveliest delineations of other minds; our own perceptions are the world to us.

4th August—Mary told me that this was my birthday. I thought it had been the 27th of June.[1]

They visited the Louvre and Notre Dame, then met a Frenchman who could speak English and who took them out of their way so that he could tell them of his adventures during the Bonaparte régime.

Journal 5th August—He made us sit down in the garden of the Tuileries, and there . . . with a smile of abundant & overflowing vanity . . . confessed that he was an author & a poet. We invited him to breakfast, hoping to derive from his officiousness a relief from our embarrassments.

7th August—(. . .) The morning passes in delightful converse. We almost forget that we are prisoners in Paris; Mary especially seems insensible to all future evil. She feels as if our love would alone suffice to resist the invasions of calamity. She rested on my bosom & seemed even indifferent to take sufficient food for the sustenance of life.

Shelley procured sixty pounds and went with Claire to buy an ass which it was proposed should bear each of them in turn on the road to Switzerland. Leaving Paris behind, and also Mary's box (a loss which caused her some trouble many years later), they set off; before long they were carrying the ass.

Journal 9th August—We sell our ass & purchase a mule, in which we much resemble him who never made a bargain but always lost half. The day is most beautiful. I led Mary on her mule.

1. See p. 22n.

Village after village they passed in this style without serious mishap. At one place which had been desolated by Cossack raiders, night fell before they reached their destination and Mary took fright; then, when they found a place to sleep, Claire insisted that rats were crawling over her face. Here, too, Shelley sprained his leg and was given priority with the mule all next day, telling the girls a story to pass the time. They sold the mule at Troyes and bought a carriage of sorts, which transaction made alarming inroads on their money. None the less, before leaving Troyes Shelley conceived the remarkable idea of adding his wife to the party in a non-marital capacity, and accordingly wrote off to invite Harriet.

Shelley, it must be remembered, was influenced at the outset of his independent career by Godwin's *Political Justice.* He had married Harriet for much the same reason that Godwin had married Mary Wollstonecraft: to protect the partner on whom the calumny of an irregular union would mostly fall. Therefore, obtuse and tactless as his invitation to Harriet seems, Shelley was conscious of no lapse from courtesy. Nor did Mary, secure in Shelley's love and at one with Shelley's ethics, see any harm in it. Harriet, of course, saw the matter in a more normal light.

But forgetting England and the separate furies that awaited them there, they pressed on through France. When we read of wanderers in ancient idylls we are struck by their unconcern over trivial obstacles; those legendary figures seem to have progressed in a paradoxical state of practical unreality: when night fell they slept; when they wanted to cross a river they took a boat—the procuring of bed or boat is irrelevant to their story. There is something of this idyllic procedure—something larger than life—in these first wanderings of Mary, Shelley and Claire as they are unfolded from the pages of their journal. Shortage of money, poor and dirty accommodation, which would have sent most travellers scuttling home, were accepted by these young people as part of the curious variety of things.

Journal 14th August—We rest at Vendeuvre two hours. We walk in a wood belonging to a neighbouring chateau, & sleep under its shade. The moss was so soft, the murmur of the wind in the leaves was sweeter than Aeolian music . . . we forgot that we were in France or in the world for a time.

At the village of Mort, Mary sat on a rock with Shelley and together they read Mary Wollstonecraft's first novel, *Mary*. Very often Mary was to return to her mother's work, as if to find in those pages a glimpse into part of her own nature; she was, moreover, justly proud of her parentage, and sitting on the rock with Shelley it pleased her to hear him talk about her mother's autobiographical romance.

On 19th August, the three travellers, weary now but taking immense delight in the mountain scenery, entered Switzerland. Next day they held a financial conference, but their grave situation in no way abashed them. Shelley went to see a banker who miraculously held out hope, promising an answer in two hours' time.

Journal 20th August—At the conclusion of the time, he sends for Shelley, & to our astonishment & consolation, Shelley returns staggering under the weight of a large canvas bag full of silver.

The money, they knew, would not last long but while it lasted they made the most of it. Three days later they were in Lucerne.

Journal 23rd August—After breakfast we hire a boat to take us down the lake. Shelley & Mary go out & buy several needful things, and we then embark. It is a most divine day; the farther we advance the more magnificent are the shores of the lake— rock and pine forests covering the feet of the immense mountains. We read part of L'Abbé Barruel's "Histoire de Jacobinism." We land at Bessen; go to the wrong inn, where a most comical scene ensues. We sleep at Brunnen. Before we sleep, however, we look out of the window.

It was characteristic of Mary and Shelley in their life together that in the midst of domestic or financial distractions they never neglected their reading, sometimes together, sometimes separately; or they would discuss literature as fervently as if no other immediate problem confronted them. Now, although they had difficulty in finding a house, as they had hoped, for the winter, and with small prospect of maintenance, reading and study were already an important part of their daily life. In protesting against their union, Godwin had underestimated the effect of his own training on Mary. She, as well as Shelley, could lose her sense of external things in any subject that called her mind into action; and from Shelley she derived the habit of following several lines of study at a time. In little more than a week their haphazard reading covered parts from Mary Wollstonecraft's novel, a work on the Jacobins, Tacitus's *History* and Shakespeare: Shelley moreover, managed to write parts of a projected novel named *The Assassins*.

They eventually found a two-roomed lodging in an ugly house at Lucerne, which they optimistically engaged for a period of six months. But the next day they decided their lack of funds was too acute to keep them any longer in Switzerland. Their return journey was perforce made in haste. On Mary's seventeenth birthday they were travelling up the Rhine in a far from comfortable manner. "We expect to be, not happier, but more at our ease before the year passes," says the journal, and indeed, their happiness made short work of their anxieties, for they did not fail to note, here a ruined tower, there the brilliant sunset colourings on the river; while Shelley read aloud from Mary Wollstonecraft's *Letters from Norway*. Little mention is made of Claire by Mary and Shelley in this part of their journal, but on two occasions when they had been free of Claire's company for a brief period on their return journey, they noted the fact:

> *Journal 2nd September*—Mary & Shelley walk for three hours; they are alone. At eleven we depart. (. . .)
> *3rd September*—(. . .) With much difficulty we reach Mayence at twelve. Mary & Shelley are alone. Shelley takes a place in the diligence *par eau* to Cologne.

and already, it would seem, the third member of the party was felt to be intrusive.

Reaching Holland, they made way by road to Marsluys, where Mary commenced writing a tale by the strange name of *Hate,* which never seems to have been completed. Her task, says the journal, gave "Shelley the greatest pleasure," and he too continued writing his romance.

The trio arrived at Gravesend on 13th September, with no money to pay for their passage; but they induced the captain who, indeed, had little alternative, to trust them. Making straight for London, Shelley hired a coach and took the two girls on a tour of his friends in search of money, but with no success. He then called on Harriet of all people, leaving Mary and Claire outside in the coach for two hours until he had persuaded his resentful wife, now the expectant mother of Shelley's second child, to lend him some of the money which, it is true, Harriet had very liberally drawn from Shelley's own account. Their debt to the captain then discharged, they next repaired to the Stratford Hotel in Oxford Street for a much needed night's sleep.

Shelley continued to meet Harriet during the month of September, apparently on friendly terms, although her immoderate withdrawal of money from Shelley's account had left him in grave difficulties. Mary calmly pursued her reading, accompanied still by Claire, in their new lodgings, while Shelley made his daily round of visits to his friends, to solicitors and moneylenders, writing to those he could not see, including the still unrelenting Godwin.

If Godwin was able to dislike Shelley the man while approving of Shelley the promising young progressive, Shelley was equally capable of making such a distinction in his view of Godwin. Throughout the course of his embittered relationship with the philosopher, Shelley continued to treat with respect the powerful mind that so strongly influenced him. We see Shelley, during this anxious month of his return to England, reading Godwin's *Caleb Williams* to Mary and Claire; but they were refused admittance to Skinner Street, and were treated to the parade of Mrs. Godwin with Fanny outside the windows of their home. But this did not worry the young people. Shelley's comings and goings were interspersed by plenty of reading and talk. Wordsworth's newly-published *Excursion* caused them some indignant disappointment, and Mary started to learn Greek. And the day that Godwin wrote to forbid all communication with him except through a solicitor, Mary re-read part of *Political Justice.* One day, when Charles Clairmont, Mrs. Godwin's older son, called, they discussed money affairs with him (most likely Godwin's) and also a plan for placing Claire in a convent. But as with most discussions as to ways of rendering Claire independent of Mary and Shelley, this came to nothing. The antagonism between Skinner Street and Shelley's ménage was now further aggravated by a vicious rumour then circulating, that Godwin had sold Mary and Claire to Shelley for eight hundred pounds and seven hundred pounds apiece.

At the end of September, Shelley, Claire and Mary moved to new lodgings in Somers Town, where Shelley's friends, prominent among them Thomas Love Peacock, came frequently to lighten their days with brilliant talk but not their impoverishment with ready money.

Shelley was a talented and educated young man at a time when such people were few. Could he not in some way have earned enough to tide him over a temporary embarrassment? The idea would never have occurred to Shelley and would have shocked his friends. Shelley's political views were, in any case, enough to bar his work from those periodicals which could have offered sufficient remuneration; and as for employment, his anti-authoritarian and highly imaginative nature would have been done such violence by it that it was as well, perhaps, that he was not even remotely tempted by any such consideration.[2] But Shelley was not wanting in colourful inventions for securing money. Could not his two heiress sisters, Elizabeth and Helen, be "converted and liberated"? Shelley and the girls put the question to Peacock one evening, and far into the night they turned over and relished this magnificent project for the liberation of two young daughters of a country squire, plus their money, from the leisured security of their home.

2. It would be unfair to assume that Shelley's impractical behaviour implies an essentially irresponsible outlook. To humankind, Shelley's attitude was one of overwhelming responsibility—and it is this voluntary assumption of the Atlas burden that gives his poetry universal meaning, and which, incidentally, might be said to have conditioned his premature ageing in appearance. We cannot have everything. If Shelley did not accept the responsibilities which the average man recognises, he took upon himself, in a deeper sense, those which the average man could not conceive, far less bear.

But next day, when Peacock called, it was a "running away scheme" that occupied their conversation.

Mary's affection for Shelley had increased with intimacy. Shelley, too, felt his troubles as nothing compared with his delight in Mary. "How wonderfully I am changed!" he wrote to Hogg in October. "Not a disembodied spirit can have undergone a stranger revolution! I never knew until now that contentment was anything but a word denoting an amusing abstraction. I never before felt the integrity of my nature, its various dependencies and learned to consider myself as an whole accurately united—rather than an assemblage of inconsistent and discordant portions."

Mary should be properly credited with the integrating influence she exerted over Shelley, to which he himself admitted. The wonderful spirit of understanding which existed at the outset of their life together had a most unifying effect on Shelley's later work; and students of the creative mind might do well to consider Shelley in this light. For in Mary, Shelley found for the first time combined erotic and intellectual elements. She was a woman with a mind.

In face of the strong bond between the two lovers, Claire now began to feel herself neglected, and so drew as much attention upon herself as possible, half-consciously perhaps. One of the ways in which she made her presence felt was in a series of spectacular nightmares which resulted in convulsive fits of varying degrees of severity. Claire was an unbalanced, excitable woman at the best of times and on many occasions Shelley's love of horrific conversation egged her on to displays of hysteria. One night Shelley's weird talk went on till the small hours of the morning; Claire eventually went to bed.

> *Journal 7th October*— . . . Shelley unable to sleep, kissed Mary
> & prepared to sit beside her & read until morning, when rapid
> footsteps descended the stairs.
>
> Jane [Claire] was there . . . her countenance was distorted
> most unnaturally by horrible dismay—it beamed with a white-
> ness that seemed almost like light; her lips & cheeks were of
> one deadly hue; the skin of her face & forehead was drawn into
> innumerable wrinkles—the lineaments of terror that could not

be contained; her [ears?] were prominent & erect; her eyes were wide & starting, drawn almost from their sockets. (. . .) This frightful spectacle endured but for a few moments—it was displaced by terror & confusion, violent, indeed, & full of dismaying significance, but human. She asked me (Shelley) if I had touched her pillow (her tone was that of dreadful alarm). I said, "No, no! if you come into the room I will tell you." I informed her of Mary's pregnancy; this seemed to check her violence.

Someone, Claire told Shelley, had touched her pillow. Shelley and Claire sat up all night by the fire, unable to resist continuing the "awful conversation" which had started the nerve-racking evening.

. . . Just as the dawn was struggling with moonlight, Jane [Claire] remarked in me [Shelley] that unutterable expression which had affected her with so much horror before; she described it as expressing a mixture of deep sadness & conscious power over her . . . her horror & agony increased even to the most dreadful convulsions. She shrieked & writhed on the floor. I ran to Mary; I communicated in few words the state of Jane [Claire]. I brought her to Mary. Her convulsions gradually ceased, & she slept.

But about this time, Mary seems to have realised the practical inconvenience of having Claire and her temperament constantly with them. Claire looked upon Shelley then, as she did in her old age, as part of her property, and did as much as she could to obtain what she considered her fair share of his attention. Shelley, for his part, maintained an attitude of friendship towards this girl, to whom he never seems to have been more than companionably attracted. (Much later, it was rumoured that a Neapolitan child registered under Shelley's name was Claire's baby by Shelley. But there is no proof, and the story is very unlikely.) Shelley's energies were, indeed, at this time, bent on sorting out the complexities in which his own life was involved.

Harriet sent a message to say she was ill; and Shelley sent her a doctor, meanwhile consulting with Mary as to whether they should both call on her—a step they wisely did not take. Following this gesture, Shelley received a "good-humoured" letter from Harriet, and at the same time a message of graver humour from Harriet's creditors, which caused Shelley to anticipate arrest. Mary and Shelley came to several decisions at once; they would leave London—they would stay. Eventually they decided to send for five pounds from Shelley's friend, Hookham, then saw a play and spent the night at the Stratford Hotel in case the creditors should call at their lodgings.

Shelley's difficulties, then, were not assisted by Claire's behaviour. He became impatient with her.

Journal 14th October—Jane's [Claire's] insensibility & incapacity for the slightest degree of friendship. The feelings occasioned by this discovery prevent me (Shelley) from maintaining any measure in my severity. This highly incorrect; subversion of the first principles of true philosophy; characters, particularly those which are unformed, may change. Beware of weakly giving way to trivial sympathies. Content yourself with one great affection—with a single mighty hope; let the rest of mankind be the subjects of your benevolence, your justice, &, as human beings, of your sensibility; but, as you value many hours of peace, never suffer more than one even to approach the hallowed circle.

So Shelley now advised himself. That same day the tension between Shelley and Claire exploded. ". . . How hateful it is to quarrel—to say a thousand unkind things—meaning none—things produced by the bitterness of disappointment!" Claire wrote in her own diary with that self-insight that she had occasional access to. On Shelley's initiative the quarrel was amended in the evening. Claire walked in her sleep that night, until Shelley, hearing her "groan horribly" for two hours, took her once more to Mary—a firm and positive enough gesture of rejection to the unfortunate Claire, who, in her self-confessed "bitterness of disappointment," had intended, consciously or otherwise, to win Shelley for herself.

[35]

Between 23rd October and 9th November, Shelley's financial position had become so precarious that he was forced to stay away from home for days at a time to elude the duns who were then at their doors. On this, their first parting, Mary's love for Shelley was intensified, and she met him by appointment at City coffee-houses, to enjoy a few brief and secret hours with him. "You may meet me with perfect safety at Adams', No. 60 Fleet Street," wrote Shelley to Mary on 24th October, "I shall be in the shop precisely at twelve o'clock. I cannot support your absence. I thought that it would be less painful to me; but I feel a solitariness and a desolation of heart where you have been accustomed to be." But Shelley was unable to keep this appointment, and Mary, anxious about him, wrought upon by the cares and privations no less than the novelties of the last few weeks, and in her first pregnancy, yet had her youth and dramatic love for Shelley to sustain her. A short meeting with Shelley was contrived after all, that day. "For what a minute did I see you yesterday—is this the way my beloved that we are to live till the sixth" Mary wrote him, "in the morning I look for you and when I awake I turn to look on you—dearest Shelley you are solitary and uncomfortable   why cannot I be with you to cheer you and to press you to my heart   oh my love you have no friends why then should you be torn from the only one who has affection for you—But I shall see you tonight and that is the hope that I shall live on through the day—be happy dear Shelley and think of me —Why do I say this dearest & only one I know how tenderly you love me and how you repine at this absence from me—when shall we be free from fear of treachery? (. . .)"

Meanwhile, Shelley was straining to raise funds from lawyers, stockbrokers and Harriet. His messages to Mary alone show how fortified he was by her, during his fugitive state. "Oh my dearest love, why are our pleasures so short and so interrupted," he asked her. "Know you, my best Mary, that I feel myself, in your absence, almost degraded to the level of the vulgar and impure. I feel their vacant, stiff eyeballs fixed upon me, until I seem to have been infected with their loathsome meaning. . . ." And later, "My beloved Mary, I know not whether these transient meetings produce

[36]

not as much pain as pleasure . . . I will not forget the sweet moments when I saw your eyes—the divine rapture of the few and fleeting kisses . . . Mary, love, we must be re-united. I will not part from you again after Saturday night. . . ." In Mary's notes to Shelley there is never the least hint of resentment or accusation. In all ways, the seventeen-year-old girl stood firmly by Shelley. To raise some ready cash for her own needs Mary pawned Shelley's microscope, but when her lover sent an urgent request for money she sent back word, "By a miracle I saved your £5 & I will bring it—I hope indeed; oh my loved Shelley we shall indeed be happy. I meet you at three and bring heaps of Skinner Street news—Heaven bless my love & take care of him—his own Mary."

"Skinner Street news" was bleak enough; both Godwin's financial problems and his cold disapproval of Shelley and Mary had increased. Mary was wounded deeply by her father's attitude; ". . . hug your own Mary to your heart," she wrote to Shelley, "perhaps she will one day have a father till then be every thing to me love—& indeed I will be a good girl and never vex you any more   I will learn Greek and—but when shall we meet when I may tell you all this & you will so sweetly reward me. (. . .)"

During Shelley's absence Mary had occupied her time—when not contriving a clandestine meeting with him, or walking "up & down Fleet Street" in the hope of seeing him—in fobbing off "Shelley's old friends," the bailiffs, in reading, and writing letters. Among her correspondents was her sister Fanny, who, subjugated by Mrs. Godwin, did not possess sufficient courage to visit Mary as she wished to do. Another letter Mary addressed to Isabel Baxter, one of the daughters of the Scottish family with whom she had been staying only the year before. Isabel did not reply, but her fiancé sent a letter of such cold bitterness as to upset Mary considerably. This was one of her first encounters, as Shelley's mistress, with the orthodox world, but while the first feelings of hurt stabbed her, Mary could still write generously of Isabel to Shelley: "I know her unexampled frankness and sweetness of character."

The young lovers remained separated well into November. It was a period Mary was never to forget and so deep an impression did it make upon her that in the novel she wrote many years later, *Lodore,* she was to reproduce the exact situation (but without the magic of the original story).

Despite the desperateness of their position, Mary went to spend a night with Shelley at an inn. "Those that love cannot separate" says the journal. She intended to stay for one night but she remained for a few days, until the innkeeper demanded payment and refused to send up dinner. Claire called to see them, and they were "all very hungry." Claire was sent on a fruitless quest for money; then a message was sent for food to Peacock, who was out. At last, Shelley set off himself for Peacock's, and with an impracticality reminiscent of Marie Antoinette's apochryphal remark, returned with cakes on which they feasted until Hookham sent enough money to pay the innkeeper.

By 8th November, Shelley's affairs had reached some state of abeyance which now released him from immediate danger of arrest. "My dearest, best love," he wrote to Mary, "only one day more, and we meet. Your affection is my only and sufficient consolation. I find that I have no personal interest in any human being but you, and you I love with my whole nature." Next morning Mary, Shelley and Claire moved into new lodgings in Nelson Square and on this day of Shelley's freedom Claire sulked. "Well never mind, my love—we are happy," the journal states.

Mary was beginning to feel the physical effects of these anxious weeks. "Mary is unwell" appears frequently in the journal, and she was not soothed by the frequent visits of Charles Clairmont, an envoy from Skinner Street, nor by Claire's continued tantrums. She was ill off and on, until the end of the year, but enjoyed the visits of Hogg, who had replaced Peacock as their most constant caller. At first, Mary had not taken greatly to Hogg, but soon the gaiety and brilliance of his personality began to impress her. The journal tells of his conversations with them on law, on "the different intercourse of sexes," and of his "funny account of Shelley's father, particularly of his vision & the matrimonial morning," among other inscrutable topics.

Mary continued with her reading and writing as assiduously as ever, but two subjects of discontent assailed her towards the end of the year. Confined to bed as she was for a greater part of her time, she was irritated by Claire's frequent jaunts with Shelley to visit, as Mary remarked, "heaps of places." A second, more serious source of resentment was the birth of Harriet's son.

> *Journal 6th December*—Very unwell. Shelley & Clary walk out, as usual, to heaps of places. Read "Agathon," which I do not like so well as "Peregrine." Shelley reads "Moore's Journal." . . . A letter from Hookham to say that Harriet has been brought to bed of a son and heir. Shelley writes a number of circular letters on this event, which ought to be ushered in with ringing of bells, etc., for it is the son of his *wife*. Hogg comes in the evening; I like him better, though he vexed me by his attachment to sporting. A letter from Harriet confirming the news, in a letter from a *deserted wife!!* & telling us he has been born a week.

This extremely telling journal entry epitomises a great many of the factors that conditioned Mary's feelings at this time. It shows not only her natural resentment that Shelley was finding the companionship in Claire which her own pregnancy prevented her from giving him, but also her impatience with Shelley's quite natural enthusiasm over Harriet's baby; we learn, too, that Mary sincerely believed Harriet and Shelley to have parted by mutual consent, and in her indignant exclamation "from a *deserted wife*" she attempted to justify with scorn her dislike of Shelley's attitude. Significant, also, are the words in this context, "Hogg comes in the evening; I like him better. . . ." But we should remember, before assuming that this journal fragment denotes any serious rift between Shelley and Mary, that the journal itself was open to both of them; Mary nursed no secret grudge but merely recorded an opinion of which Shelley was aware, and which she knew would not deeply annoy him.

Hogg had returned to Shelley's life at a time when his welcome was mixed: on the one hand, the young lawyer was able to assist Shelley financially and to bear the poet company in those evening conversations he so dearly enjoyed; but on the other, Shelley was somewhat tentative regarding a friendship which was associated with so much pain. It was Hogg who, after his spectacular expulsion with Shelley from Oxford, for publishing *The Necessity of Atheism,* had made apparently unwelcome advances to Shelley's wife, Harriet. But then it was Hogg who had supplied that newly-married pair with money. "Perhaps he still may be my friend in spite of the radical deficiencies of sympathy between us," wrote Shelley in the journal when Hogg called in mid-November.

Hogg was "pleased with Mary." But it was not until her frequent ailments prevented her from sharing in Shelley's activities that she began to look forward to Hogg's daily visits. Shelley's rapture over his son seems to have decidedly set in motion some workings of Mary's feelings in Hogg's favour; he amused and consoled her.

The New Year of 1815 brought news of the death of Shelley's grandfather. It was welcome news, for his bequest meant an alleviation of Shelley's financial anxieties. The first transactions ensured Shelley an income of one thousand pounds a year, two hundred of which he settled on Harriet; but these transactions were not completed until June of that year, and meanwhile Hogg, among others, became Shelley's creditor. Whether or not Shelley was in a position to dispense with Hogg's friendship at this moment, whether he did not wish to do so, and what Mary's real views were can only be guessed. The facts tell us that Hogg remained in close touch with Shelley's household; that he supplied them with money; that Mary wrote a series of love letters to Hogg; and that Shelley knew and approved of, if he did not even suggest, the affair.

Different commentators have interpreted these letters[3] in different ways. Professor Betty T. Bennett gives a balanced account of the "love" relationship between Mary Shelley and Hogg at this date in her 1980 edition of Mary Shelley's letters.[4]

Indeed, the letters posit a number of questions vital to the interpretation of Mary's character, no less than of Shelley's philosophical

3. The letters were not published until 1944: W. S. Scott, *Harriet and Mary* (The Golden Cockerel Press, London, 1944), and later in Mr. Scott's edition of *New Shelley Letters* (The Bodley Head, London, 1948). Earlier biographers, however, had access to the letters, but neither Professor Dowden nor Mrs. Marshall could have known of them.

4. Betty T. Bennett, ed., *The Letters of Mary Wollstonecraft Shelley* (The Johns Hopkins University Press, Baltimore and London, 1980), vol. 1, pp. 6n and 7n.

attitude to love. The points in question are admirably assembled by Mr. F. L. Jones, who was unfortunately unable to include these letters in his collection.[5] Mr. Jones writes:

> These eleven love letters from Mary to Hogg are nothing less than amazing. They reveal a situation which not even Shelley's enemies have ever believed existed. The letters make it plain (by inference) that Shelley advocated a sort of communal love and that Mary was making a great effort to put his idea into practice. That Hogg made love to her and that she attempted to return his love, all with the approval of Shelley, is evident. There is nothing secret or underhanded in the whole affair; all the while, to Hogg himself, Mary asserts her devotion to Shelley. Mary and Shelley's journal shows that since their return from Switzerland Hogg was a daily visitor; often he spent days together with them and frequently spent the night on other occasions. In Mary's letters are several expressions that seem strongly to suggest that Mary included, or meant eventually to include, sexual relationship with Hogg; but there is no absolute proof of this. It may be significant that from Mary's journal covering these early months of 1815 a number of pages at various points have been removed. In 1815 Mary was trying to force herself to love Hogg. Even then she saw evidence of that quality which by 1817 and thereafter made her dislike Hogg, although she remained on amicable terms with him: namely, Hogg's selfishness, his self-centredness, and his love of comfort.

Miss Glynn Grylls[6] very acutely observes that this was not the first time Hogg was attracted to a woman to whom Shelley was attached, nor was it to be the last. ". . . [H]e came," writes Miss Glynn Grylls, "to make love to Mary as he had made love to Harriet and as he was to enter later into a still more intimate relationship with another woman of Shelley's finding." This is not the place to pursue the line of thought suggested by this interesting

5. F. L. Jones, ed. *The Letters of Mary W. Shelley* (University of Oklahoma Press, Norman, 1944).
6. R. Glynn Grylls, *Mary Shelley* (Oxford University Press, London, 1938).

point, but students of Shelley and of Hogg may find it profitable to consider Hogg's possible identification-by-proxy with Shelley as manifest in his preoccupation with Shelley's women.

For Mary's part, Miss Glynn Grylls suggests that Mary was "not particularly attracted to Hogg, but conscientiously willing to take a lover for the sake of Free Love in the abstract"; that it was *Political Justice* rather than Mary's own inclinations that directed her responses to Hogg. In the present writer's view, this is a sound argument in its negative aspect; that is, Mary's acceptance of her father's principles clearly made it possible for her to enter upon a course of conduct without the deterrent influence of orthodox opinion. But it must be remembered that *Political Justice* in no sense contained a plea for licentiousness between the sexes; and Mary must have known that no possible interpretation of Godwin's views on this question could have supported her alliance with Hogg in her present circumstances.[7] If abstract principles influenced Mary, the evidence is perhaps more inclined to show that it was Shelley's peculiar brand of Godwinism, his exceptionally impracticable theorising, which informed her views. And we are reminded of the much-quoted passage which Shelley was to write years later to suit an occasion of his own:

> I never was attached to that great sect
> Whose doctrine is that each one should select
> Out of the world a mistress or a friend,
> And all the rest, though fair and wise, commend
> To cold oblivion. . . .
>
> (from *Epipsychidion*)

What is quite obvious is that Mary was not wholehearted about her flirtation with Hogg; but what is not clear is why she entered upon it at all. Mr. W. S. Scott, under whose editorship these documents, which are our only evidence, first appeared, offers another clue to Mary's true feelings, in pointing to the dissatisfaction Mary felt at the time with Claire and her absorption of Shelley's attention.

7. Shelley's invitation to Harriet to join Mary, Claire and himself in Switzerland was more properly in keeping with Godwin's doctrines, since here there was no question of Harriet's living with Shelley as his wife.

"She was . . . intensely jealous of Claire," writes Mr. Scott. ". . . This jealousy, I would suggest, was the chief cause of the tone of the letters which she wrote to Hogg at this time." And Mr. Scott makes the further suggestion that "Mary was unquestionably anxious to get money out of Hogg, and was offering a somewhat valueless 'quid' for a solid financial 'quo'." Though Mr. Scott, whose sympathies are with Hogg, may have expressed his view of Mary somewhat forcibly, there is certainly much in what he says to supply a practical answer to a human question. It is true that Mary was resentful of Claire when Hogg made his timely appearance. It is true, too, that her letters to Hogg are not without reference to expenses incurred by herself and Shelley, which Hogg was expected to meet.[8]

The idea of a *ménage à trois* might not, moreover, have been intellectually abhorrent to Mary—her mother, as she knew, had suggested the same arrangements to her lover, Imlay, but in far different circumstances. In the present case Mary was in love with Shelley alone, and emotionally the idea of sharing herself went against the grain.

But people seldom act from one motive alone; if they do they are said to be obsessed. Mary had no obsession about Hogg as a potential lover; nor about money; nor for absolute principles. It is more probable that a mixture of all the opinions outlined above represents the true state of Mary's motives. She felt bitter about Claire; she was in love with Shelley; they needed money; and Hogg appeared at a favourable time to offer financial assistance and amorous consolation. Mary, with Shelley's frank approval, gladly accepted the more harmless of Hogg's attentions and his much-needed money, meanwhile delaying indefinitely the physical culmination of the flirtation.

At first she fobbed Hogg off with a plea for time to get to know him better, and hints of future bliss: "You love me, you say—I wish I could return it with the passion you deserve—but you are very good to me and tell me that you are quite happy with the affection

8. But Betty T. Bennett wisely comments on this passage that if money was to be got out of Hogg, Shelley certainly could have done so: Mary's character would argue strongly against the suggestion that she sold herself.

[43]

which from the bottom of my heart I feel for you—you are so generous, so disinterested, that no one can help loving you. But, you know, Hogg, that we have known each other for so short a time, and I did not think about love, so that I think that *that* also will come in time & then we shall be happier, I do think, than the angels who sing for ever. . . ."

A few days later Mary was begging Hogg's company in the absence of Shelley and Claire: "Perhaps you can come and console a solitary lady in the mean time—but I do not wish to make you a truant so do not come against your conscience.

"You are so good & disinterested a creature that I love you more & more.

"By the bye when Shelley is in the country we shall never be alone so perhaps this is the last opportunity for a long time, but still I do not wish to persuade you to do that which you ought not."

And later, ". . . My affection for you, although it is not now exactly as you would wish, will I think dayly become more so— then, what can you have to add to your happiness. I ask but for time, time which for other causes beside this—phisical causes—that must be given—Shelley will be subject to these also, & this, dear Hogg, will give time for that love to spring up which you deserve and will one day have."

"Time, time" seems to have been her entreaty—time to get to know each other, time to wait till her baby was born, time for her love to "spring up." It is clear from her remark "phisical causes . . . Shelley will be subject to these also" that Hogg understood that Shelley was to remain Mary's lover, sharing her with Hogg when Mary's pregnancy was over. But Mary never cast doubt on the fact that the preservation of Shelley's love was her dearest consideration, and a most important point in these strange letters is brought out in Mary's references to Shelley in the passage below. Still holding out the future as bait, Mary told Hogg:

I know how much & how tenderly you love me, and I rejoice to think that I am capable of constituting your happiness. We look forward to joy & delight in the summer when the trees are green, when the sun s[hines] brightly & joyfully when,

[44]

dearest Hogg, I have my little baby, with what exquisite pleasure shall we pass the time. You are to teach me Italian, you
know, & how many books we will read together, *but our still
greater happiness will be in Shelley—I who love him so tenderly &
entirely, whose life hangs on the beam of his eye; and whose whole soul
is entirely wrapped up in him* [italics, present author].

Mary's baby was born, a seven-month girl, on 22nd February.
Hogg slept at Shelley's lodgings that night, making himself useful
in a kind and practical way, and remained all next day. On 2nd
March, the family moved to new lodgings, with disastrous results
to the delicate premature child, who died four days later. Mary sent
immediately for Hogg, who indeed proved a good friend in these
matters: "My dearest Hogg my baby is dead—will you come to me
as soon as you can," wrote Mary, "I wish to see you—It was
perfectly well when I went to bed—I awoke in the night to give it
suck it appeared to be *sleeping* so quietly that I would not awake it.
It was dead then, but we did not find *that* out till morning—from
its appearance it evidently died of convulsions—Will you come—
you are so calm a creature & Shelley is afraid of a fever from the
milk—for I am no longer a mother now."

For many weeks Mary was haunted by thoughts of her baby. She
would dream about the child, and then despondently "think about
the little thing all day." Shelley took Mary to Salt Hill for a few days
in mid-April, from where Mary wrote three letters to Hogg in a
persuasive tone, half-apologising for the expense of their holiday
and the consequent expense to Hogg. These letters are as provocative as ever, but Mary made no secret of her joy in being alone with
Shelley in the country. But since the death of her baby, a much
more playful tone was introduced into her correspondence with
Hogg, as if she realised that the time had now arrived when she
must either become Hogg's lover—which she did not wish—or
reject him. Mary compromised by investing the whole affair with
a smoke-screen of flippancy, behind which Hogg might save face
and vanity, and she make her escape.

But Shelley, always ready to interpret to the earnest letter any
theoretical way of life which he approved—whether it was vegetari-

anism, Godwinism or love—seems to have been quite prepared, now, to see his theory put to the test. "I attach little value to the monopoly of exclusive cohabitation," he had once before told Hogg during their quarrel over Harriet. So, during this spring of 1815, he left a message in Hogg's chambers in the Temple: "I shall be very happy to see you again, & to give you your share of our common treasure of which you have been cheated for several days. The Maie[9] knows how highly you prize this exquisite possession, & takes occasion to quiz you in saying that it is necessary for me to [be] absent from London, from your sensibility to its value. Do not fear. A few months [three words crossed out]. We will not again be deprived of this participated pleasure."

Their "common treasure," however, slid slyly out of the transaction, and turned her attention to Ovid; and also to Shelley's health, which had suffered from the strain of many recent anxieties, not the least being, most probably, his attempt to square his philosophy of human relationships with his natural desire to have Mary to himself.

9. "The Maie" was one of Mary's few nicknames. She was also known as "The Dormouse," possibly because of her shyness with strangers. (In November 1822 she wrote to Byron when intervening in a business matter on behalf of Leigh Hunt, ". . . my years of apprenticeship must begin. If I am awkward at first, forgive me. I would, like a dormouse, roll myself in cotton at the bottom of my cage, & never peep out.")

Chapter 4

I heard, as all have heard, life's various story,
And in no careless heart transcribed the tale; . . .
SHELLEY, *The Revolt of Islam*

Up to this time, Mary and Shelley had been actively engaged with their own destiny; they had seemed to be conscious protagonists asserting their life together. But for the next eighteen months, they were to occupy the observers' role, no less involved in what was enacted before them, than if they had been themselves the actors.

Mary, we have now seen as a woman in whom an instinctive wiliness mingled with the stoical independent and thoughtful qualities she had inherited. For Shelley, however, she preserved a simple sincerity. This frank disposal of her affections into Shelley's hands speaks plainly from a letter she wrote him from Bristol, where Shelley had left her to attend to affairs in London; Claire, meantime, had taken herself off to Lynmouth. Mary's only anxiety seems to have been lest Claire had followed Shelley to London.

"... We ought not to be absent any longer indeed we ought not

—I am not happy at it—when I retire to my room no sweet Love —after dinner no Shelley. . . .

"Pray is Clary with you? for I have enquired several times & no letters—but seriously it would not in the least surprise me if you have written to her from London & let her know that you are there without me that she should have taken some such freak. . . .

"Tomorrow is the 28th of July[1]—dearest ought we not to have been together on that day—indeed we ought my love. . . ."

Relations with the Godwin household had not improved. Shelley, though extremely provoked by Godwin, nevertheless fulfilled what he considered his duty to the older man by placing one thousand pounds at his disposal in June, and he continued to trouble himself endlessly over Godwin's difficulties. But since it is so often remarked to Godwin's disadvantage that the older man did not seem to evince the slightest gratitude and continued to write to Shelley in the most bitter terms, it might be just to quote those very facts in Godwin's favour. For if Godwin had been quite the hypocrite he is so often accused of being, surely he would have softened his tone towards his benefactor? As it was, his disapprobation remained as inflexible as when he had told the poet in 1814 ". . . I could not have believed that you would sacrifice your own character and usefulness, the happiness of an innocent and meritorious wife, and the fair and spotless fame of my young child, to fierce impulse of passion. . . ."

In August 1815 Mary and Shelley settled at Bishopsgate near Windsor Park where the summer drifted as peacefully past as the river on which they spent many a leisured afternoon. Claire was not present to try Mary's patience, and Mary tells us, in her posthumous notes on Shelley's poems, of his improved health, of the fine warm days, and the tranquil happiness of that summer.

Peacock lived nearby at Marlow, and joined them, with Charles Clairmont, at the end of August on a voyage in a wherry from Windsor to Cricklade; and at Letchdale Shelley wrote *A Summer Evening Churchyard*—a poem of uncharacteristic placidity. On their

1. The anniversary of their elopement.

return, Shelley started composing *Alastor,* that vision of the unattainable ideal which marks his first mature poetic achievement. That prolonged and quiescent season was, in fact, the high summer of existence in Mary's life with Shelley; they were not again to know such days, and it seemed as if all pacific elements accumulated before an approaching thunderbolt. Shelley sensed the transience of their present contentment: "The Poet's self-centred seclusion was avenged by the furies of an irresistible passion pursuing him to speedy ruin," he wrote in his preface to *Alastor.* The furies arrived in force with the New Year of 1816.

There is a type of person who, having glimpsed the glories attendant upon the life dedicated to creative achievement, and who is yet unqualified to create, pursues in a vague sort of way not the achievement itself but its accoutrements. Such a person was Claire Clairmont, the type of young woman who today would be known as "arty." Brought by her mother's marriage into a society of luminary spirits, she envied the high pitch of their existence but lacked its justification, a capacity for vision and performance; and there can be no more insidious or inconvenient company for the truly creative mind as this parasitic type of *manqué* individual.

Determined to assert herself in some spectacular way, Claire took herself to London and hunted down Lord Byron, who was then connected with Drury Lane Theatre. She wanted to become an actress, she told Byron, who very soon had her with child. Not that he found Claire particularly enchanting: she had found him in a state of boredom; "I was fain to take a little love (if pressed particularly) by way of novelty," Byron told his half-sister.

Claire returned to Shelley, who as yet was unaware of her pregnancy, but who had worries enough to beset him from Godwin. It was time, by now, for Godwin to have realised that Mary and Shelley were making a successful match of it. But the ageing man, harassed by his wife's narrowness and spite and by his own debts, was slithering into an intellectual decline. Shelley was infuriated by Godwin's lack of sympathy. "Do not talk of *forgiveness* again to me," he wrote, "for my blood boils in my veins, and my gall rises against all that bears human form, when I think of what I, their benefactor

[49]

and ardent lover, have endured of enmity and contempt from you and from all mankind." He spoke for Mary as well as for himself, for she felt Godwin's harshness cruelly.

"The spirit of restlessness came over him," writes Peacock of Shelley at this time. They decided to go abroad once more, and urged by Claire, fixed on Geneva where, as they knew, Byron was to spend the summer.

On the second anniversary of their elopement, Mary and Shelley, their child William who was born early in the year, and Claire had been established in Geneva for two months. They occupied a small house near the lake, above which lay Byron's larger residence, the Villa Diodati. Byron and Shelley took immediately to each other, finding in their temperamental difference as great a stimulus as their common intellectual alertness. Mary was somewhat intimidated by Byron. His personality, which may be summed up as one large gesture, overwhelmed and inhibited her less expressive nature, and she often sensed that Byron did not care for her company. As we have seen from her relationship with Shelley and Hogg, Mary was not wanting in gaiety; but admire Byron though she might, she could not find it in her to conform to his conceptions either of the witty, declassed and emancipated female, nor of the clinging, sweet and acquiescent woman, for she was neither of these.

Shelley and Byron spent most of their time on the lake, sometimes for days at a time, while Mary read at home; but when the disappointing weather prevented boating expeditions, the party, which included Byron's physician Polidori, would gather in the evenings at Byron's villa to talk. It was on one of these evenings, when their conversation turned on Shelley's much-loved topics, the supernatural and the potentialities of science, that Byron declared, "We will each write a ghost story." The suggestion was adopted with enthusiasm. Mary produced the best of these efforts, her marvellous *Frankenstein*. Her preoccupation with this ghoulish theme was further enlivened by the visit to Byron of the famous writer of supernatural stories, "Monk" Lewis, who, says the journal, told them "many mysteries of his trade."

But Shelley and Mary could never remain for long unplagued by affairs in England. Mary's half-sister Fanny, trailing out her unobtrusive, unsatisfactory existence with the Godwins, wrote a long letter to Mary in which she indulged much political and literary talk without revealing any taste above the ordinary; there was news of Coleridge and Lamb; and Fanny hinted briefly at her own plans to join her aunts, Mary Wollstonecraft's sisters, at their school in Ireland. She did not, in fact, seem much inclined to dwell on the future so far as her own "unhappy life" was concerned, but came at last to the real substance of her letter: "I left it to the end of my letter to call your attention most seriously to what I said in my last letter respecting Papa's affairs. They have now a much more serious and threatening aspect than when I last wrote to you."

So, through Fanny and Mary, Godwin made his needs known. Involved in debt, anxious to proceed with a novel he was writing, he did not observe the deepening depression suffered by his adopted daughter Fanny, who, related neither to Godwin nor his wife, felt herself a burden on the household. Mary and Shelley sensed Fanny's desolation throughout her letter, and the day after they received it they wrote to her and went to buy her a present.

By the beginning of September 1816 they were back in England. Byron had shelved Claire, and her pregnancy now being in an obvious state, she became an even greater liability to Shelley. They settled in lodgings at Bath where Claire's pregnancy could be kept secret, especially from the Godwins, and from where Shelley occasionally escaped for business trips to London, and to seek a house. Mary, too, managed to absent herself for a few days from Claire's increasing tiresomeness, joining Shelley at Marlow; and on their return to Bath they seemed to experience a deceptive lull in their present storms. In comparative tranquillity they set about their daily study and writing, and even a deal of intimate nonsense:

Journal 6th October—On this day Mary put her head through the door & said, "Come & look; here's a cat eating roses; she'll turn into a woman; when beasts eat these roses they turn into men & women."

But distressing letters from Fanny began to worry them. Fanny was distracted by the continual irritation of her home life where money matters had become the first consideration.

"You know," wrote Fanny, "the peculiar temperament of Papa's mind (if I may so express myself); you know he cannot write when pecuniary circumstances overwhelm him; you know that it is of the utmost consequence, for *his own* and the *world's sake* that he should finish his novel; and is it not yours and Shelley's duty to consider these things, and to endeavour to prevent, as far as lies in your power, giving him unnecessary pain and anxiety?"

Fanny, of course, was thinking not of "the world's sake" but of her own. To her disturbed mind, she saw her own misery brought about by the household's lack of money. Godwin was a bad manager of money, and would never have enough; it had become vastly important to this man who had once held it in such contempt. Nothing is so detrimental to the behaviour of a family as financial worry, and Fanny knew this to be the cause of her own discontent. She believed, also, in Godwin's pre-eminence as a writer, forgetting that Shelley, too, had his vocation—how great a one, she was unable to foresee—and that Mary and Shelley were still expending valuable energy and time in obtaining money for Godwin.

It is worth comparing Godwin's difficulties with those Mary and Shelley had experienced the previous year, when, seriously threatened by creditors, harassed in miserable lodgings, they had never for a moment lost sight of their real purpose, maintaining always a fundamental nobility of outlook. But they had youth and love to foster them; Godwin had neither.

Fanny, too, was loveless. Had she been as favoured as Mary, she might have found some tolerable interest in life, although her mother's melancholy was strong within her. As it was, even her plans to join her aunts in Ireland had failed through their prudish objection that she was contaminated by her sister's irregular life. On 9th October Fanny left home, and that day Mary and Shelley received a letter from her:

Journal 9th October—In the evening a very alarming letter comes from Fanny. Shelley goes immediately to Bristol.

Fanny had gone to a room at an inn in Swansea, where she took her life. A laudanum bottle was found beside her with a note:

I have long determined that the best thing I could do was to put an end to the existence of a being whose birth was unfortunate, and whose life has only been a series of pain to those persons who have hurt their health in endeavouring to promote her welfare. Perhaps to hear of my death will give you pain, but you will soon have the blessing of forgetting that such a creature existed as. . . .

She had removed her signature, possibly out of respect for Godwin's name. Her suicide was Fanny's only decisive gesture; she was right in anticipating the pain her death would cause, and right, too, in thinking that her memory would soon be forgotten.

In the first shock, Shelley and Mary were stricken with remorse, feeling they had neglected Fanny in many ways. The Godwins hushed up the affair, allowing it to be believed that she had died from an illness in Ireland. But Godwin felt the calamity keenly, though he maintained a dignified calm, and an understandable desire to shield Fanny's reputation and his own name from a sordid public scandal.

"Go not to Swansea," he advised Mary, "disturb not the silent dead; do nothing to destroy the obscurity she so much desired that now rests upon the event. It was, as I said, her last wish; it was the motive that led her from London to Bristol and from Bristol to Swansea. . . .

". . . do not expose us to those idle questions, which to a mind in anguish is one of the severest of all trials.

"What I have most of all in horror is the public papers, and I thank you for your caution, as it might act on this.(. . .)

"Our feelings are less tumultuous than deep. God only knows what they may become."

Claire was also afflicted by the news, and her lack of control did little to alleviate Mary's grief. By December, however, they had settled down once more to their customary life of writing and study at Bath, and Mary was taking lessons in painting. Shelley was frequently absent, and stayed for a time with Peacock at Marlow where he was negotiating for a house; and when he went to his first

meeting with Leigh Hunt, then editor of *The Examiner,* Mary wrote
to him with her usual warmth:

"Sweet Elf—I was awakened this morning by my pretty babe and
was dressed time enough to take my lesson from Mr. West and
(Thank God) finished that tedious ugly picture I have been so long
about—I have also finished the 4 Chap of *Frankenstein* which is a
very long one & I think you would like it.

". . . in the choice of residence—dear Shelley—pray be not too
quick or attach yourself too much to one spot—Ah—were you
indeed a winged Elf and could soar over mountains & seas and
could pounce on the little spot—A house with a lawn a river or lake
—noble trees & divine mountains that should be our little mouse-
hole to retire to. But never mind this—give me a garden & *absentia
Clariæ* and I will thank my love for many favours."

But *absentia Clariæ* was not in remote prospect, for she was now
awaiting the birth of her child.

Shelley returned to Bath on 14th December, encouraged by
Hunt's friendly interest in his ideas and work, but next day the
family received their second blow within a few months. Harriet had
thrown herself into the Serpentine and was dead. Shelley hastened
to London, distraught by the news, and hoping to bring back to
Mary his two children by Harriet, Charles and Ianthe. Shelley
wrote to say that Harriet's family were taking steps to deprive him
of the children, and Mary replied with generous sympathy, showing
a sincere desire to participate in his troubles and to care for his
children.

"I long more than ever," she told him, "that our house should
be quickly ready for the reception of those dear children whom
I love so tenderly then there will be a sweet brother and sister
for my William who will lose his pre-eminence as eldest and be
helped third at table—as his Aunt Claire is continually reminding
him. . . ."

Shelley's lawyers had advised him that if he married Mary, his
chances of obtaining the children would improve. Mary did not
display any particular enthusiasm for marriage, and seems to have
complied for the practical purpose of assisting Shelley's claims. So
she added to her letter, casually enough, "As to the event you

allude [to] be governed by your friends & prudence as to when it ought to take place—but it must be in London." Signing herself "Your Affectionate Companion—Mary W.G.," she appended a postscript: "Have you called on Hogg I would hardly advise you—Remember me sweet in your sorrows as well as your pleasures. . . ."

Hogg had become a mere background figure in Mary's regard. Her love for Shelley had matured, and motherhood had stabilised her. With Shelley, she had reached the conclusion that they could workably spend their lives together, and neither hesitated about undertaking their marriage. Concerning Harriet, Shelley was moved with profound pity; but he believed himself blameless. His pliable spirit embraced no feelings of remorse which might have suggested themselves to a mind more firmly established on the earth, however innocent. And Mary was as convinced as was Shelley that Harriet had been driven to suicide by the amorous complicity of her own life and by her relatives' hostile attitude.

Mary and Shelley were married on 30th December 1816 at St. Mildred's Church, Bread Street, in the presence of the Godwins.

Chapter 5

If Mary and Shelley looked upon their marriage as a calm necessity, Godwin's feelings were far otherwise. Marriage, the institution he had once condemned, had, in his second matrimonial venture, undone him. Domestic demands had begun to corrupt his vision; his need for money, which once had seemed merely the means towards the pursuit of truth, now became so imperative that he could hardly distinguish it from truth itself. And his other values had changed proportionately. The world's opinion, once scorned, now appeared as the arbiter of security to which he turned for approval; Mary had made a "good match." And, shedding a pitiful gloss over the facts, Godwin wrote of his daughter's marriage to his brother,

I do not know whether you recollect the miscellaneous way in which my family is composed, but at least you perhaps remember that I have but two children of my own: a daughter by my late wife and a son by my present. . . . The piece of news I have to tell, however, is that I went to church with this tall girl some little time ago to be married. Her husband is the eldest son of Sir Timothy Shelley, of Field Place, in the county of Sussex, Baronet. So that, according to the vulgar ideas of the world, she is well married, and I have great hopes the young man will make her a good husband. You will wonder, I daresay, how a girl without a penny of fortune should meet with so good a match. But such are the ups and downs of this world. For my part I care but little, comparatively, about wealth, so that it should be her destiny in life to be respectable, virtuous and contented.

It was true that Godwin cared a great deal for Mary's happiness, but since Shelley's elopement with her, he had never really liked the younger man. As with many people to whom reason becomes a god, his emotions played dark tricks with him and his dislike of Shelley seems to have been occasioned by sheer possessiveness where Mary was concerned.

The young couple were not deceived by Godwin's friendly overtures after the marriage ceremony, "so magical in its effects," as Shelley wrote. They continued to keep away from gloomy Skinner Street, while Shelley still helped Godwin with money even though he was in a poor financial way himself. What is more, Shelley continued to write to Godwin, and to discuss his own work with him, in the most genial terms. Mary and Shelley had other problems, however, to occupy their thoughts at this time.

Mary's year-old baby, William, had gained a greater hold on her affections than she had ever before experienced or was to know again. Between her "sweet babe" and her work in progress, *Frankenstein,* she would have been happily occupied enough. But where her journal proclaims "Four days of idleness," she was called upon to attend to Claire and her newly born baby, Alba (renamed Allegra in 1818). Mary now seems to have acquired a taste for children about her; she was hoping soon to add Shelley's two children to their family—she earnestly wanted these children, both for Shelley's happiness and as an expression of her own recently awakened maternal feelings. On the day that Shelley, in London, was awaiting the decision of Chancery concerning the suit for custody of his children, Mary wrote apprehensively,

Journal January 24th—My William's birthday. How many changes have occurred during this little year; may the ensuing one be more peaceful, and my William's star be a fortunate one to rule the decision of this day. Alas! I fear it will be put off, and the influence of the star pass away.

The protracted workings of the law demanded Shelley's presence in London for many more weeks than he expected. Mary joined him, staying with the Hunts, where their suspense was relieved by the company of Leigh Hunt's celebrated literary friends, John Keats among them. Claire and their Swiss nurse, Elise, later joined them in London with Claire's baby, occupying lodgings nearby. But still the judgment of Chancery was not delivered. The family, including Claire and her child, moved to their new home at Marlow.

"Our house," wrote Mary, inviting the Hunts to visit them, "is very political as well as poetical and I hope you will acquire a fresh spirit for both when you come here. You will have plenty of room to indulge yourself in and a garden which will deserve your praise when you see it—flowers—trees & shady banks—ought we not to be happy and so indeed we are. . . ."

Early in 1817 the Lord Chancellor's edict proclaimed Shelley to be an unfit guardian of his children, immoral in principle and conduct. The children were placed with a clergyman's family in Kent. Mary wrote years later, in her note to Shelley's posthumous poems, "No words can express the anguish he felt when his elder children were torn from him."

Shelley was indeed a sobered being now, and Mary alone could elicit, with her deep sympathetic insight into his nature, the way in which suffering drove him to seek relief in his imagination and in a sort of nervous sporting with his frustrate energy; ". . . sorrow and adversity had struck home," she later wrote. ". . . There are few who remember him sailing paper boats, and watching the navigation of his tiny craft with eagerness—or repeating with wild energy *The Ancient Mariner,* and Southey's *Old Woman of Berkeley;*

but those who do will recollect that it was in such, and in the creations of his own fancy when that was most daring and ideal, that he sheltered himself from the storms and disappointments, the pain and sorrow, that beset his life." No one who had not the interests, motives and inner well-being of the poet at heart could have been capable of such an understanding acceptance of his nature. In her capacity for love, Mary was greater than her mother, who, having made a considerable song about it, has come down to us as a model of the warm-hearted, generous, female lover. Mary Wollstonecraft, however, had never been so generous that she could allow her lover, Imlay, his own private tastes, faults and weaknesses. Mary Shelley was far different. She did not attempt to change Shelley nor to impose her own personality over his, and all her writings on Shelley provide the most forcible answer that can be offered to those who, superficially, once interpreted Mary as a selfish and cold woman. Her later writings on Shelley show, indeed, that even when the temperature of their relationship was at its coolest, she had been far from self-occupied, but had been observing and tending to the fluctuations of his being.

But in Shelley, Mary too was fortunate. He respected and fostered her intellect as well as her person.

Journal 14th May—Shelley reads "History of the French Revolution" and corrects "Frankenstein." Write Preface. Finis.

Her first novel now completed, Mary went up to London to seek a publisher, staying with the Godwins. Her father, with his money neurosis, depressed her, and a sensation of nostalgic sadness overcame her when she attempted to while away a few hours reading *Childe Harold:* "It made me dreadfully melancholy," she wrote to Shelley. "—The lake—the mountains and the faces associated with these scenes passed before me—Why is not life a continued moment where hours and days are not counted. (. . .)" But Godwin was delighted with Mary's visit, and enjoyed talking to his daughter who, though not yet twenty, possessed so alert and promising a mind.

Mary returned to Marlow at the end of May 1817, resuming her duty as hostess to the Hunts and their children who had been staying with Shelley, and taking up again her usual round of reading and writing. She was now awaiting the birth of her third child, and her tenderest maternal feelings were aroused by the Hunt children. "Adieu, little babes," she added to a letter to the Hunts when they were gone. "Take care not to lose one another in the streets for fear one of you should be kidnapped, but take hold of one another's hands & walk pretty." Claire's little girl, however, much as they loved her, was causing the Shelleys some embarrassment, for malicious rumours were being spread that Allegra was Shelley's child by Claire. Shelley had written to Byron in Italy, urging him to make plans for the child, but the lordly poet remained aloof so long as Shelley seemed willing to support her. Claire, too, was apathetic.

But while the summer passed Shelley's main attention was fixed on his poem *The Revolt of Islam.* He was too engrossed even to spend much time with Mary, but spent long hours floating under the beeches in his boat, as Mary informs us, or wandering the countryside. On the completion of this long poem, Shelley felt free to attend once more to the troubles which he seemed to draw about his person like a magnet. Other poets have told of the anguish of returning from the visionary world to the visible. But it was to Mary that Shelley returned, with a kind of exhausted relief; and he dedicated his poem to her:

> So now my summer task is ended, Mary,
> And I return to thee, mine own heart's home;
> As to his Queen some victor Knight of Faëry,
> Earning bright spoils for her enchanted dome;
> Nor thou disdain, that ere my fame become
> A star among the stars of mortal night,
> If it indeed may cleave its natal gloom,
> Its doubtful promise thus I would unite
> With thy beloved name, thou Child of love and light.

The house continued occupied by visitors, first Mary's former host, Mr. Baxter, and then the Hunts again. But Shelley was ill: his physique began to demand retribution for his six-month's dedication to a highly-tensed creative effort. Mary's child, Clara, was born on 2nd September, and soon after, Shelley went to London with Claire to give his poem to his publisher and to consult a doctor. Mary was low-spirited after her confinement, and with the added anxiety of Shelley's ill-health; "(. . .) ah! my love," she wrote, "you cannot guess how wretched it was to see your languor and encreasing illness. I now say to myself perhaps he is better—but then I watched you every moment & every moment was full of pain both to you and to me. (. . .)"

Claire's return, alone, to Marlow, "in a croaking humour," did nothing to aid matters or to allay Mary's fears for Shelley. Added to the gravity of his health, Mary learned, Shelley was once more being tracked down by Harriet's creditors. "You are teazed to death by all kinds of annoying affairs—dearest—how much do I wish that I were with you (. . .)," Mary wrote, and tried to cheer him with family gossip and a light-hearted account of herself "surrounded by babes." But Mary's thoughts were heavy, despite Shelley's tender letters to her, as it became clear that the threat of imprisonment for debt was upon him again. (The theme of debt throughout the nineteenth century is a social study by itself: debt was the equivalent of fraud; debt had its own prisons, its own police. Debt was a psychosis and by its dangerous nature positively mesmerized its victims.) Shelley could not risk arrest by returning to Marlow, but remained in London seeking here and there to raise loans. As was usual when affairs in England pressed him, he began to think of escaping abroad; he had been advised by his doctor to go either to the sea-coast or to Italy, and the latter now seemed the most convenient place. "Now, dearest, let me talk to you," Shelley wrote. "I think we ought to go to Italy. I think my health might receive a renovation there. . . ." Another factor in favour of Italy was Byron's residence there, and Shelley felt that the only way to raise Byron out of his lethargy about Allegra was to take the child to him.

This decided, Shelley remained meantime precariously in London.

"So you do not come this night—Love—nor any night—you are always away and this absence is long and becomes each day more dreary," was Mary's pathetic message to him. But when at last

Shelley was expected at Marlow she was forced to warn him, "Mr. Wright [a creditor] has called here today, my dearest Shelley and wished to see you. I can hardly have any doubt that his business is of the same nature as that which made him call last week—You will judge but it appears to me that an arrest on Monday will follow your arrival Sunday. My love—you ought not to come down—a long—long week has past and when at length I am allowed to expect you I am obliged to tell you not to come—(. . .)"

All the same, Shelley arrived at Marlow, accompanied by Godwin, on Sunday the 19th October, and Mary was undoubtedly relieved to see her father with Shelley, for she knew that Godwin was against the proposed visit to Italy. There was always a very close bond between Mary and Godwin—much closer than she perhaps knew—and she had confided to Shelley her feelings about Godwin's disapproval of their leaving England: "I know not whether it is early habit or affection but the idea of his silent quiet disapprobation makes me weep as it did in the days of my childhood."

As soon as the danger of Shelley's arrest was over, however, they began making plans for departure. In the next few months Mary and Shelley busied themselves in disposing of their damp house at Marlow where their books were all mildewed, but this dreary business and what Mary later described as their "uncomfortable residence in London" were mitigated by much talk and frivolity with their friends, Hunt, Hogg and Peacock. On 12th March 1818, the Shelleys, with Claire and the three children, made their third crossing to Calais. "We now depart for Italy," Mary wrote to Hunt, "with fine weather & good hopes."

By the time they reached Milan, Shelley's health had already improved noticeably, and their new colourful surroundings revitalised them. Shelley and Mary made a trip to Lake Como in a vain search for a house; they read Italian literature and wrote to their friends in enthusiastic terms. Claire, however, was in misery. Byron, in Venice, would not enter into any communication with her, and it fell to Shelley to write letter after letter on the subject of Allegra. Byron professed himself ready to accept his daughter under his own protection, provided Claire should relinquish any claim on her, or indeed all sight of the little girl. To Mary and

Shelley, no less than to Claire, this seemed monstrous, and Shelley resisted Byron's offer as firmly as possible. But at length, impressed by the illusion that Allegra might after all benefit by an upbringing in the aristocratic, Byronic atmosphere, Claire agreed to part with her child.

The Shelleys and Claire lost no time in resuming their wanderings, always observing, always reading, until they arrived at Leghorn. Here, with an introduction by Godwin, they met Mrs. Gisborne, formerly Mrs. Reveley, who had been an old friend of Mary Wollstonecraft and Godwin; she had, in fact, rejected a proposal of marriage from Godwin after his first wife's death. Mary recorded in the journal "a long conversation with her about my father & mother," and the long friendship between the Shelleys and the Gisbornes dates from this meeting.

On 11th June, Claire, Mary and her two children joined Shelley, who had taken a house at the Bagni di Lucca where, though they stayed but two months, they were so tranquilly happy that Shelley was reminded of the summer days at Marlow.

"We live very comfortably," Mary told Mrs. Gisborne, "and if Paolo did not cheat us he would be a servant worth a treasure. (. . .) So we lead here a very quiet pleasant life—reading our Canto of Ariosto—and walking in the evening among these delightful woods. (. . .)" Mary, having "attained a very competent knowledge of Italian," as Shelley reported to Godwin, was able to read Italian literature with him; the erudite Shelley himself translated Plato's *Symposium* here, in the space of ten days; while Mary was enlivened by news of *Frankenstein*'s reception—much of it condemnatory but none indifferent to its power.

Mary was now looking for a plot for her next novel, and at first considered, at Shelley's urging, using the theme which Shelley later dramatised in *The Cenci,* at Mary's suggestion.

They were thus encouraging each other to further creative efforts, while Claire was hankering daily with pitiful distress for her child, whom Byron had placed with Mrs. Hoppner, wife of the British consul at Venice. Mary and Shelley were naturally moved by her grief, and determined to persuade Byron to relent in his proviso that Claire should not see her daughter. In mid-August,

Shelley and Claire set out for Venice with this intent. From Florence Shelley wrote exhorting Mary to begin her next story; but Mary was not long free to work at her will; her baby Clara was taken ill, and she herself was unwell. Just as the Gisbornes arrived to bear Mary company, Shelley wrote summoning her to join him, and Mary departed in haste with her two children.

When Byron had found himself face to face with Shelley, he had not proved unreasonable and had readily agreed to Allegra's spending a week with her mother. This touchy subject quickly dispensed with, Byron had taken Shelley on his gondola to an island where they rode and discussed literature to their hearts' content. Nor did Shelley find Allegra's guardian, Mrs. Hoppner, in the least formidable. She had "hazel eyes and sweet looks—rather Maryish," Shelley said.

When Mary was expected to join them, Byron offered Shelley his villa at Este, and after four days' hot, tedious travel Mary arrived with her two children. The baby girl's teething ailment had developed on the journey into a serious illness, and little more than a fortnight later the Shelleys were forced to take her to Venice for medical attention. The child was ill all the way there, and Mary took her straight to an inn while Shelley hastened to fetch a doctor. He was unsuccessful; but meantime Mary had procured a medical man. It was too late; that evening of 24th September, their baby girl died —"an infant in whose small features," Mary wrote many years later, "I fancied that I traced great resemblance to her father."

Mary behaved stoutly so far as their friends could see. Only Shelley perceived, as he told Claire, that "this unexpected stroke reduced Mary to a kind of despair." The kind-hearted Hoppners immediately took the couple to their home, where Mary, after a day of weary idle retrospect, braced herself to avoid putting her friends out of their way; she joined them in their activities, visited the Academy and read. As soon as the baby was buried, Mary applied herself to persuade Byron to let Allegra remain some time longer at Este. She had still her boy, William, to console and occupy her, and Byron provided her with the task of transcribing one of his manuscripts. Still, she must have felt emotionally cheated, if rationally in credit, when her father wrote in response to the news:

"[The affliction] I may consider as the first severe trial of your constancy and the firmness of your temper that has occurred to you in the course of your life; you should, however, recollect that it is only persons of a very ordinary sort, and of a pusillanimous disposition, that sink long under a calamity of this nature. . . . We seldom indulge long in depression and mourning except when we think secretly that there is something very refined in it, and that it does us honour."

At the beginning of November the Shelleys and Claire rendered up Allegra to the Hoppners, and quitted Venice. After a fortnight's travelling and sightseeing, they entered Rome. In one whirlwind week they "did" Rome somewhat like modern tourists, endeavouring in this nervous kind of way to keep their spirits up, for Claire now was yearning for Allegra again, and Mary and Shelley missed their own child sadly. Their journey to Naples was undertaken at a more leisurely pace, and Mary and Shelley rejoiced in the classical associations of their route.

> *Journal 29th November*—We see the Promontory of Circe, and, on the rocks behind, the ruins of the Temples of Jupiter & Apollo. (. . .)
>
> *30th November*—(. . .) As we approach Gaeta, the little plain at the foot of the hills is covered with a wood of olives, festooned by vines. By the roadside, overlooking the Bay of Gaeta, we see the Tomb of Cicero, erected on the place where he was murdered, in the midst of the olive wood. (. . .) The whole bay is sanctified by the fictions of Homer, and the garden in particular by the ruins of the Villa of Cicero, which overlook the sea. A Poet could not have a more sacred burying place.

At Naples, they went on a further sightseeing tour, the memory of which later provided Mary with her opening scene in *The Last Man*. Their journal for this period shows Mary and Shelley occupied incessantly, as if afraid to stop and examine their thoughts. They read Livy, Dante, Virgil and other of the classics; they visited Virgil's tomb and went up Vesuvius, observing "the rivers of lava gush from its sides." Mary had not really recovered from the shock of her child's death, and this breathless pursuit of activity seems to have been a symptomatic safety-valve measure against despair. Shelley too, was ill, and sought medical advice, but the prescribed treatment was painful. Exhausted by this, and by the enervating effect of his renewed creative work—he had begun *Prometheus Unbound* at Este and wrote a great deal of it at Naples—Shelley none the less tried to seem cheerful for the sake of Mary and Claire.

Claire had anxieties enough too; she worried continually about Allegra, for Byron's notorious mode of life in Venice was in no way commensurate with the elegant way of life she had fancied Allegra would profit by; and Claire realised, now, that Allegra had better have remained with her. Mary received word from Mrs. Hoppner confirming Byron's "dreadful debauchery" and giving disquieting news of Allegra's progress.

Another source of trouble was their servant Paolo. He had formed an alliance with the nurse, Elise, who was now expecting a child. By the Shelleys' intervention, strangely enough, Paolo was induced to marry Elise; their desire to see this working girl respectably married was evidently for her own protection in the cause of which they were ever willing to waive principle.

A great amount of subdued melancholy prevailed at this time, yet the shadows did not fall between Shelley and Mary, but around them, rather. It was a reflective sadness induced by misfortune and low health, not bitterness, that informed their mood. Shelley's main work, *Prometheus Unbound,* occupied most of his thought, but he was aware of the uneven pattern their life had assumed, and his shorter poems no less than the major one, reflect it:

> Many flowering islands lie
> In the waters of wide agony,

he had written at Este; and this was still his theme, when he invoked the figure of Misery, not as a perpetual visitation, but as a temporary intruder on the basic peace of life.

> I am happier far than thou,
> Lady whose imperial brow
> Is endiademed with woe.

Mary and Shelley began now to make greater efforts to induce some cheerfulness into their lives. In March 1819, they were back in Rome. Here their spirits brightened: Mary took drawing lessons and Claire engaged a singing master.

Journal 9th March—Shelley & I go to the Villa Borghese. Drive about Rome. Visit the Pantheon. Visit it again by moonlight, & see the yellow rays fall through the roof upon the floor of the Temple. Visit the Coliseum.

11th March—Read the Bible.

12th March—Go to hear Messe, & the Padre Pacifico. (. . .) See the Pope. Visit the Capitol.

15th March—Write; read Montaigne & Livy. Go to the Villa Albano and the Villa Borghese. Shelley reads Lucretius.

Mary tried to recount all the wonders she had seen, in a letter to Marianne Hunt. "But my letter would never be at an end," she admitted, "if I were to try [to] tell a millionth part of the delights of Rome—it has such an effect on me that my past life before I saw it appears a blank & now I begin to live—In the churches you hear the music of heaven. . . .

"Shelley is *suffering* his cure—he is teazed very much by the means but it certainly does him a great deal of good. William speaks more Italian than English—When he sees anything he likes he cries O Dio che bella. (. . .)"

Mary was expecting another child in the late autumn, and had regained some enthusiasm for life; she loved Rome, which was always to be her favourite city, and with Shelley she had made some friends there. One of their closest friends in the early summer of 1819 was Amelia Curran, a painter whose father Godwin had known. Each of the Shelley party in turn sat for Miss Curran, and having found this new interesting friend, the Shelleys decided to stay in Rome longer than they had intended.

But the early heat of Rome rapidly affected three-year-old William, who became ill towards the end of May.

". . . [I]t is only yesterday & today that he is convalescent," Mary wrote to tell Mrs. Gisborne. "We are advised above all things to pass the summer in as cool a place as possible. (. . .) We should like of all things to have a house near you by the seaside at Livorno but the heat would frighten me for William who is so very delicate—and we must take the greatest possible care of him this summer—. (. . .)"

Before they could leave Rome, William's health grew worse. He had fallen victim of malaria. Fears for him haunted Mary for a week before they were rapidly confirmed. On 5th June Mary sent a distracted message to Mrs. Gisborne. "William is in the greatest danger—We do not quite despair yet we have the least possible reason to hope—Yesterday he was in the convulsions of death and he was saved from them. (. . .) The misery of these hours is beyond calculation—The hopes of my life are bound up in him—"

William died on 7th June 1819, and was buried in the Protestant Cemetery at Rome.

Chapter 6

We are accustomed to regard the nineteenth-century woman, married or unmarried, as a terribly frustrated being. The wife and mother, we often hear, was frustrated by a lack of erotic interest and the spinster by the lack of both lover and children. But by far the greatest sense of frustration was experienced by those mothers of large families who so frequently watched all or most of their children droop and die in infancy. This was a psychological disappointment of a very profound order, and had a more disastrous effect on women than did other emotional and physical deprivations.

So it was with Mary Shelley. She was loved, had borne three children, and lacked no intellectual stimulus. Her friends were all emancipated, and there was plenty of fulfilment in the air. Yet, deeper than her natural grief at the death of her last child lay the root exasperation and balk of three unfulfilled lives, extensions of her own being.

There was little comfort for her in the thought of the child she was soon expecting, for she foresaw no more than another blighted hope. Other women of her time might have found some comfort in religion, but Mary's frustration took the form of despondent pessimism from which she suffered more frequently from that time onward: " . . . in truth," she was to write in retrospect, "after my William's death this world seemed only a quicksand, sinking beneath my feet. . . ."

Shelley, too, was stricken by William's death, but when his sorrow dwindled and he did not see Mary recover from it, he was bewildered and disturbed by her melancholy:

> My dearest Mary, wherefore hast thou gone,
> And left me in this dreary world alone?
> Thy form is here indeed—a lovely one—
> But thou art fled, gone down a dreary road.

But Mary had retired within herself, and it was a long time before the communicating spirit was restored between them.

The Shelleys and Claire had moved to Leghorn after William's death, but still these new surroundings could not drive the child from Mary's thoughts.

"I feel it more now than at Rome—," she wrote to Miss Curran, "the thought never leaves me for a single moment—Everything on earth has lost its interest to me."

Godwin's insensibility is unbelievable. Shelley informed Leigh Hunt,

> I wrote to this hard-hearted person (the first letter I had written for a year), on account of the terrible state of her mind, & to entreat him to try to soothe her in his next letter. The *very* next letter, received yesterday, & addressed to her, called her husband (me) "a disgraceful & flagrant person"—tried to persuade her that I was under great engagements to give him *more* money (after having given him £4,700), & urged her if she ever wished a connection to continue between him & her to force me to get money for him. He cannot persuade her that

I am what I am not, nor place a shade of enmity between her & me—but he heaps on her misery, still misery.

But so far as his daughter was concerned, Godwin was well-meaning enough, and he wrote her another letter, exhorting her to see herself in her role as one of the elect, and offering sage though cheerless advice:

". . . do not put the miserable delusion on yourself, to think there is something fine, and beautiful, and delicate, in giving yourself up, and agreeing to be nothing. Remember too, though at first your nearest connections may pity you in this state, yet that when they see you fixed in selfishness and ill humour, and regardless of the happiness of every one else, they will finally cease to love you, and scarcely learn to endure you. . . ."

Shelley, however, was the more inclined to see the hard-hearted father heaping misery on Mary, since he was then engrossed in his composition of *The Cenci,* that tragedy of supremely wicked parenthood. "This tragedy," Mary wrote in her note to the poem, "is the only one of his works that he communicated to me during its progress."

It was during the August and September of 1819, while Shelley's *Cenci* was still being written, that Mary completed a short novel entitled *Matilda.* This, like *The Cenci,* deals with an incestuous father. Perhaps the fact that she did not publish the story during her lifetime shows that she perceived, on reflection, that she had been merely relieving her feelings by over-dramatising her situation. She was later to comment in her journal, ". . . when I wrote Matilda miserable as I was, the *inspiration* was enough to quell my wretchedness temporarily."

On the small roofed terrace at the top of their villa which Shelley made his study, Mary now found some degree of peace, discussing Shelley's work with him, and looking out on the wide vista of country and sea. Here they heard the peasants singing at their work, and in later years she recalled the associations of this place and time with that nostalgic pathos in which even sad times past present themselves: ". . . in the evening the water-wheel creaked

[71]

as the process of irrigation went on, and the fireflies flashed from among the myrtle hedges: Nature was bright, sunshiny, and cheerful, or diversified by storms of a majestic terror, such as we had never before witnessed."

The Shelleys saw much of Mrs. Gisborne who lived near, especially when her husband, whom Shelley thought a bore, left for England. Shelley learnt Spanish and read Calderón with Mrs. Gisborne, and by the time Claire's brother, Charles Clairmont, joined them, the party approached something like its former spirit.

Shelley hoped that the birth of Mary's child would put an end to her melancholy, and at the end of September they moved to Florence to be near the Scottish surgeon of their choice. On the way they stopped at Pisa, where a former pupil of Mary's mother was staying: this was Lady Mountcashell, who also knew Godwin. She and a Mr. Tighe were living as Mr. and Mrs. Mason. Mary was always delighted to be able to talk of her mother and father to anyone who had known them. Mrs. Mason conceived a warm regard for the Shelleys, and was to prove a good friend.

On 12th November 1819, at Florence, the Shelleys' son, Percy Florence, was born.

"Poor Mary begins (for the first time) to look a little consoled," was Shelley's report to Hunt. Mary's spirits were indeed cheered by her little child, and her letters convey something of her lightheartedness.

"Now my confinement is well over," she wrote to Mrs. Gisborne, "& I am getting well & strong I hope you are beginning to consider your promised visit which was to take place about this time —It would give me so much pleasure & would be so very agreeable to see you here. . . . The little boy is nearly three times as big as when he was born—he thrives well & cries little & is now taking a right down earnest sleep with all his heart in his shut eyes."

With renewed hope, Mary turned to her reading again, and to her third novel, *Valperga,* and though troubled by Shelley's health, which did not flourish in the climate of Florence,[1] by Claire's mournful hankerings after Allegra, by Godwin's harping demands

1. Shelley was very often at a low physical ebb after the completion of a major poem.

for money, and by money difficulties themselves, they had become inured, to some extent, to these ever-present daemons of fortune.

Early in 1820 the family moved to Pisa, near the Masons. Here further anxieties awaited them and in the spring they were obliged to go to Leghorn to consult an attorney. A scandal about them had been circulated by Paolo, their former servant who had married Elise; Paolo, it seems, was now accusing Shelley of disposing of an illegitimate child he was supposed to have had by Claire, in a foundling home at Naples.

It is apparent that Shelley, with his customary philanthropic disregard for personal consequences, did make some arrangements for someone's illegitimate child at Naples. The timing makes it improbable that this infant was Shelley's or Claire's. The baby girl, Elena Adelaide, was born December 1818 and was registered in the Shelleys' name. She died in June 1820. It appears that Shelley made provisions for the infant in Naples and that Mary was preparing to accept her in the family.[2] But Mary affirmed when the story was later repeated maliciously by Elise, that there was no truth in his own alleged involvement with Claire in any such matter. Paolo was temporarily silenced, and though Shelley was naturally disturbed by this rumour—especially that he was capable of abandoning a baby—he was essentially carefree enough to write, while at Leghorn, his *Letter to Maria Gisborne* and the *Ode to the Skylark*.

In August 1820 the hot weather drove them to the Baths of S. Giuliano at Pisa where Mary continued well occupied with her baby, her reading and her new novel. Mrs. Mason rendered Mary a good service by finding Claire a situation as governess in Florence. Shelley accompanied her there in October, returning with Tom Medwin, a cousin and former school-fellow, now a retired Indian officer.

Medwin occupied most of Shelley's time, but Mary was happily engaged in her work until they both discovered that Medwin was a bore. The Gisbornes had gone to England, and Mary was looking forward to their return, to relieve the weight of Medwin's company.

2. For a full account of various theories about this baby girl whom Shelley called his "Neapolitan charge," see Betty T. Bennett's *The Letters of M.W.S.,* vol. 1, p. 149n.

The Gisbornes, however, were annoyed with Shelley, who had engaged with Mrs. Gisborne's son, Henry Reveley, on a characteristic project of public benevolence which proved impracticable. This scheme aimed to provide, mainly at Shelley's expense, a steamboat service between Leghorn and Marseilles for the public; and for Henry Reveley, some profitable employment in the construction of the vessel. As Mary described it, an "unforeseen complication of circumstances"—no rare impediment to Shelley's plans—forced them to abandon the project. The Gisbornes were soon to be estranged from the Shelleys, not only on this account but, more seriously, because they let themselves be influenced by the disparaging stories which were being repeated by the Godwins about Shelley. On their way to England, the Gisbornes passed through Pisa but did not call, and it was some time before the friendship was mended.

So long as Mary had Shelley, her child and her work, she was satisfied. Claire was now absent and apart from Medwin they had little company at first. But Shelley was a more restless being than Mary: he could rarely stay long in one place, and when he did his mental appetite for change craved for new faces. An influx of new acquaintances began to invade the Shelleys, and Mary, for Shelley's sake, found amusement in some, while she could not conceal the tedium that others brought with them. The first of these visitors was Pacchiani, a professor at the University of Pisa, who set about introducing the intelligentsia of Pisa to the couple. Pacchiani was something of a clerical charlatan: the Shelleys did not take kindly to him and his coarseness often offended them. Another new friend, Sgricci, an improvisator who had made a name for himself, delighted and entertained them, however, while Prince Alexander Mavrocordato, a young Greek patriot who was to play an important part in the subsequent Greek revolution, was warmly respected by the liberty-enamoured Shelleys. Mavrocordato soon undertook to help Mary with her Greek studies in return for English lessons which he scarcely needed; Mary was pleased and flattered by his attentive companionship. "This is the result of an acquaintance with Pacchiani," she had remarked to Mrs. Gisborne. "So you see, even the Devil has his uses."

This particular Devil, however, had his less happy uses, so far as Mary was concerned, for through him they made a friendship which served Mary with some trying months. "There is another acquaintance of ours," she wrote to Leigh Hunt, "romantic and pathetic, a young girl of nineteen years of age, the daughter of a Florentine noble; very beautiful, very talented, who writes Italian with an elegance and delicacy equal to the foremost authors of the best Italian epoch. She is, however, most unhappy. Her mother is a very bad woman; and, as she is jealous of the talents and beauty of her daughter, she shuts her up in a convent where she sees nothing else but the servants and idiots. She never goes out, but is shut up in two small rooms which look out on the not very picturesque kitchen garden of the convent. She always laments her pitiful condition. Her only hope is to get married, but even her very existence is nearly a secret—and what a rare marriage!"

From the beginning of December the Shelleys paid daily visits to Emilia Viviani, the lovely Italian girl who was made the more interesting by her plight. Shelley himself conceived a marvellous if transient passion for Emilia, and indeed, considering Shelley's susceptibility to the ideal image of all life's manifestations, the setting was, for this purpose, a perfect one—Emilia was beautiful, ardent and eloquent; and she was in captivity. Shelley could have loved her for her captivity alone. But the fact that her convent prison rendered her unattainable and suggested untold mysteries which in reality Emilia did not possess, sent the poet into high raptures. There can be no doubt that Shelley had an erotic interest in this woman, but his erudition came to the rescue, and squared this with a Platonic view of love. But it is passion, not erudition, that informs the poem he wrote to her:

> Seraph of Heaven! too gentle to be human,
> Veiling beneath that radiant form of Woman
> All that is insupportable in thee
> Of light, and love, and immortality!

Thus Shelley addressed her in the *Epipsychidion;* while the Seraph of Heaven herself, relying less on her plumage of thought than on her woman's instinct, played her elevated part for all she was worth.

[75]

To a great extent, Shelley wrote Emilia out of his system with the *Epipsychidion,* and although early in January 1821 he had told Claire, "She continues to enchant me infinitely," by the middle of that month he was writing, "There is no reason that you should fear any mixture of that which you call *love.* My conception of Emilia's talents augments every day. Her moral nature is fine—but not above circumstances; yet I think her tender and true which is always something." In other words, Shelley was getting to know Emilia, and to do this is always to partly solve a mystery.

But Emilia had no intention of allowing Shelley's interest to flag. She wrote to him, as she did to Mary and Claire, in the most effusive terms.

"O my incomparable Friend, *angelica creatura,* did you ever suppose that I should be the cause of so much anguish to you?" she wrote to Shelley; and to Mary:

"My dearest Sister, I send you back *Corinne* with my liveliest thanks. It is a beautiful story, though sad, and such as to make a soul sensitive and *passionée* like mine shed tears. . . . Hide this sad letter from my friend. But salute him tenderly for me."

But she was in no concern to conceal her sadness from Shelley when she declared to him, "You say well; in *friendship* everything must be in common; few, indeed, very few, are the persons who know this sublime and sweet Divinity; but we know it, and that is enough. . . . Mary does not write to me. Is it possible that she loves me less than the others do: I should be very much pained by that. I wish to flatter myself that it is only her son and her occupations which cause this. Is not this the case?"

In mid-February, Shelley sent the *Epipsychidion* to his publisher, with the instruction that it should be printed anonymously.

". . . [I]ndeed," he asserted, "in a certain sense, it is a production of a portion of me already dead."

Mary, meanwhile, stood her ground, and took everything calmly. She knew Shelley's temperament; she was aware of her own uniqueness; and she did not deign to compete.

"It is grievous," she placidly informed Leigh Hunt when the affair was at its height, "to see this beautiful girl wearing out the best years of her life in an odious convent where both mind and body are sick from want of the appropriate exercise for each." And writing to Claire, who was watching the event with avid interest, Mary was non-committal:

"Of Emilia I have seen little since I last wrote, but she was in much better spirits when I did see her than I had found her for a long time before."

"Pray write to Emilia," she added.

Mary was helped to sustain her pride by the attentions of the fascinating Prince Mavrocordato.

"Do you not envy my luck," she enquired of Mrs. Gisborne, "that, having begun Greek, an amiable, young, agreeable, and learned Greek prince comes every morning to give me a lesson of an hour and a-half?"

By the beginning of summer, Mary and Shelley were visiting Emilia about twice a week, and Shelley was acting as mediator between the fair captive and one of her suitors.

"I have contrived," he informed Claire, "to calm the despairing Swain, much to the satisfaction of poor Emilia: who in that Convent of hers sees everything as through a mist, ten times its natural size."

The farcical aspect of this affair is enhanced by the fact that Shelley, at this time, conceived a distaste for Mary's self-appointed tutor, Mavrocordato.

"The Greek Prince," he added in this letter to Claire, "comes sometimes, and I reproach my own savage disposition that so agreeable accomplished and ammiable a person is not more agreeable to me." Even Shelley's spelling (less erratic, on the whole, than Mary's) suffered from his bewildered inability to locate his feelings of resentment at the young Greek's attentions to Mary.

It was not until the following spring that Mary broke her restraint on the subject of Emilia, and permitted herself the luxury of a few sardonic observations to Mrs. Gisborne:

"Emilia married Biondi—we hear that she leads him & his mother (to use a vulgarism) *a devil of a life*— The conclusion of our friendship *à la Italiana* puts me in mind of a nursery rhyme which runs thus—

As I was going down Cranbourne lane,
Cranbourne lane was dirty,
And there I met a pretty maid,
Who dropt to me a curt'sey;
I gave her cakes, I gave her wine,
I gave her sugar candy,
But oh! the little naughty girl!
She asked me for some brandy.

Now turn Cranbourne lane into Pisan acquaintances, which I am sure are dirty enough, & brandy into that wherewithall to buy brandy (& that no small sum *pero*) & you have [the] whole story of Shelley's Italian platonics.''

But the year in which the Emilia Viviani disturbance throve and then dwindled was not without its other distractions. In January 1821, the Williams', an attractive young couple (not officially married) who were anxious to join Shelley's party, arrived in Pisa. In many ways they were welcome, providing a relief from the company of Tom Medwin, who made a continual nuisance of himself by interrupting the Shelleys' writing or studies to read his own dreary effusions.

Of Edward and Jane Williams, Mary informed Claire:

"Jane is certainly very pretty but she wants animation and sense; her conversation is *nothing particular,* and she speaks in a slow monotonous voice: but she appears good tempered and tolerant. *Ned* seems the picture of good humor and obligingness, he is lively and possesses great talent in drawing so that with him one is never at a loss for subjects of conversation. (. . .) Of course they have somewhat helped from our shoulders the burthen of <u>Tom</u> which was beginning to be very heavy. (. . .) M[edwin] has no sympathy with our tastes or conversation—he is infinitely commonplace and is as silent as a fireskreen but not half so useful; except that he sometimes mends a pen.''

Shelley's circle at Pisa was now widening. It was as if, in response to some dramatic law, the actors were assembling on a stage, each a unit of suspense in attendance on the tragic dénouement. Keats, now in the last year of his life, was invited to join the Shelleys, but did not come.

In March 1821, Claire learnt that Byron had placed Allegra in a convent at Bagnacavallo. This convent was not far from Byron's establishment at Ravenna, where, with his latest and last lady, the Countess Guiccioli, he was living, as he claimed, in "the strictest adultery." Byron had been extremely taken with Allegra.

"She is very pretty," he wrote to his half-sister, "remarkably intelligent, and a great favourite with every body; . . . she has very blue eyes, and that singular forehead, fair curly hair, and a devil of a spirit." That had been two years ago.

Claire had always regretted parting with her daughter, and had made every endeavour to get her back. But the more she plied Byron with this demand, the more obstinate did he become. He disapproved of Claire, and most of all, of the Shelleys' mode of life and their vegetarian diet. The child, he said, should not be permitted "to perish of starvation, and green fruit, or be taught to believe that there is no Deity."

"Claire writes me the most insolent letters about Allegra," he complained to Hoppner, Allegra's former guardian; "see what a man gets by taking care of natural children! Were it not for the poor child's sake, I am almost tempted to send her back to her atheistical mother, but that would be too bad: . . . If Claire thinks that she shall ever interfere with the child's morals or education, she mistakes: she never shall. The girl shall be a Christian and a married woman, if possible. As to seeing her, she may see her—under proper restrictions; but she is not to throw every thing into confusion with her Bedlam behaviour."

From Byron's point of view, this seemed reasonable enough, though there was more than a hint of a deep-rooted distaste for Claire motivating his apparent solicitude for Allegra. Claire, unbalanced and sensational as always, could not control her own passionate need for the child; and so they had wrangled until Byron's domestic arrangements made it more convenient to dispose of his daughter in the convent. His argument, devised to sound like sense, was addressed once more to Hoppner. The child, he said, was now four years old and beyond the servants' control; he was himself unable to attend to her, and had no woman at the head of his house who could do so. The Countess Guiccioli, however, who was very much at the head of his house, he did not mention in this context. But, he continued, reasonably enough:

"It is also fit that I should add that I by no means intended, nor intend, to give a *natural* child an *English* education, because with the disadvantages of her birth, her after-settlement would be doubly difficult. Abroad, with a fair foreign education and a portion of five or six thousand pounds, she might and may marry very respectably. (. . .) It is, besides, my wish that she should be a Roman Catholic. (. . .)"

Mary and Shelley comforted Claire as best they could, but Shelley was absorbed in his new friends and his work, Mary in her child, her novel and her Greek studies; and they did not feel the urgency of Claire's anxiety as they had when she was living with them. But they tried to cheer her with news of their friends. When Prince Mavrocordato came one day in April with news which gladdened Mary as if it had been her personal triumph, she wrote immediately to Claire,

"Greece has declared its freedom! Prince Mavrocordato had made us expect this event for some weeks past. Yesterday he came *rayonnant de joie*—he had been ill for some days, but he forgot all his pains. Ipselanti, a Greek general in the service of Russia, has collected together 10,000 Greeks & entered Wallachia, declaring the liberty of his country. . . . The worst part of this news for us is that our amiable prince will leave us—he will of course join his countrymen as soon as possible."

The Williams lived but four miles away from the Shelleys' villa at San Giuliano di Pisa, and they all met constantly. "It was a pleasant summer," Mary wrote later, "bright in all but Shelley's health and inconstant spirits; yet he enjoyed himself greatly, and became more attached to the part of the country where chance appeared to cast us."

They had bought a small boat which used daily to bear them up and down the canal between the Williams's house and their own, and on many pleasant excursions. The news of Keats's death, however, caused a temporary pause in their happiness, and Shelley felt it deeply.

But in spite of these distractions, when Claire's misery became acute, Mary found time to write her a long letter, and tried to reason with her. Mary and Claire, in fact, were never on more friendly terms than when they were separated.

"Your anxiety for A[llegra]'s health is to a great degree unfounded," she wrote; "Venice, its stinking canals & dirty streets, is enough to kill any child; but you ought to know, & any one will tell you so, that the towns of Romagna, situated where Bagnacavallo is, enjoy the best air in Italy. (. . .)"

Claire had a plan in mind for snatching and running away with the child, but Mary counselled against this.

"No one can more entirely agree with you than I in thinking that as soon as possible A. ought to be taken out of the hands of one as remorseless as he is unprincipled. But at the same time it appears to me that the present moment is exactly the one in which this is the most difficult—time cannot add to these difficulties for they can never be greater. (. . .)"

Mary proceeded to warn Claire of the impossibility of penetrating the convent where high walls and bolted doors enclosed Allegra. Even were Claire successful, she asserted, the regular habits of the convent would cause the child to be missed immediately; and she warned Claire about Byron's character:

he vowed that if you annoyed him he would place A. in some secret convent, he declared that you should have nothing to do with her & that he would move heaven & earth to prevent your interference. L. B[yron] is at present a man of 12 or 15 thousand a year, he is on the spot, a man reckless of the ill he does others, obstinate to desperation in the pursuance of his plans or his revenge. What then would you do having A. on the outside of the convent walls? (. . .) You probably wish to secret yourself. But L. B[yron] would use any means to find you out —& the story he might make up—a man stared at by the Grand Duke—with money at command—above all on the spot to put energy into every pursuit, would he not find you?

[81]

Mary let her imagination dwell on the possibility of a duel between Byron and Shelley—the idea of retrieving Allegra without Byron's consent, she told Claire, must be abandoned for the present. Another reason why Claire should be patient occurred to Mary:

Another thing I mention which though sufficiently ridiculous may have some weight with you. Spring is our unlucky season. No spring has passed for us without some piece of ill luck. Remember the first spring at Mrs. Harbottle's.[3] The second when you became acquainted with L. B.[yron] the Third we went to Marlow—no wise thing at least—The fourth our uncomfortable residence in London—The fifth our Roman misery—the sixth Paolo at Pisa—the seventh a mixture of Emilia & a Chancery suit—Now the aspect of the Autumnal Heavens has on the contrary been with few exceptions, favourable to us—What think you of this? It is in your own style, but it has often struck me.

This argument, "in her own style," calmed Claire meantime. The Shelleys pitied Claire, but they both felt that Allegra was, at least, safe. Their relationship with Byron was, however, a strange one; he repelled them in his absence and fascinated them in his presence, as he did many who crossed his path. And suffer as they did at his hands, over other matters than this of Claire, and though Mary and Shelley professed themselves sickened by Byron's blatant immorality, they could never bring themselves to break with him. Shelley, of course, could always find common ground with Byron in conversation. None the less, the Shelleys were numbered among those many friends of Byron who feared as much as they admired him.

For Byron's part, he sought to justify himself in his behaviour over Allegra by making a great deal of scandal about Claire's lack of morals; while she retaliated in like measure, but without the forces of title and fortune to support her.

In the spring, Byron invited Shelley to stay with him. When the invitation was renewed in August, Shelley decided to go to him at

3. When Mary's first baby died in 1815.

Ravenna, for he now learned that Byron was leaving the vicinity of Allegra's convent, and was anxious to see what plans were being made for her.

Mary, at home, had now reached the copying stage of her novel *Valperga* and was sitting for a miniature portrait by Edward Williams which he was hoping to finish for Shelley's birthday. The proceeds of *Valperga* were to go to Godwin, and the fact relieved Mary's mind a little. But she was not happy at heart. Once Claire had gone, she had hoped to have some peace with Shelley, but it was not so. More and still more people surrounded them; others were to come.

Journal 4th August—Williams all day. Read Homer. Walk. (. . .) Williams finishes my miniature. Shelley's birthday. Seven years are now gone; what changes! what a life! We now appear tranquil; yet who knows what wind—I will not prognosticate evil, we have had enough of it. When I came to Italy, I said all is well if it were permanent; it was more passing than an Italian twilight. I now say the same. May it be a Polar day; yet that, too, has an end.

Chapter 7

The Magus Zoroaster, my dead child,
Met his own image walking in the garden.
SHELLEY, *Prometheus Unbound*

Mary was always conscious of
the transience of things. Experience had endorsed this awareness,
and in every appearance of tranquillity she saw, and saw correctly
so far as her own life was concerned, an approaching turmoil. It
often seems that such people invite the Furies by their own apprehension, that misfortune gains confidence, as a fierce animal will at
the sense of a stranger's fear.

It was not long before Mary's "prognostications of evil" took
shape. From Ravenna, Shelley wrote to say that he had sat up with
Byron all night, talking "a great deal of poetry, and such matters."
The other subject of their conversation was one that caused Mary
terrible distress.

The rumour about Shelley's "Neapolitan charge" was spreading,
with elaborations. "It seems that Elise," Shelley disclosed, "ac-
tuated either by some inconceivable malice for our dismissing her,
or bribed by my enemies, or making common cause with her infa-

mous husband, has persuaded the Hoppners of a story so monstrous and incredible that they much have been prone to believe any evil to have believed such assertions upon such evidence. Mr. Hoppner wrote to Lord Byron to state this story as the reason why he declined any further communications with us, and why he advised him to do the same. Elise says that Claire was my mistress; that is very well, and so far there is nothing new; all the world has heard so much, and people may believe or not believe as they think good. She then proceeds to say that Claire was with child by me; that I gave her the most violent medicine to produce abortion; that this not succeeding she was brought to bed, and that I immediately tore the child from her and sent it to the Foundling Hospital. I quote Mr. Hoppner's words—and this is stated to have taken place in the winter after we left Este. In addition, she says that both I and Claire treated *you* in the most shameful manner, that I neglected and beat you, and that Claire never let a day pass without offering you insults of the most violent kind, in which she was abetted by me."

Shelley urged Mary to write to Mrs. Hoppner. "I need not dictate what you should say," he added.

Mary, in a cold rage, wrote at once to Mrs. Hoppner, enclosing her letter in one to Shelley.

"Shocked beyond all measure as I was," she exclaimed to Shelley, "I instantly wrote the enclosed. (. . .) I wrote to you with far different feelings last night—beloved friend—our bark is indeed tempest tost but love me as you have ever done & God preserve my child to me and our enemies shall not be too much for us."

To Mrs. Hoppner, she told something of Elise and her past knowledge of the girl, continuing:

"I am perfectly convinced in my own mind that Shelley never had an improper connexion with Claire—at the time specified in Elise's letter, the winter after we quitted Este, I suppose while she was with us, and that was at Naples, we lived in lodgings where I had momentary entrance into every room, and such a thing could not have passed unknown to me."

After some words in defence of Claire, Mary added:

"Need I say that the union between my husband and myself has ever been undisturbed. Love caused our first imprudences, love which improved by esteem, a perfect trust one in the other, a confidence and affection which, visited as we have been by severe calamities (have we not lost two children?)[1] has encreased daily, and knows no bounds."

And she reproached Mrs. Hoppner for her gossip-mongering:

"You ought to have paused before you tried to convince the father of her [Claire's] child of such unheard-of atrocities on her part. If his generosity & knowledge of the world had not made him reject the slander with the ridicule it deserved what irretrievable mischief you would have occasioned her!"

But Byron had not made the generous rejection of the story that he had in fact claimed when reporting it to Shelley. When Hoppner had told him the slanderous tale, Byron had replied:

"Of the facts (. . .) there can be little doubt; it is just like them."

Byron had, however, promised Hoppner not to repeat the tale to Shelley—a promise which was soon overcome, when he met Shelley, by his love of scandal. And so, when Shelley, at Mary's request, handed her letter to Byron to read and pass on to the Hoppners, Byron realised that his indiscretion would thus be revealed. The letter was found among Byron's papers after his death, and it is not immoderate to assume that he never sent it to the Hoppners, but allowed a serious and unjust charge against Shelley to stand rather than suffer a well-deserved minor stain on his own honour.[2]

1. They had actually lost three children, but Mary was not prepared to weaken her defence of Shelley by enlightening Mrs. Hoppner as to their first, illegitimate child.

2. Miss Glynn Grylls very justly quotes a defence of Byron in this matter, from *Lord Byron's Correspondence*, edited by John Murray (John Murray, London, 1922), with the remark, "The vexed question must remain open. Only the discovery of further Hoppner papers can settle it." In the passage she quotes in full, a case is made for Byron on the grounds that the letter has come down to us opened, the seal broken. The editor believes that the Hoppners did receive the letter and broke the seal themselves. Byron, he argues, had been shown the letter by Shelley, and could hardly have wished to read it again; whereas John Cam Hobhouse, who had access to Byron's papers after his death, is said to have been too "honourable and punctilious" to open a letter addressed to someone else, and must have found the letter open.

In the present writer's view, this argument has serious flaws. Apart from the question as to why Byron should be in possession of a letter that had been seen

Shelley was now doing his best to come to some arrangement about Allegra with Byron, who was talking of leaving Italy with his Countess; but Shelley had fallen under Byron's spell, was enjoying his company, and could not press too hard.

"You will be surprised to hear that L[ord] B[yron] has decided upon coming to *Pisa*, in case he shall be able, with my assistance, to prevail upon his mistress to remain in Italy, of which I think there is little doubt," Shelley told Mary. "He wishes for a large and magnificent house. (. . .)"

Shelley spent three hours with Allegra at her convent, and sent home a full description of her appearance and manner.

"Her light and airy figure and her graceful motions were a striking contrast to the other children there. She seemed a thing of a finer and a higher order."

Shelley found her unnaturally obedient, and was surprised when she shared the sweets he had brought her with the other children. "This is not much like the old Allegra," he mentioned sadly. But before he left, Allegra made him run all over the convent with her, "like a mad thing."

The Shelleys decided to stay in Pisa for the winter, and moved from the Baths into the top flat of the Tre Palazzi, a large villa on the Lung'Arno, while the Williams' took a lower flat in the same house.

"So here we live," wrote Mary to Mrs. Gisborne, "Lord Byron just opposite to us in Casa Lanfranchi. (. . .) So Pisa, you see, has become a little nest of singing birds. You will be both surprised and delighted at the work just about to be published by him; his *Cain*, which is in the highest style of imaginative poetry. It made a great impression upon me, and appears almost a revelation, from its power and beauty. Shelley rides with him; I, of course, see little of

and opened by Hoppner, we cannot suppose that Byron would not have broken the seal himself, for if, as is likely, he sealed the letter in Shelley's presence, he might well have wished to re-read it before deciding not to send it. And also, we cannot assume that Hobhouse was entirely "honourable and punctilious," since he was not above literary jugglery in other circumstances connected with Byron —in his collaboration with the Italian poet, Foscolo, for example—and should not be too readily presumed incapable of opening the letter if it were sealed when he found it.

him. The lady *whom he serves* is a nice pretty girl without pretensions, good hearted and amiable. (. . .)"

Mary and Shelley were now anxious about Leigh Hunt, whom Shelley and Byron had invited to Italy to edit a periodical which was to publish mainly the work of their circle. Hunt had reported, ". . . about the 21st of October we shall all set off, myself, Marianne, and the six children." But no further news had reached them yet.

Mary spent much time with Byron's mistress, referred to in her journal as "the Guiccioli." With her, Mary rode almost daily though she saw little of Byron, to their mutual satisfaction. Shelley, however, saw a great deal of Byron and the Countess's brother, who had accompanied the lovers to Pisa.

Only two journal entries between September and December show a departure in Mary's routine from the often-repeated "Call on the Guiccioli. Ride out with her. . . ." or "The Williams' and Medwin in the evening." The first of these is,

> *Journal 29th November*—† I mark this day because I begin my Greek again, and that is a study which ever delights me. I do not feel the bore of it, as in learning another language, although it be so difficult, it so richly repays one; yet I read little, for I am not well.

and the second,

> *9th December*—Go to church at Dr. Nott's. Walk with Edward & Jane to the Garden.

It was with relief that Mary had laid down her task in finishing *Valperga*, for the past year had been full of irritations from which she had been forced to wrest whatever quiet hours she could, necessary to creative work. Her renewed study of Homer soothed her spirits, although her health was far from good.

Her first visit to "church" was followed by others; the services were held on the ground floor of the house they occupied. These visits were undertaken, as Mary told Mrs. Gisborne, "for good neighbourhood's sake," on the invitation of the presiding minister, Dr. Nott, though they made a rare stir among the English at Pisa who knew Shelley's views on religion. Mary suspected that on one occasion when she was present, Dr. Nott preached a sermon directly against Shelley, but when she taxed the clergyman she was assured this was not so.

Undertaken "for good neighbourhood's sake" or no, these visits to church show that Mary was beginning to branch out on fields of enquiry for herself, where hitherto she had followed Shelley's route. But at this stage in her development, Shelley's own growing tolerance encouraged her independence of thought.

By the end of the year they had heard from Hunt and his family, whom it was proposed to lodge in Byron's palace, that their passage had been delayed first by storms and then by Mrs. Hunt's illness. It was not until 13th May 1822 that the family left England.

But in the New Year another wanderer had encamped at Pisa. This was Edward John Trelawny, a friend of the Williams' and Medwin, and a Cornish adventurer. He was delighted with Shelley, of whom he had heard so many frightful tales.

"Was it possible this mild-looking beardless boy could be the veritable monster at war with all the world?" he wrote of his meeting with Shelley, whose marvellous powers of conversation soon convinced the visitor that he was indeed the poet.

Mary found their new friend a bracing addition to their party.

Journal 19th January—Copy. Walk with Jane. The Opera in the evening. Trelawny is extravagant—un giovane stravagante (though not as the Venetian Gondoliere meant) partly natural & partly perhaps put on—but it suits him well, & if his abrupt but not unpolished manners be assumed, they are nevertheless in unison with his Moorish face (for he looks oriental yet not Asiatic) his dark hair his herculean form. And then there is an air of extreme good nature which pervades his whole countenance, especially when he smiles, which assures me that his heart is good. He tells strange stories of himself, horrific ones, so that they harrow one up, while with his emphatic but unmodulated voice, his simple yet strong language, he pourtrays the most frightful situations; then all these adventures took place between the ages of 13 & 20. I believe them now I see the man, &, tired with the everyday sleepiness of human intercourse, I am glad to meet with one, who, among other valuable qualities, has the rare merit of interesting my imagination.

Meantime Jane Williams charmed Shelley with her sweet grace and lovely singing voice. She would play the piano in the evenings, or the guitar which Shelley had given her. Mary, too, felt warmly towards their pretty friend whom she saw almost daily.

Except for the Hunts, the Pisan circle was complete. Mary felt particularly aware of their present tranquillity, and as usual, began to apprehend the climacteric of fortune. Some of her journal entries are unusually introspective.

Journal 7th February—Read Homer, Tacitus, "Emile." Shelley & Edward depart for La Spezia. Walk with Jane, & to the Opera with her in the evening. With E. Trelawny afterwards to Mrs. Beauclerck's ball. During a long, long evening in mixed society, dancing & music—how often do one's sensations change, and, swift as the west wind drives the shadows of clouds across the sunny hill or the waving corn, so swift do sentiments pass, (. . .) painting—yet, oh! not disfiguring—the serenity of the mind. It is then that life seems to weigh itself, and hosts of memories and imaginations, thrown into one scale, makes the other kick the beam. You remember what you have felt, what you have dreamt; yet you dwell on the shadowy side, and lost hopes and death, such as you have seen it, seems to cover all things with a funeral pall. The time that was, is, & will be, presses upon you, &, standing in the centre of a moving circle, you "slide giddily as the world reels." You look to Heaven and would demand of the everlasting stars that the thoughts and passions which are your life may be as everliving as they. You would demand from the blue empyrean that your mind might be as clear as it, and that the tears which gather in your eyes might be the shower that would drain from its profoundest depths the springs of weakness and sorrow. But where are the stars? Where are the blue empyreans? A ceiling clouds that, and a thousand swift consuming lights supply the place of the eternal ones of Heaven. The enthusiast suppresses her tears, crushes her opening thoughts, and—

[90]

But all is changed; some word, some look excite the lagging blood, laughter dances in the eyes & the spirits rise proportionally high.

> "The Queen is all for revels, her light heart,
> Unladen from the heaviness of state,
> Bestows itself upon delightfulness."

8th February—Sometimes I awaken from my ordinary monotony & my thoughts flow until, as it is exquisite pain to stop the flowing of the blood, so it is painful to check expression & make the overflowing mind return to its usual channel. I feel a kind of tenderness to those, whoever they may be (even though strangers), who awaken this train & touch a chord so full of harmony & thrilling music, when I would tear the veil from this strange world & pierce with eagle eyes beyond the sun; when every idea, strange & changeful, is another step in the ladder by which I would climb the—.[3]

Read "Emile." Jane dines with me, walk with her, E. Trelawny & Jane in the evening. Trelawny tells us a number of interesting & amusing stories of his early life. Read the third canto of "L'Inferno."

They say that Providence is shown by the extraction that may ever be made of good from evil, that we draw our virtues from our faults. So I am to thank God for making me weak. I might say, "Thy will be done," but I can never applaud the permitter of self-degradation, though dignity & superior wisdom arise from its bitter & burning ashes.

25th February—What a mart this world is! Feelings, sentiments—more invaluable than gold or precious stones—are the coin, & what is bought? Contempt, discontent & disappointment, if indeed the mind be not loaded with drearier memories. And what say the worldly to this? Use Spartan coin, pay away iron & lead alone, & store up your precious metal. But alas! from nothing, nothing comes, or, as all things seem to degenerate, give lead & you will receive clay—the most con-

3. Mary was probably interrupted at this point.

temptible of all lives, is where you live in the world & none of your passions or affections are called into action. I am convinced I could not live thus, & as Sterne says, that in solitude he would worship a tree, so in the world I should attach myself to those who bore the semblance of those qualities which I admire. But it is not this that I want; let me love the trees, the skies & the ocean, & that all encompassing spirit of which I may soon become a part—let me, in my fellow creatures, love that which is—& not fix my affections on a fair form endued with imaginary attributes; where goodness, kindness & talent are, let me love & admire them at their just rate, neither adding or diminishing, &, above all, let me fearlessly descend into the remotest caverns of my own mind, carry the torch of self-knowledge into its dimmest recesses: but too happy if I dislodge any evil spirit or enshrine a new deity in some hitherto uninhabited nook.

Mary was now finding her own inward reservoir of certitude; she was attempting to formulate for herself a philosophy distinct from Godwin's or Shelley's, and this new degree of self-perception was stimulated both by her Greek studies and, in a sense, by the new bevy of friends who surrounded her and forced her in upon herself, to analyse and compare. In the past, Shelley's friends had for the most part been people whose interests coincided with his literary ones; she had lived then on a level of compressed, if narrow, absorption in literature and ideas. But these new acquaintances, diverting as she found them, had no immediate sense of vocation; their interests were wider and somewhat shallower, they were more active, than those Mary had experienced in her previous associates. This now brought Mary to recognise that she perforce occupied two worlds, and she began to notice some of the consequent disadvantages: "(. . .) it is painful to check expression and make the overflowing mind return to its usual channel."

Mary might have felt resentful towards Shelley for casting out invitations far and wide; but she understood something of his present agitated mood and need for activity. She was, as ever, willing to accept all manifestations of his personality as it existed, and not merely as she wished it to be: "(. . .) let me, in my fellow creatures, love that which is—& not fix my affections on a fair form endued with imaginary attributes; where goodness, kindness & talent are, let me love & admire them at their just rate, neither adding or diminishing. (. . .)" This was her practical manifesto of love; and as such, was one which held potentialities for an enduring alliance between herself and Shelley.

Self-examination of this order made Mary more placid and kindly. When Claire wrote to say she was unhappy, and wished to leave Italy, Mary wrote to her with some tenderness, bidding her come to Pisa:

"I think in every way it would make you happier to come here —and when here, other views may arise—at least discuss your plans in the midst of your friends before you go. . . ."

When Claire heard that Byron's mother-in-law had died, leaving him a substantial fortune, she once more approached him with a request to see Allegra, mentioning her intention to leave Italy.

"I assure you," she pleaded, "I can no longer resist the internal inexplicable feeling which haunts me that I shall never see her more."

But Byron was in no haste to consider Claire's forebodings, and meantime she became more and more frantic. She arrived at Pisa in response to the Shelleys' summons, and while they endeavoured to calm her, they spoke of the summer and their future plans.

Shelley had just returned with Williams from a house-hunting trip to La Spezia, having found only one house available. They had hoped to find several houses for their colony, which, Mary informed Mrs. Gisborne, "will be a large one, too large I am afraid for unity—yet I hope not—there will be Lord Byron, who will have a large & beautiful boat built on purpose by some English navy officers at Genoa—there will be the Countess Guiccioli and her brother—the Williams whom you know—Trelawny—a kind of half Arab Englishman. (. . .) We are to have a smaller boat. (. . .)"

Mary was expecting another child, and as always during her pregnancies she was frequently ill, and was prevented from undertaking much activity. So on a second trip in search of a house, the Williams' went, accompanied by Claire, leaving Shelley with Mary —mercifully, for she was to need his presence.

The Williams' party had no sooner left than a message arrived to say that Allegra had died of typhus fever at her convent. Their first anxiety, after receiving this shock, was to find a way of keeping this news from Claire until she should be established somewhere remote from Byron; for they had every reason to fear that in her passion of grief she might be driven to any wild revenge on the child's father.

They knew of only one furnished house, the Villa Magni at San Terenzo, a fishing hamlet on the Bay of Lerici; and as soon as the Williams' party had returned, Claire was induced to accompany Mary to San Terenzo with little Percy Florence and Trelawny. Shelley and the Williams', who had remained behind to pack, hastily joined them, and as no other house was to be found in the neighbourhood the two couples had to share. Here Shelley broke the news to Claire that her child was dead.

"You may judge," Mary told Mrs. Gisborne in June, "of what was her first burst of grief and despair; however she reconciled herself to her fate sooner than we expected; and although, of course, until she form new ties she will always grieve, yet she is now tranquil—more tranquil than when prophesying her disaster; she was forever forming plans for getting her child from a place she judged but too truly would be fatal to her. She has now returned to Florence, and I do not know whether she will join us again."

Allegra's death was the tragedy of Claire's life, but the effect on Mary, though less profound, was enough to tell on her precarious health. She had known Allegra from babyhood, and this child's death, following on the fate of Mary's own children, plunged her once more into that abysmal gloom which had followed William's death.

She tried to take an interest in her friends and all their doings. Byron, fortunately, had not joined them, and Trelawny, who was to command his vessel, had gone to Leghorn. Their own boat had arrived, and Mary duly reported their new acquisition to Mrs. Gisborne:

Shelley's boat is a beautiful creature; Henry would admire her greatly; though only 24 feet by 8 feet she is a perfect little ship, and looks twice her size. She had one fault, she was to have been built in partnership with Williams and Trelawny. Trelawny chose the name of the *Don Juan,* and we acceded; but when Shelley took her entirely on himself we changed the name to the *Ariel.* Lord Byron chose to take fire at this, and determined that she should be called after the Poem; wrote to Roberts to have the name painted on the mainsail, and she arrived thus disfigured. For days and nights, full twenty-one, did Shelley and Edward ponder on her anabaptism, and the washing out the primeval stain. Turpentine, spirits of wine, buccata, all were tried, and it became dappled and no more. At length the piece has been taken out and reefs put, so that the sail does not look worse. I do not know what Lord Byron will say, but Lord and Poet as he is, he could not be allowed to make a coal barge of our boat.[4]

The Shelleys were well and truly sick of Byron.

Mary went out in the boat occasionally, but she was too ill to enjoy sailing. Domestic arrangements were annoying her, for it was one thing to spend the evenings with Jane and Edward Williams relaxing in Jane's melodious sweetness, and another to share an uncomfortable house with her. Today, a lively village has grown up around the Casa Magni, Shelley's last house. But in those days food could only be obtained from a distance, transported by sea or across mountain paths. Mary confided to her faithful Mrs. Gisborne,

"(. . .) the Williams have taken up their abode with us, and their servants and mine quarrel like cats and dogs; and besides, you may imagine how ill a large family agrees with my laziness, when accounts and domestic concerns come to be talked of."

4. It appears that the real cause of the grievance was the vulgar painting of the name on the sail, and not the name itself. The boat was referred to by Shelley, Williams and others as *Don Juan.* But it seems clear at least from Mary's letter that the "anabaptism" of the boat was in question at first. It is possible that the vessel was renamed but was referred to as the *Don Juan* from habit. It is also possible that Shelley was content with refitting the sail and did not trouble, after that, about removing the name from the prow, or with the "anabaptism" of the boat.

Shelley, entranced with his new boat, could not easily tolerate Mary's melancholy. When she could not sail with him he took Jane Williams, whose conversation, with him at least, was not soured by domestic discussions. Shelley was extremely attracted to Jane, but his feelings for her were coloured by nothing of the passion-in-the-void which had marked his brief infatuation with Emilia Viviani. Jane was gracious, feminine and pleasing, and she exerted these qualities, without effort, at the very time when Mary could not do so. Shelley was hurt by Mary's apparent coldness, which was a symptom of the very poor state of health she was then enduring. The hasty departure from Pisa with Claire following the horror of Allegra's death had a disastrous effect on her, and Shelley felt sorely her lack of participation in his interests and was bewildered by her withdrawn aspect. He envied the Williams' mutual contentment, and in a poem addressed to Edward Williams declared,

> When I return to my cold home, you ask
> Why I am not as I have ever been,
> *You* spoil me for the task
> Of acting a forced part in life's dull scene—

Many a tender lyric, too, he addressed to Jane, who was flattered by Shelley's manner towards her; however, she made no serious attempt to come between Mary and Shelley. His feelings for her, in any case, were not deep ones, and if Mary had been her normal self, Shelley would not have paid Jane undue attention. And his observations on Jane were by no means unequivocal.

"I like Jane more and more; . . . she has a taste for music and an elegance of form and motions, that compensate in some degree for the lack of literary refinement," he remarked to John Gisborne, while to Claire he confessed:

"Jane is by no means acquiescent in the system of things, and she pines after her own house and saucepans to which no one can have a claim except herself. It is a pity that any one so pretty should be so selfish."

And two days later:

"Jane the other day was very much discontented with her situation here, on account of some of our servants having taken something of hers, but now as is the custom, calm has succeeded to storm. . . . Mary, though ill, is good."

Mary's "goodness" had followed upon some "hysterical affections" which Shelley had mentioned in a previous letter. Actually Mary was distracted by Jane's domestic tantrums and her own symptoms of a serious impending illness. On 16th June she had a miscarriage and was not alone in believing herself to be dying. She was rescued only by Shelley's resourcefulness in procuring a bucket of ice in which he promptly made Mary sit. The doctor they had summoned arrived belatedly, by which time Mary had passed the critical stage. It was to this illness and her sense of the imminence of death that Mary referred many years later, when she wrote,

> My feeling . . . was, I go to no new creation, I enter under no new laws. The God that made this beautiful world (& I was then at Lerici, surrounded by the most beautiful manifestations of the visible creation) made that into which I go; as there is beauty & love here, such is there, & I felt as if my spirit would when it left my frame be received & sustained by a beneficent & gentle Power. I had no fear, rather, though, I had no active wish—I had a passive satisfaction in death. Whether the nature of my illness—debility from loss of blood, without pain—caused this tranquillity of soul, I cannot tell; but so it was, & it had this blessed effect, that I have never since anticipated death with terror, and even if a violent death (which is the most repugnant to human nature) menaced me, I think I could, after the first shock, turn to the memory of that hour, & renew its emotion of perfect resignation.

It was some time before Mary recovered; her spirits were lethargic and low, but Shelley showed her great consideration, and began to understand her a little better. When Godwin started to harry them again, Shelley concealed her father's letters from Mary, but knew he would have to discuss them with her before long. This concealment, and the anxiety he had suffered when Mary was in danger, placed Shelley himself in a state of nervous tension; always prone to harrowing dreams and waking hallucinations, Shelley was at this moment more than ever susceptible to them.

These were young people. It should be remembered that they were all—Shelley, Mary, Claire, Edward and Jane—still in their twenties. They were isolated in a small, and at that time quite savage, fishing community on the Ligurian coast. On the night of 22nd June 1822 Mary was awakened by Shelley's scream as he rushed into her sick room. He had dreamt, he told her, that the Williams' had walked naked into his room, their skins torn and bloodstained. Edward had said, "Get up, Shelley, the sea is flooding the house & it is all coming down." And when Shelley had looked out on the terrace, he had seen, in his dream, the sea pouring in. Then the dream changed and he saw the figure of himself strangling Mary, and, on waking, had rushed shrieking into Mary's room. Next morning he told Mary that he had recently experienced many "visions," as Mary later recounted: "He had seen the figure of himself, which met him as he walked on the terrace, & said to him, 'How long do you mean to be content?' "

An atmosphere of tautness pervaded the Villa Magni during these weeks. Even the phlegmatic Jane had a waking visionary experience; she "saw" Shelley walking on the terrace when in fact he was not in the house. And Edward Williams' journal records how he and Shelley were talking one night on the same terrace by moonlight when Shelley "grasped me violently by the arm and stared steadfastly on the white surf that broke upon the beach under our feet . . . and declared that he saw, as plainly as he saw me, a naked child, Allegra, rise from the sea, and clap its hands as in joy, smiling at him."

In mid-June the Hunts arrived in Genoa, and Shelley's circle was complete. On 1st July Shelley and Williams, with a sailor-boy, Charles Vivian, set out in the boat for Leghorn to meet them. Shelley was worried about Hunt; he was rightly uneasy about how Byron would receive their friend, after so long a delay, and with such an entourage of a family. Shelley was inclined to bring the Hunts back with him, and Mary feared this above all things. She was ill and exhausted and could not face the trial of having another, and at that a large, family thrust upon her. In desperation she wrote a distracted note to Hunt, pleading with him not to come: "I wish I could write more—I wish I were with you to assist you—I wish I could break my chains & leave this dungeon. . . ."

The news Shelley sent her of the Hunts was depressing. Byron, on whose invitation and for whose purpose Hunt had made the journey, now proposed to leave Italy. Marianne Hunt was ill and the doctor pronounced her case to be hopeless—wrongly, as it transpired.

"How are you, my best Mary?" Shelley enquired after his news had been recounted. "Write especially how is your health and how your spirits are, and whether you are not more reconciled to staying at Lerici, at least during the summer.

"You have no idea how I am hurried and occupied; I have not a moment's leisure but will write by next post. Ever, dearest Mary, Yours affectionately—S.

"I have found the translation of the 'Symposium.' "

On Monday 8th July, Shelley and Edward were to return, but the bay was so stormy that Mary and Jane entertained no thoughts of their having set out. But on Tuesday and Wednesday it was calm, and when no sight of the well-known sails appeared, the women believed that some business had detained their husbands, and awaited letters from them. The day when the post usually arrived was Friday, and on that day they received only a letter from Hunt to Shelley asking how had he got home, for there had been bad weather after they had sailed on Monday.

Only then did Jane and Mary realise the truth, though snatching at hope that the men had returned to Leghorn. Hunt had no news, nor Trelawny, nor Byron, except that Shelley and Williams had sailed on the Monday for Lerici.

Trelawny accompanied the widows to their home and there left them, setting out to explore the remote hope that the men had been cast alive on some farther shore. It was not until 19th July that Trelawny returned, with the final, ghastly information that the bodies of Shelley and Williams had been washed ashore.

Chapter 8

A cold heart! Have I a cold heart? God knows! But none need envy the icy region this heart encircles—And at least the tears are hot. . . .
MARY SHELLEY, *Journal,* 17th November 1822

For many months after Shelley's body had been burnt on the funeral pyre, and the wrangle about Shelley's heart, snatched from the flames by Trelawny, had died down, Mary lived half her life in retrospect, the other half in preparing herself to face an uncertain future. "My life is chalked out to me—it will be one of study only—except for my poor boy—," she wrote to Medwin.

To Mary's regret, Jane Williams left in September to join her friends in England. Claire had gone to her brother in Vienna, while Mary, anxious to help Hunt with his new paper, *The Liberal*—a service she was the better enabled to perform since she possessed Shelley's manuscripts—and having no wish to face London and the poverty which the high cost of living there would enforce on her, took a house with the Hunts in Genoa. But Mary was unsettled during the months she remained in Italy with the Hunts; in their badly-managed household she could not apply herself to study or writing which alone, she knew, could direct her thoughts from constant reflection upon her past life and present tragic situation.

She was surprised at first that Hunt's manner towards her was cool. As she recalled her past life with Shelley, she thought of the sum total of eight years, a companionship of the rarest order. But Hunt focussed his attention only on the last weeks of Shelley's life, sadly embittered, as Shelley had confided to Hunt in those last tragic days, by Mary's low spirits and withdrawal.

When Mary discovered the reason for Hunt's coldness, she too began to accuse herself and to repent her latter moodiness. This repentance was greatly to Hunt's satisfaction, but Mary need not have obliged him; and it would be a mistake, as it was then, to judge Mary's relationship with Shelley on the strength of a temporary and superficial estrangement occasioned by her illness. Edmund Blunden[1] takes a further factor into account, overlooked by Hunt and even by Mary:

"As she reviewed the position, she did not remember, and it is too easily forgotten, that both of them were of the race of artists; both were pursuing inner designs which demanded much of them; that like Shelley she herself was married as much to the intellectual life as to a person."

It was a long time before Mary could rid herself of this torturing sense of guilt which Hunt provoked in her.

On those occasions when Mary could bring herself to write, she poured forth in her journal the emotions she dared not express to those around her, knowing too well they would tire of her complaints.

Journal 2nd October—For eight years I communicated, with unlimited freedom, with one whose genius, far transcending mine, awakened & guided my thoughts. I conversed with him; rectified my errors of judgment; obtained new lights from him; and my mind was satisfied. Now I am alone—oh, how alone! The stars may behold my tears, & the winds drink my sighs; but my thoughts are a sealed treasure, which I can confide to none. (. . .) But can I express all I feel? Have I the

1. Edmund Blunden, *Shelley: A Life Story* (Collins, London, 1946).

talent to give words to thoughts & feelings that, as a tempest, hurry me along? Is this the sand that the ever-flowing sea of thought would impress indelibly? Alas! I am alone. No eye answers mine; my voice can with none assume its natural modulation; all is show—& but a shadow—What a change! Oh my beloved Shelley! (. . .) How often during those happy days—happy, though chequered—I thought how superiorly gifted I had been in being united to one to whom I could unveil myself, & who could understand me! Well, then, now I am reduced to these white pages, which I am to blot with dark imagery. . . . Literary labours, the improvement of my mind, & the enlargement of my ideas, are the only occupations that elevate me from my lethargy; (. . .) all events seem to lead me to that one point, & the coursers of destiny having dragged me to that single resting-place, have left me. Father, mother, friend, husband, children—all made, as it were, the team that conducted me here; & now all, except you, my poor boy (& you are necessary to the continuance of my life), all are gone, and I am left to fulfil my task. So be it.

Mary was to live by her pen. This was, as always, a precarious situation. Although Sir Timothy Shelley, her father-in-law, was finally to assist her with an allowance repayable from the estate her son was to inherit, at this moment Mary's livelihood was involved in her decision to continue with her literary life. And equally, she knew that peace and sanity could be obtained by diverting her grief, her loneliness and the sum of her passions along a creative channel.

At the time of Shelley's death, then, she was in serious economic difficulties. Byron, who had proved generous so far as his intentions went, had been negotiating with Sir Timothy Shelley on behalf of Mary and her son, but without success. Shelley's father refused to interest himself in Mary's circumstances; her child he offered to support in a small way, provided Mary would take him to England and hand him over to some guardian approved by Sir Timothy.

"You may guess," Mary wrote to Hogg, "that I do not make it a question whether I will part with my boy. He is my all. My other children I have lost, & the pangs I endured when those events happened were so terrible, that even now, inured as I am to mental pain—I look back with affright to those periods of agony. (. . .) I could not live a day without my boy."

But Byron had assured Mary, in October 1822, "I will be your banker until this state of things is cleared up." This, however, like so many of his generous impulses, had cooled by the following July. At first, Mary had busied herself in transcribing Byron's poems, and many visits passed between her and Byron's establishment in Genoa. Mary found in Byron, as in no other of Shelley's friends, a quality which evoked an acute memory of Shelley. When he spoke she was inevitably reminded of her first weeks with Shelley and Byron in Geneva, when she had listened with rapt attention to the conversation of the two poets, "(. . .) & thus as I have said," she wrote in her journal, "when Albè[2] speaks & Shelley does not answer, it is as thunder without rain. (. . .)" But Mary examined this phenomenon and knew it was merely a product of association. She admired, but did not like Byron—"(. . .) my feelings," she wrote in her journal, when observing how his voice moved her, "have no analogy either with my opinion of him, or the subject of his conversation."

In the summer of 1823, Byron was turning his thoughts towards the struggle in Greece, which he hoped to join. Mary's decision to leave Italy found him less prepared than formerly to part with his promised loan, and he conveniently discovered that he did not like Mary, anyway, nor Shelley either for that matter, and told Hunt as much. Whereupon Hunt reminded Byron that he owed Mary one thousand pounds for a wager which Shelley had made with him (on the longevity of Byron's mother-in-law and Shelley's father respectively) and which Shelley had won. But Mary was too wounded by these insults to Shelley's memory to pursue the matter, and refused what aid Byron sulkily offered her. Trelawny, whom she looked upon as her truest friend, supplied Mary's wants from his small capital before sailing off with Byron for Greece—"Lord Byron with £10,000, Trelawny with £50," as Mary observed.

Mary set out from Genoa on her journey to London on 25th July

2. The Shelleys' name for Byron.

1823. It was with some relief and some foreboding that she took her leave of the Hunts and their children—those veritable "little blackguards" that Byron had termed them. In the latter months, Hunt had made amends to her for his earlier coldness, perceiving how silent and genuine was her sorrow. They had become "the best friends in the world." Mary wrote gaily to the Hunts from all along the route.

"After you receive this letter," she told them at last, "you must direct to me to my fathers—(pray put W. G. Esq. since the want of that etiquette annoys him—I remember Shelley's unspeakable astonishment when the author of *Political Justice* asked him half reproachfully why he addressed him "Mr." G.). (. . .)"

Godwin had moved to 195 Strand, and there Mary went, intending to stay until her future was settled in some respect. She had written to Lady Shelley, whom she had heard was virtually directing Sir Timothy's affairs, and soon after she arrived she heard from Sir Timothy's lawyers, on whom she called with Godwin. No permanent arrangement was made, but the solicitor advanced her one hundred pounds with the advice of patience. Mary was now in a position to leave the Godwins whose house she could not look upon as her home, though she continued to maintain close contact with them.

"My lodgings are neat & quiet," she reported to the Hunts, "—my servant good—my boy in delightful health & very happy & amiable."

Her time was fully occupied at first. She discovered, soon after her arrival, that *Frankenstein* had been staged. (It was then possible to present a "play of the book" without the author's permission or entitlement.) Mary attended a performance and was greatly amused; Godwin had done his best for Mary by having a new edition of *Frankenstein* published to coincide with the dramatic version.

Mary also renewed two friendships—one with Isabel Baxter of her girlhood days, whose husband had previously objected to her seeing Mary. Now, in view of Mary's marriage, Isabel was free to acknowledge her. Mary was delighted with Isabel. The other friends were the Vincent Novellos, the famous musician's family, whom she had not seen since 1818 and to whom she was very greatly drawn. Mary saw Jane Williams, too, and felt as affectionately as ever towards her, though Mary did not yet know that Jane had engaged in disparaging gossip with Hunt about her.

Altogether, Mary's first weeks in England left her little time to think. Apart from attending to her own affairs, she had undertaken to negotiate for Hunt with his brother, on account of some financial differences between the two. This was not, however, an unrewarded kindness on Mary's part, for through John Hunt, she was approached by Bryan Waller Procter (Barry Cornwall) with the suggestion that an edition of Shelley's poems should be published. He, together with the poets Beddoes and Kelsall, was an admirer of Shelley and undertook to arrange for the expense of publication. Wishing to keep her own name as far as possible from Sir Timothy's eye, Mary applied to Hunt for a biographical introduction to the work, but she busied herself with editing the manuscripts.

Her evenings were seldom lonely. Mary experienced once more the engaging atmosphere of Godwin's circle, narrower now as it was, but adorned still by the sages of her youth—Hazlitt, the Lambs and eloquent, ageing Coleridge. The Novellos made her welcome, while the invalid Procter's gentle interest in her awakened a tender response; Mary was very sensitive to voices, and Procter's voice, she said, reminded her of Shelley's.

She met Hogg again; but there was no question of renewing their former intimacy. She saw Mrs. Gisborne; and she saw Peacock.

But the hubbub of her return died down, and Mary could not afford to continue her social rounds, for she had few means ("Poor un-dinner-giving as I was," as she informed Miss Curran later) of returning hospitality.

Early in 1824 she confided to her journal, "I have now been nearly four months in England and if I am to judge of the future by the past and the present, I have small delight in looking forward."

Shelley's poems were published and sold extremely well—"Shelley has celebrity even popularity now," Mary observed bitterly to Hunt. But the popularity embittered Sir Timothy in a different way, and he threatened to stop the small allowance he was making Mary on her child's behalf, if any biography of Shelley, or the poet's works, were published during his lifetime. The volume of poems was suppressed, at Sir Timothy Shelley's insistence, after the sale of three hundred and nine copies. Mary was also obliged to suppress a proposed volume of Shelley's prose.

Mary meanwhile struggled with a new novel she had started, determined to succeed in literature for her son's sake as well as her own. But a dark mood had overtaken her in reaction to her first diverting months in England; she could not write. "My imagination is dead, my genius lost, my energies sleep," she wrote in her journal.

It was not till 15th May 1824 that she heard the news that subdued the most unyielding spirits in England—Byron had died at Missolonghi.

Byron's last Greek venture had won him the reputation of a popular hero, though but a few months back, Hunt's brother had been heavily fined for printing Byron's *Vision of Judgment*. For Byron the poet, none but the intelligentsia grieved—and even they were divided as to his merits. But for the lordly adventurer and hero of liberty, all England mourned.

Mary was roused out of her lethargy by the blow. "Albè—the dear, capricious, fascinating Albè (. . .)," she said in her journal, forgetting his errors in the flood of associations his death evoked. But the effect of this news strangely stirred her creative powers. Once more she applied herself to her novel, *The Last Man*.

In the summer of that year, Mary had gone to live in Kentish Town to be near Jane Williams. The young women consoled each other, talked often of the past and more often of the future. Neither of them was secure from financial worry, but when their pending affairs were settled, they promised each other, they would return to Italy.

"I love Jane better than any other human being," Mary wrote in her journal, "but I am pressed upon by the knowledge that she but slightly returns this affection. I love her, and my purest pleasure is derived from that source—a capacious basin, & but a small rill flows into it."

Mary herself needed affection, and she found compensation for the lack of it in the bestowing. We are reminded of the passage she had written two years earlier: ". . . as Sterne says, that in solitude he would worship a tree, so in the world I should attach myself to those who bore the semblance of those qualities which I admire."

She had perceived for some time that Hogg was in love with Jane; knowing Hogg as she did, she took a cool view of the prospects for Jane's happiness in the affair. But she wrote to Hogg frequently, always mentioning Jane.

"My evenings are for the most part spent with Jane. You ask me news of her. There she dwells in her flower adorned bower, sometimes gay, sometimes sorrowful, always gentle, always dear. Your last letter appeared to annoy her. (. . .) I think with your great understanding you might contrive to please instead of to annoy 'the fair one,' & to make her smile instead of frown. (. . .)"

But there was, none the less, a hint of patronage in Mary's remark, reminiscent, however, of some of Shelley's words on the subject of Jane:

"If during the last twenty years she had cultivated her mind while living with a person superior to herself, what would she not have become?—petty cares and deference to the judgment of one so entirely her inferior, have narrowed many of her views; still she is a charming personage."

These were unnecessary words, perhaps. Jane was simple, selfish, pretty and graceful with no intellectual pretensions, and apart from her gossip-mongering—that pursuit common to men and women with nothing better to do—she was harmless enough. Mary was to suffer considerably from Jane's gossip, but Jane was the type of woman whose best qualities are to be measured, not by her achievements, but by the influence of her charm. Jane extracted love from the flintiest quarters, and quite effortlessly induced an atmosphere of sympathy and elegance wherever she appeared.

She was warm and kind towards Mary while they were living at Kentish Town, but she had no genuine love of Mary's company—intent on her work and serious as Mary was; and when in the summer of 1826 the two friends spent a month together in Brighton, Mary was horrified to hear Jane thank God it was over.

Jane was not free to marry Hogg, nor, indeed, had she been

married to Williams; her first husband was still alive. But five years' devotion on Hogg's part gave Jane a sense of security; she needed a protector and had proved by close association with Hogg from the time of her arrival in England that he was likely to remain constant. This association had, in fact, been much closer than Mary had suspected, and Hogg's disapproval of Mary's return to England was well-grounded in his own interests, since no doubt he feared her intervention.

Meanwhile, since Byron had died, Trelawny, in Greece, had been corresponding with Mary, who was overjoyed to hear from her friend, and she confided many of her inmost feelings to him. Her present position, she told him, depressed her.

"I am under a cloud," she wrote, "& cannot form new acquaintances among that class whose manners & modes of life are agreeable to me—& I think myself fortunate in having one or two pleasing acquaintances among literary people. (. . .)"

She admitted this quite frankly, for she disliked being the outcast from society that her early elopement with Shelley had made her. She also told Trelawny that she hoped—a vain hope as it proved —soon to have an independent income from Sir Timothy of three or four hundred pounds a year, when her first action would be to liberate Claire, who had gone to be a governess-companion with a family in Moscow.

Trelawny sent Mary a draft of an article, "The Cavern Fortress of Mount Parnassus"—a resistance hide-out in the mountains to which he and some followers planned to retire if the Greek cause were lost. This he requested Mary to turn into an article for *The Examiner,* which did not come to its intended fruition; but from this and Trelawny's letters, her interest in Greece was revived and she was able, in *The Last Man,* to present as authentic a picture of Greece as if she had been there herself.

While she was completing *The Last Man* Mary saw few people apart from Jane. Those few included the Godwins, whom she visited once a week; and occasionally she attended the theatre with some friends, among whom was Count Gamba, brother of Byron's Countess. Mary was, however, to receive great pleasure from a new acquaintance which she had made in 1824. This was John Howard

Payne, an American-born actor some six years older than herself, and who was now engaged in adapting plays for the stage. With him he had brought to England his friend Washington Irving, and Mary was even more impressed by this brilliant man of letters than she was by Payne. Irving showed some interest in Mary, and when he went back to Paris, promised to visit her on his return to England.

To these welcome intrusions on her solitude Mary did not give undue thought; for the moment she was occupied by problems of her very existence. On the publication of *The Last Man* in 1826, Sir Timothy's allowance, now two hundred pounds a year, was stopped, for although the novel was published anonymously, as "by the author of *Frankenstein,*" Mary's name had been mentioned in reviews, a circumstance the old man could not tolerate. At length he was persuaded that Mary was not at fault and that he could hardly prevent her from earning her living.

In the September of that year, Charles Shelley, the poet's eldest son, died, leaving Mary's child, Percy, the heir to the Shelley fortunes.

"Percy is well—grown tall and taller and thrives," she told her friends. Her son consoled her and anchored her to life; but even this comfort could not thaw the icy grief within her. Her sorrow had been still and unspectacular, and few who knew her could have suspected her feelings, when in the autumn of 1826 she wrote in her journal: "My head aches. My heart (. . .) is deluged in bitterness."

Chapter 9

. . . thus on the way
Mask after mask fell from the countenance
And form of all. . . .
SHELLEY, *The Triumph of Life*

If Mary had not perceived how close was Jane's association with Hogg during his courtship, when the two women were seeing each other daily at Kentish Town, Jane, for her part, had no idea that Mary, too, was turning over in her mind the question of matrimony. Many of her friends expected Mary to marry again; she was young and talented, and her appearance had changed from that of the attractive verve of her early youth into a mature and rare beauty. A daughter of Mary's friend Novello (Mary Cowden Clarke) described Mary in her early widowhood, speaking of:

Her well-shaped, golden-haired head, almost always a little bent and drooping; her marble-white shoulders and arms statuesquely visible in the perfectly plain black velvet dress, which the customs of that time allowed to be cut low, and which her own taste adopted (for neither she nor her sister-in-sorrow ever wore the conventional "widow's weeds" and "widow's cap"); her thoughtful, earnest eyes; her short upper lip and intellectually curved mouth, with a certain close-compressed and decisive expression while she listened, and a relaxation into fuller redness and mobility when speaking; her exquisitely formed white, dimpled, small hands, with rosy palms, and plumply commencing fingers, that tapered into tips as slender and delicate as those in a Vandyke portrait.

Jane Williams knew, of course, that Mary had met John Howard Payne with Washington Irving in 1824, and she must have known, too, that Payne was deeply interested in Mary, who was constantly receiving books and theatre tickets from him. In fact, Jane accompanied Mary and Payne on many an evening's entertainment. Jane may have wondered if Mary was serious in her assertion that her association with Payne meant friendship and nothing more, but the presence of another man in Mary's thoughts she did not guess.

It was true that Mary did not consider Payne in any other light but as a welcome friend. A writer of drama and himself an actor, he had that flexibility of personality peculiar to theatre people; he could provide an evening's exuberance but not the mental consistency against which Mary needed to pit her talents. Payne, as he admitted, fell in love with Mary at the outset of their acquaintance, and in the summer of 1825 asked her to marry him. Mary refused Payne quite firmly. Having been Shelley's wife, she said, none but a man of equal genius could satisfy her. But where was a man approaching Shelley's stature? The name of Payne's friend Washington Irving occurred in this extraordinary conversation, for indeed at that time Irving's fame had established itself far beyond Shelley's.[1]

Payne gave serious consideration to the idea then suggested, namely that Washington Irving might make a future husband for Mary. Payne was ardently in love with Mary but unselfish enough

1. This affair is described with the supporting letters of Payne and Mary in F. B. Sanborn, ed., *The Romance of Mary Shelley, John Howard Payne and Washington Irving* (Boston Bibliophile Society, Boston, 1907). It is further discussed very fully by F. L. Jones in Appendix II of his edition of Mary Shelley's letters, and by Betty T. Bennett, *The Letters of M. W. S.,* vol. 1, pp. 493n and 494n.

to desire her happiness on her own terms, and theatrical enough to envisage himself as the magnanimous dispossessed lover. Could he not, he wondered, bring about a match between his two closest friends? Mary, he knew, was interested in all Irving's activities, and had gratefully accepted the letters from Irving to Payne which the latter had lent her to read.

Mary was well aware of Payne's intention to approach Irving. Payne made this clear in a letter to her on 29th June 1825. It seems that Mary inwardly welcomed this move, for she said nothing to really prevent it; but she adopted the most dignified attitude she could in the circumstances, making some ineffectual protestations from time to time, even to the extent of claiming that she did not remember the prominence of Irving's name in her conversation with Payne on the subject of marriage.

But it is highly improbable that Mary expected him to go to the lengths he decided upon in order to secure her happiness, and she would have been greatly embarrassed had she known that in August 1825 Payne gave Washington Irving the letters he had received from Mary—in which Irving was frequently mentioned—and also copies of the love letters he had written himself to Mary, his intention being to make clear Mary's rejection of himself, and her predilection for Irving—to "act the hero," as he expressed it.

Irving did not learn anything startling from these letters of Mary's. She had mentioned him playfully on one occasion, and when Payne had placed a serious construction on her remark she had suggested the joke had gone too far. Irving learnt, too, that Mary had read some of his correspondence with Payne, with such interest that she had pleaded for more; he learnt that Mary admired him and desired his friendship.

"As to friendship with him—," Mary had written, "it cannot be —though every thing I hear & know renders it more desirable— How can Irving surrounded by fashion rank & splendid friendships pilot his pleasure bark from the gay press into this sober, sad, enshadowed nook?"

Only once did Mary commit herself—and then it was only half-seriously, when she had told Payne,

"(. . .) As for my favourite I[rving]—methinks our acquaintance proceeds at the rate of Antedeluvians who I have somewhere read thought nothing of an interval of a year or two between a visit— Alack I fear that at this rate if ever the Church should make us one it would be announced in the consolatory phrase that the Bride & Bridegrooms joint ages amounted to the discreet number of 145 and 3 months."

But Mary had repented this remark when Payne threatened to disclose it; she begged him not to make her "appear ridiculous to one whom I like & esteem," gaily ending her letter, "Give my love, of course Platonic, to I[rving]."

All this, then, was read by Irving, who was further enlightened by an explanatory letter from Payne, extolling Mary's virtues and pleading that the correspondence should not be made light of. To Payne, deeply in love with Mary, it seemed impossible that his friend should not feel likewise. But Irving did not respond, and Mary, happily, never learned of Payne's misguided heroism. The friendship of Payne, however, she retained; he returned to America in 1832. No evidence of Mary's imaginative adventure was allowed to awaken the suspicions of her other friends; and the only trace of her admiration for Irving after 1825 occurs in a footnote commending one of Irving's works in her novel *Perkin Warbeck*. If, as is probable, she nourished no high hopes in the matter, her disappointment was proportionately slight.

In the October of 1825 the Hunts had returned to England, and during the next year Mary's friendship with Hunt was somewhat strained due to an article he had written on Shelley in which he stated that the poet had parted from his first wife by mutual consent.

"They did not part by mutual consent," Mary insisted, "and Shelley's justification, to me obvious, rests on other grounds." But at the time of her elopement with Shelley, Mary had clearly been under the impression that he had parted from his wife "by mutual consent." Was Mary, then, guilty of extreme injustice to the dead woman? It would appear not, for after Harriet's suicide there had been talk between Godwin and Shelley of "evidence" of Harriet's infidelity before her separation from Shelley. Shelley inclined to grasp at these statements, true or otherwise as they might be, probably in self-justification; and Mary accepted her father's and Shelley's representation of the matter. There is every evidence to show that Mary bore Harriet no grudge, for in later years she did all she could to avert publicity from Harriet's character for the sake of Shelley's daughter, Ianthe.

Mary's quarrel with Hunt was patched up, though he did not alter this statement. He did, however, remove some passages in which Claire was mentioned, to which Mary took exception on Claire's behalf. Therefore, when the death of Charles Shelley made Percy heir to the Shelley fortunes, Mary wrote generously to Hunt who was then enduring financial stress, offering him what comfort she could, and reminding him that Shelley had intended to include him in his will to the extent of two thousand pounds. This intention of Shelley's, she confirmed, she would honour when Shelley's inheritance should fall to her disposal on Sir Timothy's death. At that time Mary seemed justified in anticipating that event to be not far off, and few of her friends could have thought that Shelley's father would, in fact, endure for another eighteen years.

Mary was always anxious, sometimes over-anxious, to keep her friends, and when she received a dispirited letter from Trelawny after a long silence, she wrote pressing him to return to England.

"Come, dear friend, again I read your melancholy sentences and I say, come!"

In the summer of 1827 Mary found a new friend and lost an old one.

Journal 26th June—I have just made acquaintance with Tom Moore. He reminds me delightfully of the past, and I like him much. There is something warm & genuine in his feelings & manner. . . .

Mary felt the fascination of this man whose social talents had charmed the most distinguished men of his time. Moore spoke of Byron and she of Shelley; "(. . .) It is an evanescent pleasure," she wrote characteristically, "but I will enjoy it while I can." Before long, she was helping Moore with notes for his Life of Byron, which the publishers John Murray were bringing out.

Her pen was rarely idle. When she was not engaged on a novel, she was doing bread-and-butter work in the shape of articles for

The Westminster Review and short stories which appeared in a popular annual, *The Keepsake*.

That summer, Jane Williams, who was pregnant, went to live with Hogg as his wife. Mary missed Jane when she had left Kentish Town, but was delighted for her friend's sake that she had taken this step; and she wrote round to her friends expressing her own pleasure in the match, speaking in praise of Hogg despite his pronounced coldness to her in the early years of her widowhood.

Mary left Kentish Town, and indulged in a country holiday with Percy. But her pleasures were evanescent indeed. Soon after Jane's departure she heard that her friend had been gossiping about her, boasting of her last-minute ascendancy over Shelley, and spreading tales of Mary's insufficiency as a wife. Mary was wounded on her most vulnerable point of pride:

> *Journal 13th July*—My friend has proved false & treacherous! Miserable discovery. For four years I was devoted to her, & I earned only ingratitude.
>
> Not for worlds would I attempt to transfer the deathly blackness of my meditations to these pages. Let no trace remain save the deep bleeding hidden wound of my lost heart, of such a tale of horror & despair.
>
> Writing, study, quiet, such remedies I must seek. (. . .) What deadly cold flows through my veins; my head weighed down; my limbs sink under me. I start at every sound as the messenger of fresh misery, & despair invests my soul with trembling horror.

It may seem that this lamentation and misery were somewhat out of proportion to the offence, and that Mary took Jane's cattiness immoderately hard. There are two factors to be considered, however. The first is that Mary knew very well that her eight years with Shelley represented, on the whole, a successful union. She was still aware, though, of a vague feeling, inculcated by Hunt (who, in turn, had been worked up by Jane's gossip in the early days after Shelley's death), that she had let Shelley down at the last, and she knew that his flattering attentions to Jane had been nothing more than a result of her own temporary neuroticism.

But Shelley's love for Mary had survived the Viviani episode, and she was convinced it would have survived Jane's influence. But all this was a matter of her own conviction. Jane possessed the evidence of those elegant lyrics Shelley had composed to her in the last months of his life, and though Mary knew that Shelley's principal attention had been directed towards his last philosophical poem, *The Triumph of Life,* and that Jane had merely occupied his moments of recreation, this would have been difficult to explain, had Mary deigned to do so. As it was, Mary felt that the respect of all who knew her depended upon their recognition of her proud place in Shelley's life and work, and her courageous combat with countless tribulations since his death; and she felt now that a few careless words from an attractive woman had demolished the very foundations of the respect due to her.

This was a savage enough blow to Mary, but it was the more effective since it had been delivered by Jane. It should be recognised that Mary had been a little in love with Jane, if that phrase can be used about two women without implications of abnormal behaviour. Mary's repeated references to Jane in her letters and journals disclose an obsessional attitude, and to say that Mary sublimated all her emotional passion in her love for Jane is no exaggeration; nor is it a surprising phenomenon in a highly-tensed, imaginative woman with no other emotional outlet. In time, Mary came to realise this fact, and in 1835 she knew herself thoroughly enough and had sufficient self-humour to be able to confess to Trelawny:

"Ten years ago I was so ready to give myself away, & being afraid of men, I was apt to get *tousy-mousy* for women."

Mary had discovered, and was troubled by the fact, that Jane did not return her ardent devotion, but she had not dreamed that Jane, as she now thought, had hated her throughout their association. Jane, of course, neither hated nor loved Mary. She loved herself, and only for her own glorification of that personage had she put about the stories. From the evidence of the correspondence and journals which touch upon the subject, it only remains to be wondered how a group of educated people could bother to concern themselves with it; Mary was not an easy character, but at least she was not petty, like so many around her.

For many months following this revelation, Mary endured a comprehensive sense of agitation which would probably be called today a nervous breakdown. In vain did she try to comfort herself with other friendships—with Frances Wright, for instance, who was an emancipated American emigrant, a disciple of Lafayette, and an active participant in the cause of slave-liberation. Mary responded first to Frances Wright's letters, and then to the lady in person, warmly enough, but she had little desire to make common cause with this libertarian.

Her other friends, the Robinsons, a numerous family who had entered Mary's life earlier that year, took up much of Mary's attention. She went to stay with them frequently at their home in Paddington. She was especially close to Isabel Robinson, who for a time virtually replaced Jane in Mary's affections.[2]

Having been betrayed by Jane (and it was Isabel Robinson who was her informant), Mary tried to argue herself into restraint over Isabel.

> *Journal 26th September*—Arundel (. . .) But now my desire is so innocent. Why may I not hover a good genius round my lovely friend's path? It is my destiny, it would seem to form rather the ties of friendship than love—the grand evil that results from this is—that while the power of mutual Love is in itself a mighty destiny—friendship though true, yields to the adverse gale—& the vessels are divided far which ought never to part company.

At the end of July 1827, when Mary and her son, Percy, were on holiday in Sussex, one of the Hunt daughters and Isabel Robinson accompanied her. After moving their lodgings they settled near Arundel. Isabel was seriously ill; she suffered from acute attacks of asthma. Mary nursed her assiduously.

On 28th August Mary wrote to Jane Williams, "I am glad for pretty Isabel's sake that D. now seriously thinks of les culottes

2. Little has been known about the Robinsons, but thanks to Professor Betty T. Bennett's more recent scholarship, (*The Letters of M. W. S.*, vol. 2), much more can now be written about this friendship that throws an important light on Mary's character.

[breeches]—I do not expect this person—as Isa names D—for two or three weeks."

To decode this enigmatic sentence we have to refer back to an older acquaintance of Mary's: Maria Diana Dods, a writer whose pseudonym was David Lyndsay and whose works Mary had admired in her Pisa days. She was known to Mary's circle as "Doddy," and is the "D" of the above letter. Doddy was the illegitimate daughter of the Earl of Morton. She is described by a contemporary as looking more like a man than a woman, indeed like a man dressed as a woman. She is described as "grotesque-looking." She wore her hair cropped short. She held Mary Shelley in high esteem and appears to have been a woman of considerable intelligence and culture.

From the evidence of Mary's letter of 28th August—"I am glad for pretty Isabel's sake that D[oddy] now seriously thinks of les culottes"—it seems plain that Mary and her intimate acquaintance were aware of a close relationship between Doddy and Isabel. On 17th September Mary wrote again in a letter to Jane, "We do not know yet when to expect Doddy. I hope Isabel will be a little in good looks for the Sposo."

From this time Doddy now took on a male guise and changed her name to Walter Sholto Douglas. With Mary's help and connivance, Doddy and Isabel left England under the name of Mr. and Mrs. Douglas and lived thereafter in France, accepted as man and wife.

Professor Bennett's ample documentation of this strange case includes a possible explanation of it. "While the motivations for this charade are not fully known," writes Professor Bennett, "one reason may have been to give legitimacy to Isabel Robinson Douglas's apparently illegitimate infant daughter."[3]

I think this a very reasonable answer to the questions that arise from the affair. There are probably several answers. But Mary's

3. Betty T. Bennett, *The Letters of M. W. S.*, vol. 2, p. 7n.

Is it also possible that Doddy was a man all along, registered at birth, for reasons of family inheritance, as a girl? This might account for Isabel Robinson's child, and the fact that Doddy was accepted in France without question as a man.

declared gladness "for pretty Isabel's sake" that Doddy had decided to pose as her husband on their leaving England seems to point to a sensible well-laid plan, however strange. It was a scheme that reconciled both Isabel's need for a nominal husband and Doddy's need to look the man she presumably felt herself to be.

So far as Mary is concerned, my view is that this episode shows her at her most practical, staunch, rational and broadminded. It must be remembered, too, that she was risking her own reputation, should anything have gone wrong with the scheme.

Julia Robinson, Isabel's sister, for a time took Isabel's place in Mary's affections. The friendship with the family was to disintegrate early in 1841, when Julia, with incredible hypocrisy, complained to Claire Clairmont that her family had "sacrificed a brilliant society" on Mary's account.[4]

Late in 1827 Mary returned to London to live in Somerset Street, Portman Square. Suffering still from the mighty impact of Jane's betrayal, she was induced by Moore to speak to Jane on the subject. Jane wept, of course, and Mary was forced to pursue her case by letter.

"If I revert to my devotion to you," she asserted, "it is to prove that no worldly motives could estrange me from the partner of my miseries—the sweet girl whose beauty, grace & gentleness were to me so long the sole charms of my life—Often leaving you at Kentish Town I have wept from the overflow of affection—often thanked God who had given you to me—could any but yourself have destroyed such engrossing & passionate love? And what are the consequences of the change?—When I first heard that you did not love me—every hope of my life deserted me—the depression I sunk under, and to which I am now a prey, undermines my health —How many many hours this dreary winter, I have paced my solitary room driven nearly to madness. (. . .)"

Jane made excuses, denied, and prevaricated, somewhat ineffectually. The matter was never fully resolved, but Mary did not seem to care. A great disenchantment had come over her life, and the

4. See Paula R. Feldman and Diana Scott-Kilvert, eds., *The Journals of Mary Shelley* (Oxford at the Clarendon Press, 1987), p. 570, n. 3.

reserve which had always been one of her features became more pronounced; she began to develop a self-protective hardness which preserved her sanity but which as she grew older her friends interpreted as self-centredness and frigidity. Mary continued her friendship with Jane, but never on the same intimate basis. "The veil is torn now," Mary had told her.

In the spring of 1828 Mary went to Paris with Isabel Robinson's father, Joshua, and sister, Julia, to visit Isabel, now "Mrs. Douglas." Sick in mind, she felt her body sicken too, and for three weeks lay ravaged by smallpox. But still her courage asserted itself, and at the end of her illness she forced herself to face a social round, marked as she was by the disease. Ungratefully, Isabel had, like Jane, talked about Mary in an unfavourable light, an obstacle that Mary seems to have overcome when actually presented to the people who had heard Isabel's opinions.

"I was well repaid for my fortitude," she reported to a friend. "(. . .) What will you say also to the imagination of one of the cleverest men in France, young and a poet, who could be interested in me in spite of the mask I wore. It was rather droll to play the part of an ugly person for the first time in my life, yet it was very amusing to be told—or rather not to be told but to find that my face was not all my fortune."

The young poet in question was Prosper Mérimée, and pleased as she was by his amorous regard, Mary was in no flirtatious state of mind. When the author of *Carmen* wrote to express his feelings for her Mary replied that, since she was not a flirt, she was returning his letter, shrewdly observing that he would probably have repented the contents later. All the same, she enjoyed a close and confiding friendship with Mérimée for some years.

It was an altered Mary that Trelawny found when he returned to England. Her appearance had not been permanently disfigured by the smallpox, but her face had lost the clear transparency that her friends had so often remarked upon. She was changed in character, too, and Trelawny found her more than a match for him when he requested material for a *Life of Shelley*. Mary was adamant in her refusal. She knew that Sir Timothy would disapprove strongly, and that only on his good will did her son's education and her own livelihood depend.

Sir Timothy was now beginning to take a slight interest in Percy, and his allowance was gradually increasing; but it was only by a tremendous effort of tact and contrivance that Mary had gained these few concessions—it had meant repeated letters, cautiously worded, to Sir Timothy's solicitors, and continual reports on Percy's progress, besides no end of watching and waiting for her quarterly cheques. Determined that Percy should have a good education with as many advantages as she could demand for him, Mary was not going to forfeit these ends for Trelawny or anyone else. A *Life of Shelley,* appearing now, apart from infuriating Sir Timothy, would cast her own name before an untrustworthy public, and Mary judged that this would not aid her present struggles for her boy.

Trelawny left for Florence empty-handed and sulky. But Mary had no wish to quarrel with him, and managed to reinstate their friendship in subsequent correspondence. It was she who, eventually, took some trouble over, and found a publisher for, Trelawny's book, *The Adventures of a Younger Son,* concluding the arrangements in 1831.

The years following Trelawny's departure were active ones, and Mary was rapidly making a place for herself in the literary world. Her historical novel, *Perkin Warbeck,* was published in 1830, and though she was disappointed in the sum she received for this work ("Poor *Perkin Warbeck* for £150," she had exclaimed to her publisher), she was supplementing her income with a small revenue from stories and articles.

Her friendship with Trelawny was now on a footing of jocular intimacy. Mary had gone out of her way to appease him, for she could never bear to lose a friend. Her placing of Trelawny's book had increased their correspondence, and Mary gossiped easily with him.

When, however, she teased him about some of his female friends who had married—"(. . .) so you know that your ladies desert you sadly. If Claire & I were either to die or marry you would be left without a Dulcinea at all (. . .)"—Trelawny replied, "Do not you, dear Mary, abandon me by following the evil examples of my other ladies. I should not wonder if fate, without our choice, united us; and who can control his fate?"

To this Mary retorted,

"You tell me not to marry—but I will—any one who will take me out of my present desolate & uncomfortable position. Any one —& with all this do you think that I shall marry? Never—neither you nor anybody else. Mary Shelley shall be written on my tomb —and why? I cannot tell, except that it is so pretty a name that though I were to preach to myself for years, I never should have the heart to get rid of it."

But Trelawny was not satisfied.

"I was more delighted," he pursued, "with your resolve not to change your name than with any other portion of your letter. Trelawny, too, is a good name, and sounds as well as Shelley."

Now Mary, alarmed, dropped her badinage, and spoke in earnest, though somewhat forcibly:

"My name will *never* be Trelawny. I am not so young as I was when you first knew me, but I am as proud. I must have the entire affection, devotion, &, above all, the solicitous protection of any one who would win me. You belong to womankind in general, & Mary Shelley will *never* be yours."

Meanwhile Mary turned her thoughts to directing the life she had chosen. Since she had come to know the publishers John Murray through Tom Moore's introduction, she had been endeavouring to interest them in her work. Theme after theme she put up to them for books which she felt she could write—a work on Madame de Staël was suggested by the eminent publisher, but the project went no further. Then Mary became tactlessly comprehensive in the range of subjects she proposed to them, which included a "Life of Mahomet," "Conquests of Mexico and Peru," a "History of Manners and Literature in England from Queen Anne to the French Revolution," "Lives of Celebrated Women," a "History of Chivalry," and no less than a "History of the Earth in its Earlier State." It was no wonder that the publishers could not find sufficient confidence to commission a work from a writer whose interests seemed so diffuse. Mary was over-anxious to be published by Murrays' for the sake of the prestige which their name bore, but it is immoderate to suggest, as does F. L. Jones,[5] that this is "probably the most pitiful portion of Mary's correspondence" and that here "Mary came nearer to abject begging than at any other time of her life." Mr. Jones is immoderate because Mary was not begging. She was an author who had enjoyed considerable success, who had faith in her own powers, and who was offering a publisher the commodity in which publishers deal. Many an author before Mary, and many a one after her, has plagued a good publisher no less; and within the limits of this practice, Mary can only be said to have revealed her eagerness too plainly, and to have written to Murrays' with indiscreet frequency.

She found profitable work, however, and did it well, in her contributions to Lardner's *Cabinet Cyclopædia,* of a series of biographical and critical essays on Italian, French, and Spanish writers. This was a type of writing which Mary enjoyed. Her studies ranged from Dante, Petrarch, Boccaccio, Lorenzo de' Medici and important minor Italian poets to the contemporary poets including Ugo Foscolo. Mary also rescued from oblivion some early Spanish poets whose work she outlined with a reference to their historical background, moving on to Cervantes and Calderón.

This work, more than any other, serves to show a side of her temperament which cannot be detected in her letters and journals, and which remained a constant factor throughout her life. This was her propensity for scholarship, and her ability to submerge herself in objective study. Had she lived a century later, given the necessary opportunities, Mary would almost certainly have been a scholar in the vocational sense. She possessed that historical grasp which can place the phenomena of literature against the wider backcloth of human affairs, and produce therefrom a pattern.

As Mary approached her thirty-fifth year, then, she had "found herself," and had made peace with reality, to the extent of having discovered intellectual satisfaction. She also had a degree of financial security, though not a sufficiency, having come to an arrange-

5. F. L. Jones, *The Letters of Mary W. Shelley,* vol. 1, p. 371n.

ment with Sir Timothy whereby her allowance was increased to four hundred pounds a year, still conditional upon the total sum being repaid to Sir Timothy's personal estate after his death, out of the amounts she would then inherit.

Mary no longer measured her beliefs nor based her desires on the potential perfectibility of mankind. She subscribed to no specific religious doctrine, but embraced an unformulated but certain spiritual conviction of ultimate peace such as she had described in referring to her last illness before Shelley's death; and this was sufficient to sustain her. It was sufficient to sustain her, and in fact, it was this very workability of her vague philosophical outlook which made it possible for her to educate her child and to write creatively. Had she, as many wished her to do, allowed her natural pessimism to range far and wide on philosophical theoretics, she must have been ruined.

At the end of September 1832, Mary achieved a triumph over the prejudices of Shelley's family, in sending Percy to Harrow. She had immense hopes for her boy, and if he did not show signs of genius she hoped that Harrow would awaken his talent in some direction.

Percy's expenses at Harrow made difficulties for her, but she was determined he should remain there. She decided to live at Harrow, where Percy should become a day scholar with a consequent reduction in fees. It was a wrench to leave London where she had many interests, and where she had recently spent some time with Trelawny, who had returned to England:

"He is a strange yet wonderful being," she wrote of him in her journal, "endued with genius—great force of character & power of feeling—but destroyed by *being nothing*. (. . .)"

But Trelawny was soon to sail for America. Mary had her novel, *Lodore,* in hand, and after a tough struggle with Sir Timothy, through his lawyers, for the loan of ready money towards the expenses of removal, she left London.

"To go and live at pretty Harrow," she told Mrs. Gisborne, "with my boy, who improves each day, and is everything I could wish, is no bad prospect. (. . .)"

Chapter 10

. . . comfortable men
Gather about great fires, and yet feel cold:
SHELLEY, *Summer and Winter*

The climacteric of Mary's emotional life had passed with all she had endured on Jane Williams' account. Life had begun to lose its intensity, and the years that followed found in Mary a less resistant victim, a less responsive beneficiary. What hopes for the future she entertained were not passionate ones, but were none the less forceful in a practical, driving and obstinate way; for she was not allowed to vegetate: the battery of misfortune which had seemed so peculiarly to have singled her out, still held her marked; but as she had come to expect less of life, so she was less prone to disappointment.

Mary had fondly expected that as an author and a personality in her own right, and as the daughter and widow of eminent personages, the "upper" world would forget her early indiscretion and accept her. Precisely what she meant by "society" when she mentioned it, she never defined, and this notional society of hers probably never existed. She knew a great many of the distinguished intellectuals of her day and received their respect. If she had entered that other fashionable gallimaufry which she probably had in mind, she would have speedily discovered its superficiality and the fast decay of its spiritual existence. But the pity was, she was never aware of this illusion she fostered. And so far as the middle class was concerned, the conventions of the times were against Mary entering it; and here again she would never have been able to tolerate the wholesale philistinism of its members, and had no real place there.

It was, however, with a decided conviction that she was being denied admittance to "society" that she began to concede more and more, and too much, to public opinion. Social compromise was, admittedly, a wise course for Mary to adopt. But her craving was of the desperate kind, and lacked that enthusiasm which might have given new bearings to her life and work. The moderate terms she had made with life she now began to relax, until finally she forgot them and remembered only her desire for status.

It is possible to see some affinity between the forces that set Mary to write her novel *Lodore*—a work in which social compromise overreached itself—and those which, in the same year, motivated Godwin's ready acceptance of a government sinecure. There is more to it than an assumption that Godwin, to whom all forms of government had been anathema, now turned renegade; or that Mary was likewise traitor to her own convictions. Long years of never having enough money, of all kinds of material anxiety, had been at work on both father and daughter. No one is independent of material things, and stoical as they were, Mary and her father yielded to their conceptions of necessity.

Lodore was a success, but Mary took her greatest pride, after her removal to Harrow, in the *Lives* she continued to contribute to the *Cyclopædia*. She mentions these works in her letters more frequently than any of her other compositions, and obviously felt some relief in this more objective form of writing, for in the *Lives* no one could pry into Mary's own feelings, whereas her novels, Mary knew, addressed a curious, censorious and prejudiced audience.

She was miserable during the years she spent at Harrow. Isolated from her few friends, she tried hard to submerge herself in her son's welfare, and to entertain his school friends as far as her means would allow. "Sometimes," Mary wrote to Mrs. Gisborne, "he gives breakfasts to 6 or 8—& so gets a portion of popularity, despite my poverty." But Percy did not prove the consolation she had anticipated. With that amazement with which parents always regard the "otherness" of their children, Mary noted that he was neither a replica of Shelley nor herself. "(. . .) [H]e wants sensibility," she confided to her friend, "but I fancy mine at his age was almost as covert—except that Mrs. Godwin had discovered long before my excessive & romantic attachment to my Father."

The excessive and the romantic, however, were not in Percy's make-up. As Mary watched him grow into a youth of sixteen she was a little mortified to discover no signs of intellectual activity in him. Stout, indolent and placid, the Shelley squirearchy in his blood ran stronger than his father's or Godwin's genius. Mary did not foresee, then, that Percy's mediocrity had its ultimate advantages of sorts. She longed for him to shine in company, and to distinguish himself in some vocation. Instead, he was to remain loyally and negatively by her side to sustain her old age; he was to make a comfortable marriage, contract no debts, and create no trouble anywhere.

At Harrow, though, Mary still clung to the hope that Percy would develop latent talents, and when he was sixteen she managed to send him to board with a tutor pending his entrance to Cambridge. Mary left Harrow a good deal older in spirit than can be calculated by the months she spent there. Loneliness had made her more tough and she knew this. Writing to Trelawny, she admitted, "I am more wrapt up in myself, my own feelings, disasters, & prospects for Percy. I am now proof, as Hamlet says, both against man & woman."

When Godwin died on 7th April 1836, Mary did not experience a sense of calamity such as would have visited her ten years earlier. She attended his last days and nights, buried him, as he had wished, beside Mary Wollstonecraft, and set about petitioning for a pension for Mrs. Godwin. She endured a brief illness as a result of her grief and the fatigue of nursing, but though she had been passionately attached to her father, she did not pour out her heart to her friends and journals on the subject, as she had done in her disastrous youth. Godwin died in his eightieth year. There is a sentence in Mary's journals and calm references in her letters to this event, but she saw no tragedy in it. The Reform Parliament had given Godwin a sinecure as Yeoman Usher of the Exchequer, which carried an income of two hundred pounds a year, a house in New Palace Yard, and other perquisites. When later the Whigs had begun to abolish sinecures, Godwin's fears for his livelihood had been dispelled by the intervention of the Duke of Wellington and Sir Robert Peel. So that Mary had observed, with some surprise, "It is not that I am not a Whig—I suppose I am one. (. . .) I feel particularly kindly towards the Conservatives also just now as they have behaved with the greatest consideration towards my father—preserving him in his place, which was about to be abolished by the Whigs & that with a *manner* as gracious as the *deed."*

Mary, therefore, was consoled by the knowledge that the old man had enjoyed a certain belated tranquillity at last. He left a message charging Mary with the task of publishing his last work, *The Genius of Christianity Unveiled:* "I am most unwilling," Godwin had written, "that this, the concluding work of a long life, and written, as I believe, in the full maturity of my understanding, shall be consigned to oblivion. It has been the main object of my life, since I attained to years of discretion, to do my part to free the human mind from slavery. I adjure you, therefore, or whomsoever else into whose hands these papers may fall, not to allow them to be consigned to oblivion."

But Mary was reluctant to revive the calumny which had once circled round Godwin's name by publishing this refutation of Christian dogma, moderate though it was compared with his early writings. For a time, however, she considered publishing Godwin's memoirs and letters, a number of which she collected and annotated. Her principal aim was to raise money for Mrs. Godwin by these means; but in spite of some murmurings of conscience, Mary did nothing public with the papers, and explained her very sound reasons to Trelawny:

This year I have to fight my poor Percy's battle—to try to get him sent to college without further dilapidation on his ruined prospects—& he has to enter life at college—that this should be undertaken at a moment when a cry was raised against his Mother—& that not on the question of *politics* but *religion,* would mar all—I must see him fairly launched, before I commit myself to the fury of the waves.

A sense of duty towards my father, whose passion was posthumous fame makes me ready—as far as I only am concerned, to meet the misery that must be mine if I become an object of scurrility & attacks—from the rest—for my own private satisfaction all I ask is obscurity. What can I care for the parties that divide the world or the opinions that possess it? What has my life been? (. . .) One thing I will add—if I have ever found kindness it has not been from Liberals—to disengage myself from them was the first act of my freedom—the consequence was that I gained peace & civil usage.

So Godwin's manuscripts were placed aside, and his last work remained unpublished for more than twenty years after Mary's death.

Her last novel, *Falkner,* was published the year after her father died. She wrote this book with unusual facility. "My best it will be —I believe," she stated in her diary when the book was in progress. But at other times she seemed to look upon her work, now, as a breadwinning device only, and not as something necessary to her well-being. It was ten years since she had written in her diary, "Writing, study, quiet, such remedies I must seek. (. . .)" From the evidence of her frequent deep depressions, it is probable that she now intended to give up her literary work when Sir Timothy's death should render her independent, but he waxed hale and long; many a wry comment did Mary make on his continued heartiness.

She had been approached with the suggestion that an edition of Shelley's collected poems should be published, with a biography, and this she was eager to prepare. Sir Timothy stubbornly forbade the biography, "under a threat of stopping the supplies," but Mary devised a means of circumventing Sir Timothy's wrath by appending critical and biographical notes to the poems—a happy contrivance, as it has since proved to Shelley's readers and biographers.

It may seem strange that Mary was prepared to publish Shelley's work with all its provocative ideology, when only recently she had decided to suppress her father's. But Mary was conscious of the simple truth that the reading public will accept in poetic form ideas which it will reject in prose, this being, of course, a manifestation of one of the incidental powers of poetry. Mary must have recognised, too, that Shelley's poetry, unlike Godwin's prose, was more than a vehicle for polemics; that Shelley's work compressed within its aesthetic mould many layers of experience unsuspected even by the poet. And of Shelley's greatness, Mary had no doubt.

When her publisher suggested leaving out Part VI of *Queen Mab* on the grounds that it was "too atheistical," Mary felt uneasy, and explained her dilemma to Hunt: "I don't like Atheism (. . .) yet I hate mutilation (. . .)," and some days later, still worried, she wrote, "I have not yet made up my mind. Except that I do not like the idea of a mutilated edition, I have no scruple of conscience in leaving out the expressions which Shelley would never have printed in after life. I have a great love for *Queen Mab*—he was proud of it when I first knew him—& it is associated with the bright young days of both of us."

Shelley, it is true, would not have reprinted the whole, if any, of *Queen Mab*. Mary consulted Hunt, Hogg and Peacock, none of whom objected to the omission, and she decided, in spite of her scruples, to leave some parts out. She was unfortunate, if justified, however, in omitting Shelley's dedicatory poem to Harriet, which brought Hogg's fury upon her in the form of an "insulting letter."

But Mary was aware of Shelley's desire that this poem should not appear—when he had first met Mary, he had given her a copy of *Queen Mab* in which he had inscribed an ironical reference to the dedicatory "Harriet" poem. Mary remembered, moreover, that when a second, "pirated" edition had reached Shelley at Pisa, he "expressed great pleasure that these verses were omitted," as she wrote in her journal—"This recollection caused me to do the same. It was to do him honour."

Trelawny, too, added his bitter protestations about Part VI of *Queen Mab* being omitted, while some reviewers were equally severe on her.

Mary discovered now that Shelley's friends were no friends of hers.

> *Journal 12th February 1839*—In so arduous a task others might hope for encouragement and kindness from their friends—I know mine better. (. . .) I am unstable, sometimes melancholy, and have been called on some occasions imperious; but I never did an ungenerous act in my life. I sympathise warmly with others, I have wasted my heart in their love & service.

Her task, to be sure, was arduous. She was tortured by the effort of recalling, for the purpose of the Notes, so many details of her life with Shelley—"I am torn to pieces by memory," her journal records. This excavation of the past accompanied by the acrimony of her friends almost destroyed her. She fell ill, and believed herself to be dying for the second time in her life. Dying, or losing her sanity—"What an illness! (. . .) Often I felt the cord would snap, & I should no longer be able to rule my thoughts. (. . .)" She recovered slowly, but was not truly easy in mind until a second edition of the Poems bore the sentence, "At my request the publisher has restored the omitted passages of *Queen Mab.*"

Mary felt, still, the critical and watchful eyes of her "friends" upon her. Hogg she distrusted, and after receiving his insulting letter had written in her journal, "He has (. . .) done his best to give another poke to the poisoned dagger which has long rankled in my heart (. . .)," cautioning herself to give him no further opportunity. It is curious that it should have been Hogg and Trelawny—the former of whose amorous advances she had once encouraged and then rejected, and the latter of whose proposal of marriage she had treated likewise—who were the first and loudest to raise their voices against her in this matter. There was a weird mingling of jealousy and resentment in the contempt these men showed for Mary now and later—a suggestion of some score they had never paid off.

Mary had taken a furnished house in Putney in March 1839, two years after Percy went up to Cambridge. Putney was then seven miles from London. Mary felt happier there, and now started publishing a selection of Shelley's prose works. But in view of her recent experience she was in a continual state of anxiety, torn between a desire to publish every word of Shelley's and a longing to disarm the public who were now to be offered Shelley's views in unequivocal prose.

Mary was in a position to take up an imperious attitude over the publication of Shelley's work; she could have told her critics that it was her own business what she printed. But she had a profound sense of responsibility towards Shelley's admirers, and in no way did she give the impression that she considered Shelley the poet to be her exclusive property.

In dealing with Shelley's prose, Mary consulted Hunt, who proved willing to co-operate with her. It was obvious to them both that minor changes would have to be made in some of these writings if they were to pass the prevalent censorship, or, indeed, if the publisher would risk printing them at all. Shelley's translation of Plato's *Symposium,* for example, provided them with a difficult problem, until Hunt advised alterations based on John Stuart Mills's translation of *The Phædrus,* whereupon Mary altered the text, as she said, "(. . .) so that the common reader will think common love is meant—the learned alone will know what is meant." But she did not adopt all Hunt's suggestions. "(. . .) I could not bring myself to leave the word *love* out entirely from a treatise on Love," she insisted.

There were other passages in Shelley's prose, too, which they agreed to omit altogether. But thinking it over, Mary cast discretion to the air, and wrote a last-minute note to Hunt: "(. . .) I have it at heart to replace these passages—why not—we write to show *him* not ourselves. (. . .)"

It is clear from Mary's behaviour in these matters that there were limits to the concessions she was prepared to make to convention; and it must be remembered to her credit that she risked the public's disfavour, which she feared greatly, to perpetuate Shelley's fame.

The editing of Shelley's writings churned up Mary's memories. She was ill.

Journal 1839 [1]—What an illness—driving me to the verge of insanity.

In November of that year, recovered from her illness, she writes in her journal:[2]

A hope gleams through the clouds of my life. (. . .) Another hope—Can I have another hope? A friendship secure helpful —enduring—a union with a generous heart—& yet a suffering one whom I may comfort & bless—if it be so I am happy indeed—but I am no longer able to confide in fate. I can indeed confide in A's inalterable gentleness & true affection but will not events place us asunder—& prevent me from being a comfort to him—he from being the prop on which I may lean—We shall see—If I can impart any permanent pleasure to his now blighted existence, & revivify it through the force of sincere & disinterested attachment—I shall be happy —We shall see!

It has been plausibly suggested that the "A" in this entry has been identified with the recently-widowed Aubrey Beauclerk. Journal entries in 1834 leading to his first marriage that year, and on the anniversary of that marriage, might well imply a romantic relation between Mary and this obviously likeable man which was renewed after the death of his first wife. Mary had been a friend of the Beauclerk family throughout the 1830s. Major Aubrey William Beauclerk, a few years younger than Mary, was M.P. for East Surrey from 1832 to 1837. He was a reformer. If Mary was in love with him the allusions are oblique; if not, then she certainly re-

1. In *The Journals of Mary Shelley,* edited by Paula R. Feldman and Diana Scott-Kilvert, p. 563, n. 1, the editors write, "This entry for March appears in the manuscript between those for 5 October 1839 and 27 November 1839, when Mary's health suffered from the strain of preparing Shelley's manuscript for publication, and was copied into her Journal book out of place."
2. Ibid., p. 537, including nn. 1, 3; p. 544; pp. 563–64. See also p. 539, including n. 4, and p. 565 for the possible identity of "A".

ferred in her Journal entries with nostalgia to someone else.[3] Aubrey Beauclerk married again in 1841.

Shelley's prose works were published in 1840 along with a new edition of the *History of a Six Weeks' Tour*—the topographical essay written, mainly by Mary, about her first travels with Shelley. That year Percy came of age, and Mary was able, by the payments she had received for Shelley's works, to indulge in a holiday abroad with her son. Percy now received an adequate allowance from the Shelley estate. He was not to graduate from Cambridge until the following February, but in the Long Vacation of 1840 they set off. They were joined by two of Percy's college friends who, like himself, were to combine their holiday with studying for a degree. Before she left, Mary, resting at Brighton, took stock of her position and experienced a rare sense of tranquillity. Percy's equitable temperament, she felt, compensated for his want of originality, and she had hopes that this, and future visits to the Continent, would bring him amongst people who would awaken some social response in him. Mary was to take a maid to attend her, and though far from rich, she felt free from a sense of impending penury for the first time in her life. At Brighton, then, she recorded:

> *Journal 1st June*—I must mark this evening, tired as I am, for it is one among few—soothing—balmy. Long oppressed by care, disappointment, & ill health, which all combined to depress & irritate me, I felt almost to have lost the spring of happy reverie. On such a night it returns—the calm sea, the soft breeze, the silver bow new bent in the western heaven—nature in her sweetest mood, raised one's thoughts to God & imparted peace.

Their tour, which carried them up and down the waterways of Germany, to Zürich and finally to Lake Como, was recorded by Mary, together with an account of a subsequent tour, in her later *Rambles in Germany and Italy,* a work which shows that she had lost none of her keen powers of observation and her receptivity to new

3. See also *The Letters of Mary Wollstonecraft Shelley,* edited by Betty T. Bennett, vol. 2, p. 184n, with special reference to Emily W. Sunstein's advancement of this theory in *Keats-Shelley Journal* 29 (1980), p. 224.

experiences. She was happier, now, than she had been for many years, and this is apparent from the *Rambles*. Only occasionally did low spirits overtake her on this first tour. Once, when a letter containing necessary money had not arrived at Milan, she stayed behind to await it while the three young men went ahead.

> I left England [she wrote in the *Rambles*] with a merry party
> of light-hearted youngsters; they are gone, and I alone: this,
> the end of my pleasant wanderings. Such, you know, is the
> picture of life: thus every poet sings—thus every moralist
> preaches.

And when, catching up on her young companions, she passed through Geneva, Mary located, with what a distillation of memory and wonder, the landscape of times past.

> At length, I caught a glimpse of the scenes among which I
> had lived, when first I stepped out from childhood into life.
> There, on the shores of Bellerive, stood Diodati; and our
> humble dwelling, Maison Chapuis, nestled close to the lake
> below. There were the terraces, the vineyards, the upward
> path threading them, the little port where our boat lay
> moored; I could mark and recognise a thousand slight
> peculiarities, familiar objects then—forgotten since—now re-
> plete with recollections and associations. Was I the same per-
> son who had lived there, the companion of the dead? For all
> were gone: even my young child, whom I had looked upon as
> the joy of future years, had died in infancy—not one hope,
> then in fair bud, had opened into maturity; storm, and blight,
> and death, had passed over, and destroyed all. While yet very
> young, I had reached the position of an aged person. . . .

Here Byron's magnificence had first entered her imagination; here Shelley had conversed and boated with him; it was here, round the fireside of Byron's Villa Diodati, that *Frankenstein* was conceived. ". . . [A]ll my life since was but an unreal phantasmagoria," Mary wrote, "—the shades that gathered round that scene were the realities. . . ."

Percy graduated in the following February. Sir Timothy, whom

Percy had visited at the Shelleys' home, Field Place, was inclined to like the boy, but Lady Shelley, jealous for her younger son, John, did not encourage Percy's visits. He had gained from his grandfather, however, an allowance of four hundred pounds a year, without the condition of repayment which attached to Mary's income. Percy was now independent of his mother's purse, and she was free to manage for him another, longer, Grand Tour in a modest way.

In the summer of 1842, Mary and Percy travelled first to Germany, taking with them a young writer, Alexander Andrew Knox, who had been with Percy at Trinity College, and in whose talents and affairs Mary took a solicitous interest. Knox had been ill, and Mary hoped that the holiday abroad would revive him, and at the same time, he would provide a companion for Percy.

It was in keeping with Mary's nature that as soon as her financial prospects improved, she found someone in need of assistance, and for whom she willingly reduced her own means to a minimum. Mary has never been given the credit she deserves for her generosity, for even in her leaner years she never refused a request for money unless she really did not possess it. Not only did Mary deny herself in order to supply familiar quarters like the Godwins and Claire, but also such people as her aunt Everina Wollstonecraft whose disastrous refusal to help Fanny Imlay is her only claim to remembrance. Now, it was in Knox that Mary found an object of benevolence. Contributing liberally towards his expenses, her year's tour was fraught with discomforts: ". . . the perpetual recurrence of money care puts to flight every power of enjoyment—do what I will it is the same thing, & I am thoroughly tired out," Mary wrote to Claire.

At Dresden, another talented young man, Henry Hugh Pearson, a musician of some repute, joined the party, and though at first he charmed everyone and generally became the soul of the group he presently began to cause trouble between Knox and Percy, besides other mischief elsewhere. They got rid of Pearson at Florence, to Mary's open relief, though she noted that Knox was proving moody, difficult and a poor companion to Percy. With all this exhausting young talent in the air, Mary was forced to admit to Claire, "Percy is my delight—he is so good & forbearing &

thoughtful for me, that he is the greatest comfort in the world."

Mary loved Italy, and would have been content to stay there even though she was disappointed in some of the old friends she looked up. Disappointed she was, too, that for all her straining to gather the smart set round her son, Percy remained indifferent; and instead of cultivating the choice spirits of society, bought a trumpet to play upon and pined for England, where his main ambition was "to see the model of the Flying Machine."

At the end of summer, 1843, Mary stopped on her way home to stay at Paris with Claire for a few weeks, while Percy proceeded to England. Claire was established in Paris now, in modest comfort, having realised an annuity on Sir Timothy's life, in anticipation of a twelve-thousand-pound legacy she was to inherit under Shelley's will. And to help Claire to become "known as an established person" Mary had given her one hundred pounds.

At the time of Mary's visit, Claire had made friends with some young Italian political refugees, whose eloquent enthusiasm and exiled plight moved Mary to admiration and pity. One of these, Gatteschi, was exceptionally brilliant, and Mary once more adopted the role of patron. Hard pressed as she was after her long tour, she borrowed two hundred francs from Claire, which she delicately asked Gatteschi to look upon as a loan. This talented Italian seemed to compensate Mary, somehow, for her disappointment in Percy, and her feelings were more deeply involved than she suspected.

On her return to England, Mary set about contriving by all means to raise money for him. Her *Rambles in Germany and Italy* were undertaken in this cause, and Gatteschi, writing piteous and subtly flattering letters to her, agreed to supply material on Italian politics for her work. Meanwhile, Mary racked her ingenuity to serve both Gatteschi's wants and his apparent pride. "Could you not contrive," she suggested to Claire, "that some governess took lessons from him & we—or I—advance money to pay for them. The governess might think it all done from interest for *her* on your part, & his pride not hurt."

Both women were complete prey to the fascinating exile. By the next spring Gatteschi had ceased to exert himself, even to a token effort to earn his own livelihood. There is no question that Mary felt any sense of wrong in satisfying her emotions thus; but encouraged by his increasing ardour—Gatteschi even talked of marriage —she wrote him recklessly about her life, her past, her inmost thoughts. Mary did not see herself, as others would too readily have seen her, as a middle-aged woman making herself ridiculous. That she considered herself, at first, merely in the light of a patron is clear from the fact that she made no secret of her new protégé to Percy, who, indeed, approved of his mother's kindness, obliging her with money for Gatteschi, "in the most Angelic manner," as Mary expressed it.

It was not until she discovered that Gatteschi had found a richer "patron" in Lady Sussex Lennox that the benefactress in Mary gave way to the woman in her. She was kept well supplied with highly-coloured information about Gatteschi's new affair by Claire, who no doubt suspected Mary's infatuation; by the summer of 1845, Mary was confiding to Claire her doubts as to Gatteschi's character. Later, she admitted, "his affair with Lady S. [Sussex] alienated me from him entirely."

But if Mary put Gatteschi out of her heart, he was to enter her thoughts again somewhat violently.

Sir Timothy died at last, "falling from the stalk like an overblown flower," as Mary told Hogg. There was much to be settled, legacies to be paid, and other encumbrances on the estate to be cleared. Claire, in spite of her large inheritance, would not come to England at Mary's request to attend to her own affairs, and some sharp words were exchanged between them.

Hogg received his legacy but could not forbear to reveal his long-standing resentment of Mary. "I daresay," he taunted her, "you wish that you were a good deal richer—that this had happened and not that—and that a great deal, which was quite impossible, had been done, and so on! I should be sorry to believe that you were quite contented; such a state of mind, so preposterous and unnatural, especially in any person whose circumstances were affluent, would surely portend some great calamity."

Percy's inheritance was, indeed, less than had been expected. The repayment of Mary's income during the long years of her struggle to educate Percy prevented her from displaying the generosity her friends looked for. Hunt had to be content with an income of £120 a year instead of the lump sum Mary had promised him at a time when no one had expected Sir Timothy to live so long, and before considerable inroads had been made on the estate by Mary's income.

But Hogg's harsh and graceless expression of doubts as to Mary's contentment with her own portion had some foundation. "Heaven help us—the burthens on the estate legacies & debts, etc., etc. amount to so much that if we get £2,000 a year we may think ourselves lucky—My poor Percy is quite ruined," Mary lamented to Claire. "Ruined," she could exclaim now, with that luxurious hyperbole in which only those assured of a livelihood to the end of their days dare indulge.

But Mary was comfortably off, plead as she might the upkeep of Percy's style, his baronetcy and estates. For the time being, she remained in her cottage in Putney, but not in peace. Lack of money had been her tormentor; now it was the sufficiency of it that brought its disquiet in the form of a series of blackmails which propelled her to the verge of the grave.

The first of these originated in a bright idea of Gatteschi's to extort money from Mary with the threat of revealing, or even publishing, her very frank letters to him. Gatteschi wrote her in cautious terms, managing "himself never to ask or even to hint at getting any," and only making his demands clear through a third party. Mary, distracted, was fortunate in finding a loyal confidant in her friend Knox, whom she sent to Paris to try and recover the letters. Her agony of mind while she awaited news was intense. Dropping the note of hauteur she had recently adopted towards Claire, she declared, ". . . I am indeed humbled—& feel all my vanity & folly & pride—my credulity I can forgive in myself but not my total want of common sense—& worse—my self reproaches are indeed keen—If my folly causes you annoyance in Paris—will you come to me my heart and house are open to you—

"The blow was so terrible—for yours—my child's my name's sake—& in truth because to feel one has come in contact with a villain. . . ."

Now she experienced an overwhelming sense of guilt—not on

account of her motives: "I meant no ill—I thought I was doing so kind so good an action . . . ," she insisted; but what tore at her was the ridiculous nature of her folly—"at my age too," she wrote in her torture, ". . . I feel as if soon they will be pointing at me. . . ."

But Knox, in Paris, had the matter magnificently in hand. He knew Gatteschi's secret political activities could be used against him, and Mary, scrupulous despite her anguish, had tried to dissuade Knox from getting the Italian into serious trouble with the police: ". . . one's conscience must be clear of any betrayal of that sort," she pleaded.

Knox, however, wasted no time pondering the niceties of revenge, nor possible repercussions on the Italian cause. After considerable coaxing in terms of Mary's francs, the prefect of the Paris police seized Gatteschi's papers, ostensibly for political reasons, and Mary's letters were retrieved.

"Is not Knox a darling. . . . how clever—how more than clever he is.—Even now I can scarce believe that all is well—my letters my stupid nonsensical letters really rescued . . . ," wrote Mary in high delight.[4]

This is, perhaps, the most human incident of Mary's life; human because it reveals the flesh-and-blood susceptibilities which she normally kept under rigid control. Her infatuation, her jealousy, her panic, her remorse, and her childish pleasure at the happy issue of the affair—all might resound the experience of any woman at any time; no social accent of Godwin's, no spiritual effluvium of Shelley's, no choice literary dish, adulterates, as it were, the purity of the situation.

Barely a fortnight after the rescue of her letters, Mary was approached through Shelley's friend Thomas Hookham by a man who called himself "G. Byron,"[5] and who claimed to have some letters of Shelley's for sale. Mary suspected that these might include

4. See F. L. Jones, *The Letters of Mary W. Shelley,* vol. 2, pp. 193–94n, for a full account of the transaction between Mary Shelley and Gatteschi, so far as is known of the matter.
5. A full discussion of G. Byron's activities is presented in Theodore G. Ehrsam, *Major Byron: The Incredible Career of a Literary Forger* (John Murray, London, 1951).

Shelley's early love letters to her which were contained in the box she had left behind in Paris during her elopement in 1814. She wanted all Shelley's letters, also, because up to her last years she intended to write his biography. And letters from Shelley's first wife, Harriet, would have greatly embarrassed Mary had they been made public. She wanted her own early love letters, fearing their possible publication, and the consequent publicity to a period of her life she wished to keep in the background. But Mary now felt herself able to cope with blackmail and its variations. "In treating with a fellow of this sort a third person is so much better," she advised Hookham as one with experience, ". . . We must not show any great desire the man must feel that he can get something, but not much."

The bargaining went on for months, Mary offering higher terms for the early letters to herself than for any others. But she kept comparatively cool. The documents were hers, legally, and though she dreaded the publicity of legal proceedings, she threatened to act against any publisher who might print them. So she continued to prompt Hookham in his role: "Let him bully & threaten a little more, & feel that I will do nothing & then he may avail himself of what I will do. . . ."

When, during this same month, Claire wrote to say that Gatteschi and Lady Sussex Lennox were threatening to publish a memoir against her, Mary was not disturbed. She had her "foolish letters," and felt safe in assuring Claire that her enemies could do her no real injury.

G. Byron was a clever forger who did a great deal of damage to the manuscript market, especially that dealing with Shelley, Keats and Byron (whose son he claimed to be). So far as the material he offered to Mary Shelley was concerned, he was too cunning to invent the substance of the letters, which she would immediately have recognised as false. But, having acquired the original documents, he made word-for-word copies in forged handwriting.

Over the next months G. Byron sold Mary a number of letters, though Mary was convinced he had many more and was not surprised when he turned up again in the autumn of 1847. This time he appears to have threatened to publish copies of letters he had already sold to Mary. Her friend Thomas Hookham now obtained these copies on loan and, with Mary's authority, refused to return them. G. Byron then attempted to reclaim the papers legally. At this point, anxious "to avoid police reports & police magistrates," Mary lost interest in these copies. And though she persisted in her conviction that G. Byron had many other letters and Shelley papers in his possession, G. Byron does not seem to have put in a further appearance.

These episodes affected Mary's health and soured what should have been a period of tranquillity. But she braced herself, early in 1846, to take on a house in Chester Square, for Percy's sake. He intended to stand for Parliament, but of his prospects, Mary entertained few hopes. "As he has never cultivated any acquaintance with any one in his own rank of life—he finds himself quite alone in this first step in life . . . [he] is so thoroughly without address or quickness—that I quite despair," Mary complained to Claire. She was ill, agitated and tired, and looked forward to a holiday abroad in the autumn, before beginning to entertain for Percy.

She was not to make her escape, however, before yet another blackmailing attack descended from Shelley's cousin Thomas Medwin, who wrote to say he was writing a life of Shelley which was to relate such incidents as Shelley's Chancery suit for custody of his children. Mary replied in deprecation of this work; it would offend so many people, she pointed out, and ". . . the account of the Chancery suit above all, would wound and injure the living—and especially Shelley's daughter [Ianthe] who is innocent of all blame and whose peace every friend of Shelley must respect." Medwin next wrote to inform her he had made arrangements for publication within six weeks, which he could not be expected to cancel. Mary made no reply, and in a few weeks she received another missive from Medwin stating his explicit price for suppressing the biography: he had obtained details of the Chancery suit, he asserted, and these would be related in "justice" to Shelley, along with other matters "whose discussion" he assured her, "you would not approve of"; if Mary wanted to suppress the book, he continued, she must make some indemnity for his losses. His price was £250.

Still, Mary did not respond. She discovered that the book had not been accepted, as Medwin had claimed—on the very date of his threatening letter a publisher had rejected the manuscript. "An attempt to extort money finds me quite hardened," she told Hunt. "I have suffered too much from things of this kind. . . ." Medwin tried once more to obtain money from Mary, when in a year's time his book was actually about to be published. Then he wrote to warn her of "the hubbub it would make." Mary made no move, doubting if the book were really in the press. She was alarmed when she saw it advertised, and became ill with apprehension but firmly resolved neither to make payment nor to read the book, which, when it appeared, seems to have caused little of the threatened commotion.

Following Sir Timothy's death in 1844, the years of financial freedom that Mary had so long looked forward to were the most embittered of her life. Throughout her prolonged struggle for her livelihood, her private history had been secure; but now, against her inheritance, she had to balance an account of insult and treachery. Money she would have given away with a good heart, but she could not willingly patronise blackmailers; and these incessant attacks upon her privacy wrecked her.

When, presently, she was to find peace, it was too late, for Mary had tired of life. Early in 1848 she met Jane St. John, a young widow, and Percy's future wife, "who is a prize indeed in the lottery being the best & sweetest thing in the world," she told a friend. Jane was equally drawn towards Mary, and always in later years spoke of her mother-in-law with tenderness. In Jane's old age she remembered Mary as she had known her, describing how young and slim was Mary's form, how expressive her deep-set eyes, how gracefully and simply dressed she was, in soft grey.

Jane's affection brought out a final mellowness in Mary, who was now resigned to Percy's lack of initiative, and was content that he should give up politics and settle on his estate. Jane's personal fortune added to their comfort, and Mary accompanied the young couple wherever they went, moving between Chester Square and Field Place, acquiescent as a shadow.

At Field Place they lived quietly. "Jane dislikes society . . . & Percy has the same tastes—We have our garden & our farm—our dogs, our birds, our doves," Mary wrote drowsily in one of her now infrequent letters. Claire descended upon them once or twice to disturb the peace with her increasing hysteria, until finally she was asked to leave and not return. "She has been the bane of my life ever since I was two!" Mary exclaimed to Jane.

Mary's only anxiety now was for Jane's health, which had been affected by the damps and draughts of Field Place. In the spring of 1850 they went to Nice where Mary enjoyed her last summer in dreamy tranquillity. Percy and Jane had decided to leave Field Place very soon, and had chosen a healthier residence in Boscombe Manor, near Bournemouth. But Mary was too frail now to resist the illness which paralysed her on one side; she suffered a series of strokes towards the end of January 1851 and lay immovable in Chester Square, attended by Percy and Jane. She died on 1st February at the age of fifty-three.

There are those among Mary Shelley's critics who have condemned her as being a singularly discontented woman; and to readers of Mary's history, as to her own friends, it seems indeed as if her nature acted as a magnet to misfortune; as if, in fact, there was some force within her that repelled happiness or even an equitable state of well-being.

Yet this is not so much a manifestation of a constitutional discontent as it is of a constitutional pessimism; the first being to some extent self-controllable, the latter, not. In developing this distinction, I would suggest that an individual may maintain a satisfactory fellowship with the world, who is intellectually pessimistic—today, in fact, this type is quite common—but the emotional pessimist is rarely at ease in personal relationships.

Mary Shelley's pessimism was deeply planted in her emotions by the inhibiting hand of her rationalistic upbringing. And as the following, very revealing, statement of hers indicates, she was prey to this emotional darkness even while experiencing a sense of inner contentment. That is why she so often, in the happier moments of her life, was overcome by feelings of foreboding.

It was a few years before the end of her life that she wrote to Claire:

I have been pursued all my life by lowness of spirits which superinduces a certain irritability which often spoils me as a companion. I lament it & feel it & know it—but that does not suffice—To be as I ought to be towards others (*for very often this lowness does not disturb my inward tranquillity*) I need to be a little tipsy—this is a sad confession but a true one; any thing of emotion that quickens the flow of my blood makes me not so much a happier as a better person.

I have italicised the words "for very often this lowness does not disturb my inward tranquillity," since I believe they illustrate that paradoxical condition common to people of Mary's type—a condition of inner satisfaction, which is somehow distorted in the process of communication, and which in fact, can rarely be communicated.

But in this whole statement, Mary lit upon the source of that mighty reserve which her friends observed. Had she been able to thaw emotionally, her friends would have found her contented enough, despite the remarkable amount of trouble, quite beyond her control, which came her way.

Mary's words are significant, too, for another truth she stumbled upon about herself: "*I need to be a little tipsy* (. . .) *any thing of emotion that quickens the flow of my blood makes me not so much a happier as a better person.*"

Why then, we may ask, was she not more often a little tipsy? But Mary Shelley was never drunk, not by wine, nor literature, nor love, nor virtue. I suppose it is the function of a biographer to diagnose, and not to indulge in vain retrospective proscribing. None the less I seriously suggest that if there had been more wine in Mary's life there would have been fewer tears. But Mary was reared abstemiously, so to say, first on Godwin's iced water, and then on Shelley's self-generated health salts. So the whimsical tippling of her "sad confession" remained no more than a vicarious indulgence.

It may well be enquired of Mary, where then, are the signs of this "inward tranquillity" that she speaks of? Where, if anywhere, did this Child of Light cast her rays? Mary herself anticipated the answer when, glancing through her journal in 1834, she added to it:

It has struck me what a very imperfect picture (. . .) these querulous pages afford of *me.* This arises from their being the record of my feelings, & not of my imagination. (. . .)

(. . .) My imagination (. . .) my Kubla Khan—my Stately pleasure ground.

Mary Shelley was reticent about her own work, and disliked talking about it. Allusions to her novels in her letters and journals are few, brief and factual. In her writings themselves, then, we must seek the imaginative complement to an "imperfect picture." She was not only the daughter of William Godwin and of Mary Wollstonecraft; not only the wife of Percy Bysshe Shelley, to become the mother of Sir Percy Shelley. She was also a professional writer of lasting fame.

END OF PART ONE

AUTHOR OF 'THOUGHTS ON MAN'.

Cartoon engraving of William Godwin

Mary Wollstonecraft Godwin—a painting by John Opie

Mary Shelley—a painting by Richard Rothwell, dated 1840.

Shelley

*The house at Marlow, where Mary and Shelley lived
from early 1817 until their departure
for Italy in early 1818.*

Byron

Claire Clairmont

Jane Williams

The Villa Magni at San Terenzo on the Bay of Lerici.
Mary and Shelley were living here
at the time of his death.

PART II

Critical

Foreword to Part II

Selected for consideration in the following chapters are those works by Mary Shelley which seem best to represent the variety of her writings. Of these, *Frankenstein* and Mary Shelley's invaluable Notes to the 1839 edition of Shelley's poems are in current use. *The Last Man* has been reprinted in recent years, and also *The Fortunes of Perkin Warbeck.*

Apart from these works, which I examine at length, there remain some of which a word should be said:

Between the two major achievements of *Frankenstein* (1818) and *The Last Man* (1826), Mary Shelley published her novel *Valperga* (1823)—a romance of mediaeval Italy, of sound historical colour, which fails properly to assimilate the story within its pattern of superstition, inquisition and ancestral warfare. This lack of integration may be ascribed to the fact that the period of composition coincided with a time of grief, distraction and illness in the author's private life, for it was pieced together in the years between its conception at Marlow in 1817 and its completion at the Baths of Pisa in 1821—years which were loaded for Mary with the deaths of two children, the importunities of Claire Clairmont and uncertain relationships with Shelley's numerous friends. *Valperga* was further intruded upon by Godwin's editing of it, to what extent of patchcraft we do not know. Even so, in points of characterisation among others, *Valperga* may be favourably compared with George Eliot's *Romola*.

Matilda, a short novel, was written in the late summer of 1819. Its main interest is that it reveals Mary Shelley's state of mind at the time. And perhaps a more revealing thing about this work is the fact that she did not publish it during her lifetime. (Indeed, it was not published till 1959.) The story deals with a beloved father's incestuous passion for his daughter, her anguish, his suicide, and her subsequent wistful attachment to a gentle poet. It is a melodramatization of Mary Shelley's deepest feelings of hopelessness following the death of her son William. She had borne three children and lost all, and was pregnant again. Her relations with Shelley were strained. Her father, whom she had idolized, was dunning the Shelleys for money; to him, Mary's feelings did not count. Three years later, after Shelley's death, Mary wrote in her journal, ". . . when I wrote Matilda miserable as I was, the *inspiration* was enough to quell my wretchedness temporarily. . . ."

Part of the inspiration was the story of Beatrice Cenci, victim of an incestuous father. During the spring and summer of 1819 Shelley was writing his poetic drama *The Cenci,* finishing his final draft in August, while Mary was working on *Matilda.* Mary greatly admired *The Cenci,* and was undoubtedly influenced by her discussions with Shelley on the theme.

Since she finally decided not to publish *Matilda,* it is evident that she herself perceived that the work belonged more to her personal life-story than to literature.

Of the two other novels which I have not dealt with, *Lodore* (1835) and *Falkner* (1837), the former is notable only for providing biographical confirmation, more or less literal: Professor Dowden and other commentators have already amply illustrated the points at which *Lodore* concurs with Mary Shelley's life-story. In all other respects, *Lodore* (successful in its time) represents a misdirected effort to reconcile things as they were in Mary's life with things as they might have been—an effort to fit the unorthodox facts into an orthodox moral system; and as a creative work it has no health.

Falkner, her last novel, discloses some trace of Mary's former ability to retain suspense and handle a complicated plot. The principal character, Falkner himself, is drawn from Trelawny, but in the general theme can be detected a propagandistic attempt to exculpate Shelley from a charge of precipitating his first wife's suicide. Defects of style, however, as well as the introduction of unnecessary incident, prevent this otherwise interesting work from being worthy of preservation.

It would be incorrect, though, to judge from Mary Shelley's last novels that all her work progressively deteriorated, for while these novels were in progress, Mary was also preparing her praiseworthy *Lives* which appeared in Lardner's *Cabinet Cyclopædia.* As her creative faculty dwindled, Mary seemed to gain in critical discrimination; and these critical-biographical notes on Italian, Spanish and French literature convey her own enthusiasm for objective study, in the same way as do her latter novels her basic boredom with life. The intensified prose style and varied vocabulary of these essays, their evidence of knowledge scrupulously acquired and evaluations far from shallow, are such that I would have wished to have given them fuller attention. But I have preferred to consider Mary Shelley as critic on the basis of her Notes to the 1839 edition of Shelley's poems, towards which her work on the *Lives* was profitable experience, and which are more accessible today than Lardner's long-forgotten *Cabinet Cyclopædia.*

The short stories Mary wrote over a long period of her life, which were collected in 1976, can be classified with *Lodore* and *Falkner* as possessing no major claims. They appeared in company, usually, with stories by names that mean nothing to us now; and besides which the tales announced as "by The Author of *Frankenstein*" are indeed prominent.

The last writings by Mary Shelley, her two-volume work, *Rambles in Germany and Italy* (1844), are among those which I would like to have been able to dwell upon. These travel books have an intimate manner quite different from her earlier topographical work, *History of a Six Weeks' Tour* (1817), which is marred by the rigid impersonality of her early journals, whence it is mainly lifted. The *Rambles* gain by Mary's frank autobiographical style, and combine descriptions of landscape, people and works of art with practical information and advice. And though in one sense this is the most dated of her works, it contains more humour and liveliness than occur in anything else she wrote. But only as travel literature is it dated: we can no longer find an immediate use for the information that the rooms in a certain Bavarian inn were clean and comfortable, or that the bill for four people's dinner, Rhenish wine and rooms "was only ten florins or thirteen shillings and fourpence." But we may find some charm in the reminder that the "Knowing Traveller" is a human constant:

> . . . he pounced upon a poor little man sitting next him, today, "So you have been shopping—making purchases; been horribly cheated, I'm sure. Those Italians are such rogues! What did you buy? What did you give for the gloves?"

The *Rambles* are curiosities which would reward a student of European travel with much insight into the period's modes and methods of getting about, and the student of manners with an excellent critique upon them. It is interesting, too, to follow the Shelley routes and discover what is still there, unchanged or unchangeable, and what is no more but must have existed.

Chapter 11

Frankenstein

O_thello, Don Juan, Micawber, Becky Sharp—such characters have become popular terms; but out of that vampire-laden fug of gruesomeness known as the English Gothic Romance, only the forbidding acrid name Frankenstein remains in general usage.[1]

To call *Frankenstein* a Gothic novel is, of course, a loose definition, and one which would defeat the claim I hope to establish, that this novel was the first of a new and hybrid fictional species. But if we remember for the moment that the wayward plethora of Mrs. Radcliffe's thrillers had already captured the reading public's imagination before Mary Shelley was born, and that Shelley's delight in the weird, the horrific and the awful was enough to intensify Mary's own interest in such themes, we must recognise the

1. In "general usage" however, the name is very often misrepresented as the monster of Frankenstein's creation, and not as Frankenstein himself. For a discussion of the significance of this common error see p. 161.

primary Gothic influence on *Frankenstein.* But we can see this novel both as the apex and the last of Gothic fiction—for though many other works of the Radcliffe school were to follow, their death-stroke was delivered, their mysteries solved, by *Frankenstein*'s rational inquisition.[2]

In the year 1818, the work created a wonderful and *nouveau frisson.* The limits of the horror-novel had been reached, and old props of haunted castles, hanged babes and moonlit dagger scenes were beginning to raise a shrug rather than a shudder. Much earlier, the young though perceptive Coleridge had foreseen the crumbling of Gothic literature when he said, in reviewing *The Mysteries of Udolpho,* ". . . in the search of what is new, an author is apt to forget what is natural; and in rejecting the more obvious conclusions, to take those which are less satisfactory."

This was, of course, an eighteenth-century opinion, and what was "natural" was expected to be the rational protraction of an idea.

Frankenstein, then, was a best-seller; it occurred at the propitious moment when it was necessary for works of fiction to produce, not only repellant if vicarious sensations in the pit of the stomach, but speculation in the mind. The *Edinburgh Magazine*'s comment on the book—"There never was a wilder story imagined; yet, like most fictions of this age, it has an air of reality attached to it by being connected with the favourite projects and passions of the times"— was one of many that arrived in a blundering sort of way at this conclusion.

"Methinks," wrote Byron to John Murray, "it is a wonderful work for a girl of nineteen,—*not* nineteen, indeed, at that time." But perhaps the wonder of it exists, not despite Mary's youth but because of it. *Frankenstein* is Mary Shelley's best novel because at that age she was not yet well acquainted with her own mind. As her self-insight grew—and she was exceptionally introspective—so did her work suffer from causes the very opposite of her intention; and what very often mars her later writing is its extreme explicitness. In *Frankenstein,* however, it is the implicit utterance which gives the theme its power.

2. I except *Wuthering Heights,* which is sometimes regarded as a Gothic novel but which I believe to be only superficially so.

It was not until 1831, when Mary revised *Frankenstein,* that she wrote her Introduction to it. (The book had previously appeared with a Preface by Shelley purporting to come from the author's hand.) By this time Mary had reached a higher degree of consciousness, but even she, now, seemed aghast at the audacity of the work —her "hideous progeny" as she called it; the question she asked herself, "How I, then a young girl, came to think of, and to dilate upon, so very hideous an idea?" was one which many people had asked, and which she attempted to answer by giving an account of the circumstances of *Frankenstein*'s inception, naming the place, the people and the books which had influenced her. She took this task very seriously, and succeeded as far as (probably further than) any artist will, who tried to get at the root of his own work. The Introduction is too long to reproduce, but here are the most revealing passages:

In the summer of 1816 we visited Switzerland and became the neighbours of Lord Byron. (. . .) But it proved a wet, ungenial summer, and incessant rain often confined us for days to the house. Some volumes of ghost stories, translated from the German into French, fell into our hands. There was the *History of the Inconstant Lover,* who, when he thought to clasp the bride to whom he had pledged his vows, found himself in the arms of the pale ghost of her whom he had deserted. There was the tale of the sinful founder of his race, whose miserable doom it was to bestow the kiss of death on all the younger sons of his fated house just when they reached the age of promise. His gigantic, shadowy form, clothed like the ghost in *Hamlet,* in complete armour, but with the beaver up, was seen at midnight, by the moon's fitful beams, to advance slowly along the gloomy avenue. The shape was lost beneath the shadow of the castle walls; but soon a gate swung back, a step was heard, the door of the chamber opened, and he advanced to the couch of the blooming youths, cradled in healthy sleep. Eternal sorrow sat upon his face as he bent down and kissed the forehead of the boys, who from that hour withered like flowers snapped upon the stalk. I have not seen these stories since then; but their incidents are as fresh in my mind as if I had read them yesterday.

"We will each write a ghost story," said Lord Byron; and his proposition was acceded to. There were four of us. (. . .)

I busied myself *to think of a story*—a story to rival those which had excited us to this task. One which would speak to the mysterious fears of our nature, and awaken thrilling horror—one to make the reader dread to look round, to curdle the blood, and quicken the beatings of the heart. If I did not accomplish these things, my ghost story would be unworthy of its name. I thought and pondered—vainly. I felt that blank incapability of invention which is the greatest misery of authorship, when dull Nothing replies to our anxious invocations. *"Have you thought of a story?"* I was asked each morning, and each morning I was forced to reply with a mortifying negative.

This, then, was the atmospheric environment of *Frankenstein*'s origin. The volumes of ghost stories, the Swiss mountains rearing through the rain, and the supernatural themes of their nightly conversations—all were enough to infuse the Gothic element into her proposed story. But not enough to give it substance. "Every thing must have a beginning" are her next words as she goes on to speak of these circumstances that revealed, among her nebulous imaginings, a single embodied idea.

Invention, it must be humbly admitted, does not consist in creating out of a void, but out of chaos. (. . .) Invention consists in the capacity of seizing on the capabilities of a subject, and in the power of moulding and fashioning ideas suggested to it.

Many and long were the conversations between Lord Byron and Shelley, to which I was a devout but nearly silent listener. During one of these various philosophical doctrines were discussed, and among others the nature of the principle of life, and whether there was any probability of its ever being discovered and communicated. They talked of the experiments of Dr. Darwin (I speak not of what the Doctor really did, or said that he did, but, as more to my purpose, of what was then spoken of as having been done by him), who preserved a piece of vermicelli in a glass case till by some extraordinary means it began to move with voluntary motion. Not thus, after all, would life be given. Perhaps a corpse would be re-animated; galvanism had given token of such things: perhaps the component parts of a creature might be manufactured, brought together, and endued with vital warmth. (. . .)

When I placed my head on my pillow I did not sleep, nor could I be said to think. My imagination, unbidden, possessed and guided me, gifting the successive images that arose in my mind with a vividness far beyond the usual bounds of reverie. I saw—with shut eyes, but acute mental vision—I saw the pale student of unhallowed arts kneeling beside the thing he had put together. I saw the hideous phantasm of a man stretched out, and then, on the working of some powerful engine, show signs of life, and stir with an uneasy, half vital motion. Frightful must it be; for supremely frightful would be the effect of any human endeavour to mock the stupendous mechanism of the Creator of the world. His success would terrify the artist; he would rush away from his odious handywork, horror-stricken. He would hope that, left to itself, the slight spark of life which he had communicated would fade; that this thing, which had received such imperfect animation, would subside into dead matter; and he might sleep in the belief that the silence of the grave would quench for ever the transient existence of the hideous corpse which he had looked upon as the cradle of life. He sleeps; but he is awakened; he opens his eyes; behold the horrid thing stands at his bedside, opening his curtains, and looking on him with yellow, watery, but speculative eyes.

I opened mine in terror. The idea so possessed my mind that a thrill of fear ran through me, and I wished to exchange the ghastly image of my fancy for the realities around. (. . .) On the morrow I announced that I had *thought of a story.*

So, among the raw materials of *Frankenstein* were two forces that ultimately combined—firstly and generally that of the supernatural and harrowing; secondly and specifically, the scientific proposition:

"Perhaps a corpse would be re-animated; galvanism had given token of such things: perhaps the component parts of a creature might be manufactured, brought together, and endued with vital warmth."

It is not surprising that Mary should be excited by a scientific and rational theme; throughout *Frankenstein,* the voice of her father, Godwin, is never far off:

"I heard [says the Monster] of the division of property, of immense wealth and squalid poverty; of rank, descent, and noble blood.

"I learned that the possessions most esteemed by your fellow-creatures were high and unsullied descent united with riches. A man might be respected with only one of these advantages; but, without either, he was considered, except in very rare instances, as a vagabond and a slave, doomed to waste his powers for the profits of the chosen few!"

This was the lesson Mary knew by rote. But it had not gone for nothing that she had heard, while still a child, a rendering of *The Ancient Mariner* from the poet's own lips; and she was never released from her enthralment by the poem. Her character, Walton, who is introduced merely for the purpose of recounting Frankenstein's story, but whose vocation makes him none the less a sort of shadow-Frankenstein, informs his sister:

"I am going to unexplored regions, to 'the land of mist and snow;' but I shall kill no albatross, therefore do not be alarmed for my safety, or if I should come back to you as worn and woeful as the 'Ancient Mariner'? You will smile at my allusion; but I will disclose a secret. I have often attributed my attachment to, my passionate enthusiasm for, the dangerous mysteries of ocean, to that production of the most imaginative of modern poets. There is something at work in my soul which I do not understand."

And Frankenstein himself, in his first flight from his Monster, feels himself to be

Like one, that on a lonesome road
Doth walk in fear and dread,
And having once turned round walks on,
And turns no more his head;
Because he knows, a frightful fiend
Doth close behind him tread.[3]

And indeed, the many conversations between Coleridge and Godwin, which Mary had listened to, were not lost on her. The influential currents of these two minds—Godwin representing the scientific empiricism of the previous century, and Coleridge, the nineteenth century's imaginative reaction—met in Mary's first novel. And this imaginative reaction in *Frankenstein* is a violent one, which places her work in the category of the "horror" novel as distinct from that of "terror"—the former comprehending disgust as well as dismay (Mary repeatedly stresses the loathsomeness and filth of Frankenstein's task, no less than of the Monster himself), and the latter, merely panic and alarm.

This fusion of the ways of thought of two epochs occurred, then, in *Frankenstein,* and gave rise to the first important example of that fictional genre which was later endorsed by H. G. Wells and M. P. Shiel, and of which there are numerous examples in present-day literature.

Comparatively recent literature can probably best illustrate where *Frankenstein* and the Gothic novel parted company, for the latter was destined to lose its status as a literary genre, to be revived merely in its capacity as an influence on the surrealist movement, for which it became a focus of curiosity; and we may say that where the "Wellsian" scientific romance differs from surrealist literature, *Frankenstein* differs from the works of Horace Walpole and Mrs. Radcliffe. We can say that, although these two main arteries have moved apart, there are definite affinities between the modern scientific romance and surrealism, which point to a closer affiliation nearer their source. When the English critic Richard Church[4] wrote of *Frankenstein,* "It has in it a touch of the genius of Edgar Allan

3. Amended text—Mary Shelley misquoted the text.
4. Richard Church, *Mary Shelley* (Gerald Howe, London, 1928).

Poe," he pinpointed a phase in this affinity, despite the renunciation of Poe by the later surrealists. *Frankenstein* is not, indeed, without its moments of surrealistic effect—when, for example, Frankenstein traverses the Alps through darkness and storm, thinking of his murdered child-brother:

> I perceived in the gloom a figure which stole from behind a clump of trees near me; I stood fixed, gazing intently: I could not be mistaken. A flash of lightning illuminated the object, and discovered its shape plainly to me; its gigantic stature, and the deformity of its aspect, more hideous than belongs to humanity, instantly informed me that it was the wretch, the filthy dæmon, to whom I had given life. What did he there? Could he be (I shuddered at the conception) the murderer of my brother? No sooner did that idea cross my imagination, than I became convinced of its truth; my teeth chattered, and I was forced to lean against a tree for support. The figure passed me quickly, and I lost it in the gloom. Nothing in human shape could have destroyed that fair child. *He* was the murderer! I could not doubt it. The mere presence of the idea was an irresistible proof of the fact. I thought of pursuing the devil; but it would have been in vain, for another flash discovered him to me hanging among the rocks of the nearly perpendicular ascent of Mont Salêve.

That statement of an intuitive process in the words "No sooner did that idea cross my imagination, than I became convinced of its truth," and the final image of the fiend "hanging among the rocks of the nearly perpendicular ascent"—indeed, the entire passage, impregnated with surmise, with the larger-than-life quality of a dream—contain the general flavour and specific Gothic elements of surrealism. So far as I know, the early surrealists did not seize on *Frankenstein* for their own purposes, and I wonder why they did not.

II

Perhaps because *Frankenstein* was born of ideas not fully realised by its author but through the dream-like vision she had described, there are several ways in which it can be considered; this variety of interpretative levels is part of its artistic validity.

There are two central figures—or rather two in one, for Frankenstein and his significantly unnamed Monster are bound together by the nature of their relationship. Frankenstein's plight resides in the Monster, and the Monster's in Frankenstein. That this fact has received wide, if unwitting, recognition is apparent from the common mistake of naming the Monster "Frankenstein" and emanates from the first principle of the story, that Frankenstein is perpetuated in the Monster. Several implicit themes show these characters as both complementary and antithetical beings.

The most obvious theme is that suggested by the title, *Frankenstein—Or, The Modern Prometheus.* (That casual, alternative *Or* is worth noting, for though at first Frankenstein is himself the Prometheus, the vital fire-endowing protagonist, the Monster, as soon as he is created, takes on the role. His solitary plight—". . . but am I not alone, miserably alone?" he cries—and more especially his revolt against his creator establish his Promethean features. So, the title implies, the Monster is an alternative Frankenstein.)

The humanist symbol of Prometheus was one that occupied Shelley in many forms beside that of his *Prometheus Unbound,* and Shelley's influence on Mary had gained time to give figurative shape to Godwin's view of mankind's situation. It is curious that Shelley should have written in his Preface to *Frankenstein:*

> The opinions which naturally spring from the character and situation of the hero are by no means to be conceived as existing always in my [that is, Mary's] own conviction; nor is any inference justly to be drawn from the following pages as prejudicing any philosophical doctrine of whatever kind.

Curious, because one cannot help inferring a philosophical attitude; but not so curious when we remember Shelley's refusal to admit the didactic element in his own poetry.

Less curious, however, is the epigraph to the book (original edition):

> Did I request thee, Maker, from my clay
> To mould me man? Did I solicit thee
> From darkness to promote me?
> *Paradise Lost*

The motif of revolt against divine oppression, and indeed, against the concept of a benevolent deity, which is prominent in much of Shelley's thought, underlines the "Modern Prometheus" theme of *Frankenstein*. "You accuse me of murder," the Monster reproaches his maker, "and yet you would, with a satisfied conscience, destroy your own creature"—not the least of *Frankenstein*'s echoes from Shelley.

The Prometheus myth is one of action but not of movement; that is, the main activity of the original story is located around the tortured Prometheus himself, chained to one spot. A novel, however, demands a certain range of activity, and in *Frankenstein* the action is released from its original compression by a secondary theme—that of pursuit, influenced most probably by Godwin's *Caleb Williams*. It is this theme that endows the novel, not only with movement, but with a pattern, easily discernible because it is a simple one.

It begins at Chapter V with the creation of the Monster who becomes, within the first two pages, Frankenstein's pursuer. He is removed for a time from the vicinity of his quarry, but continues to stalk the regions of Frankenstein's imagination, until it is discovered that he has been actually prosecuting his role through the murder of Frankenstein's young brother, William. Frankenstein is then hounded from his homeland to the remote reaches of the Orkney Islands where he is to propitiate his tormentor by creating a Monster-bride for him.

If we can visualise this pattern of pursuit as a sort of figure-of-eight macaberesque—executed by two partners moving with the virtuosity of skilled ice-skaters—we may see how the pattern takes shape in a movement of advance and retreat. Both partners are moving in opposite directions, yet one follows the other. At the crossing of the figure eight they all but collide. Such a crossing occurs when Frankenstein faces his Monster alone in the mountains, and another, when Frankenstein makes his critical decision to destroy his nearly completed female Monster. Once these crises are passed, however, we find Frankenstein and the Monster moving apparently away from each other, but still prosecuting the course of their pattern. It is not until Frankenstein, on his bridal night, finds his wife murdered by the Monster that the roles are reversed. Frankenstein (to keep our image) increases his speed of execution, and the Monster slows down; now, at Chapter XXIV, Frankenstein becomes the pursuer, the Monster, the pursued.

Thenceforward, this theme becomes the central focus of the story. Motives have already been established, and we are induced to forget them, since hunter and hunted alike find a mounting exhilaration in the chase across frozen Arctic wastes, until it becomes the sole *raison d'être* of both. Frankenstein is urged in his pursuit, and in fact sustained, by the Monster:

> Sometimes, indeed, he left marks in writing on the barks of the trees, or cut in stone, that guided me and instigated my fury. (. . .) "You will find near this place, if you follow not too tardily, a dead hare; eat and be refreshed. Come on, my enemy."

And one of the most memorable passages in the book occurs where the Monster again instructs his creator:

> "Wrap yourself in furs and provide food; for we shall soon enter upon a journey where your sufferings will satisfy my everlasting hatred."

I find that "wrap yourself in furs" very satisfying; as I do Frankenstein's rationalisation of his own fanatical relish in the chase; he swears:

> to pursue the dæmon who caused this misery until he or I shall perish in mortal conflict. For this purpose I will preserve my life.

until he comes to conceive himself divinely appointed to the task, his purpose "assigned . . . by Heaven."

The whole ironic turn of events is, I think, a stroke of genius. Mary's treatment of this theme alone elevates her book above *Caleb Williams* and other novels which deal with the straight-forward hunter-and-hunted theme. By these means the figures retain their poise to the very end. No collision occurs, and the pattern is completed only by Frankenstein's natural death and the representation of the Monster hanging over him in grief. They merge one into the other, entwined in final submission.

The pattern of pursuit is the framework of the novel, a theme in itself which encloses a further theme; there, Frankenstein's relationship to the Monster expresses itself in the paradox of identity and conflict—an anticipation of the Jekyll-and-Hyde theme—from which certain symbolic situations emerge.

Frankenstein himself states:

I considered the being whom I had cast among mankind (. . .) nearly in the light of my own vampire, my own spirit let loose from the grave, and forced to destroy all that was dear to me.

We may visualise Frankenstein's doppelgänger or Monster firstly as representing reason in isolation, since he is the creature of an obsessional rational effort. The manifest change in Frankenstein's nature after the creation of the Monster can be explained by the part-separation of his intellect from his other integral properties. He becomes a sort of Hamlet figure, indecisive and remorseful too late. He decides to destroy the Monster, but is persuaded to pity him—he decides to make a female Monster, but fails at the last moment—he receives the Monster's threat of revenge and does nothing: "Why had I not followed him, and closed with him in mortal strife? But I had suffered him to depart," Frankenstein muses bitterly when the damage has been done. And he admits,

through the whole period during which I was the slave of my creature, I allowed myself to be governed by the impulses of the moment.

After the Monster's "birth," then, Frankenstein is a disintegrated being—an embodiment of emotion and also of imagination minus intellect. When, in his final reflections, Frankenstein realises that it was not always so, and exclaims,

> My imagination was vivid, yet my powers of analysis and application were intense; by the union of these qualities I conceived the idea and executed the creation of a man.

he reminds us of those eighteenth-century geniuses (the story of Frankenstein is set in that century) whose too-perfect balance of imaginative and rational faculties did in fact so often disintegrate and ultimately destroy them.

Generally speaking, therefore, it is the emotional and the intellectual that conflict in the form of Frankenstein and his Monster. The culminating emotional frustration by the intellect is reached in the murder of Frankenstein's bride by the Monster. Thereafter, Frankenstein's hysterical pursuit of his fleeting reason completes the story of his madness—a condition perceived in the tale only by the Genevan magistrate, who, when Frankenstein demands of him the Monster's arrest, "endeavoured," says Frankenstein, "to soothe me as a nurse does a child."

Richard Church recognised a parallel in Mary Shelley's life when he discussed the murder of Frankenstein's brother, William. "At the time that she was writing this book," Mr. Church remarks, "the baby William was in the tenderest and most intimate stage of dependent infancy. . . . It is almost inconceivable that Mary could allow herself to introduce a baby boy into her book; deliberately call him William, describe him in terms identical with those in which she portrays her own child in one of her letters—and then let Frankenstein's monster waylay this innocent in a woodland dell and murder him by strangling."

It *is* almost inconceivable; and Mr. Church described Mary's motives as a "miserable delight in self-torture." But another suggestion by Mr. Church might give a clue to this coincidence. The creature who murdered William "was a symbol of Mary's overtrained intellectual conscience." The conflict between the emotional and the intellectual Frankenstein was Mary Shelley's also.

Her baby, William, we know was the child Mary loved more than any; and when she began to feel her intellect grow under her new task, she automatically identified the child with her threatened emotions.

But the symbolic ramifications of the Jekyll-and-Hyde theme reach further than Mary's own life. For so far as she, like others of her time, was beginning to work out her own philosophical mind, her *Frankenstein* expresses the prevalent frustrated situation and reaction to it; the dichotomous elements in the novel are those which were tormenting the ethos. As Frankenstein clashed with his Monster, so did fixed religious beliefs with science: so did imaginative and emotional substitutes for religion with scientific rationalism; so did the intuitive and lush passions of the new era with the dialectical, material and succinct passions of the eighteenth century.

And *Frankenstein* represents, also, that unresolvable aspect of the Romantic temperament which was very soon to be expressed in the quasi-cult of Doubt. Shelley, it is true, had approached these issues with a more emphatic voice, a more perfect heart; his ideas were beliefs, not doubts, and Mary adapted many of them to her novel. But *Frankenstein,* I think, bears the signature of a less positive way of thought which nevertheless held sway in a large number of intelligent minds. Shelley, for example, would see Frankenstein, in his role of creator, as the perpetrator of human misery and therefore an object of hatred. And, Mary added, he is the sufferer from human misery and therefore an object of pity. But, she also added, he is an amoral product of nature, on whom no responsibility can be attached, towards whom no passion can logically be entertained. It was probably with some insight into the deadlock at which such propositions arrived that Shelley wrote his equivocal Preface to *Frankenstein.* [5]

Although these questions, typical of the Romantic outlook, form the moral spirit of her novel, Mary Shelley does not allow them to end in deadlock, but resolves them by introducing a process of psychological compensation, which also has a counterpart in his-

5. For a discussion of *Frankenstein* and *The Last Man* as reactions against the rational-humanism of Godwin and Shelley, see my broadcast talk "Mary Shelley: A Prophetic Novelist" in *The Listener,* 22nd February 1951.

tory. Her intellectual image, the Monster, comes to ultimate repentance. But his repentance has not the rational flavour of Calvin-
ism; for his resolve to perish by fire has all the ecstatic feeling of
Revivalism:

> I shall ascend my funeral pile triumphantly, and exult in the
> agony of the torturing flames.

The more rigid the logic, therefore, the more fervent the imaginative reaction.

III

"I wish you would strike your pen into some more genial subject
(more obviously so than your last)," Leigh Hunt wrote to Mary
after reading *Frankenstein*, "and bring up a fountain of gentle tears
for us. That exquisite passage about the cottagers shows what you
could do." The passage about the cottagers shows, in fact, what
Mary Shelley could do at her worst. Hunt was a bit of a humbug
at times, especially as regards women, and really did more harm to
Mary's conscience by disapproving of this and that than did a more
or less open hater like Hogg.

But the reviews of *Frankenstein* were nothing like so lame. The
"Author of Frankenstein" was generally taken to be a man; and the
notice in *Blackwood's*, written by Sir Walter Scott (who assumed
Shelley to be the author), was the most favourable one of any
importance:

> . . . the author seems to us to disclose uncommon powers of
> poetic imagination. The feeling with which we perused the
> unexpected and fearful, yet, allowing the possibility of the
> event, very natural conclusion of Frankenstein's experiment,
> shook a little even our firm nerves. . . . It is no slight merit in
> our eyes, that the tale, though wild in incident, is written in
> plain and forcible English, without exhibiting that mixture of
> hyperbolic Germanisms with which tales of wonder are usually
> told. . . .
> Upon the whole, the work impresses us with a high idea of

the author's original genius and happy power of expression. We shall be delighted to hear that he had aspired to the *paullo majora;* and in the meantime, congratulate our readers upon a novel which excites new reflections and untried sources of emotion.[6]

Of course *Frankenstein* received the usual blasting, reserved for works of originality, from the *Quarterly Review,* which bore the book a further grudge on account of its dedication to the deadly "Mr. Godwin." Though the *Quarterly* decided:

Our taste and our judgment alike revolt at this kind of writing, and the greater the ability with which it may be executed the worse it is—it inculcates no lesson of conduct, manners, or morality; it cannot mend, and will not even amuse its readers, unless their taste have been deplorably vitiated.[7]

It adds a grudging allowance that

The author has powers, both of conception and language, which employed in a happier direction might, perhaps (we speak dubiously), give him a name among those whose writings amuse or amend their fellow-creatures.

As *Blackwood's* pointed out, Mary Shelley's prose style, compared with other writers of horror-fiction, was very restrained. As a prose writer she never developed any idiosyncrasy which pronounced her writings to be peculiarly her own; and as she became a more conscious writer, her efforts to fetch the deepest layers of her thought up to the surface had a devitalising effect on her style. But in *Frankenstein,* her quite unremarkable, and often tedious, language is rescued by its concentration throughout on direct effect rather than elaboration. She achieved some notably lucid effects by concentrating every word on the merciless exploration of her grim subject.

6. *Blackwood's Edinburgh Magazine,* March 1818.
7. The *Quarterly Review,* January 1818.

Who shall conceive the horrors of my secret toil, as I dabbled among the unhallowed damps of the grave, or tortured the living animal to animate the lifeless clay? (. . .)

I collected bones from charnel-houses; and disturbed, with profane fingers, the tremendous secrets of the human frame. In a solitary chamber, or rather cell, at the top of the house, and separated from all other apartments by a gallery and stair-case, I kept my workshop of filthy creation.

The effect, only, is Gothic, but the language is that of realism. If we compare this, for example, with a passage from a Gothic "clas-sic":

"What!" exclaimed she; "must I lose then my tower! my mutes! my negresses! my mummies! and, worse than all, the laboratory in which I have spent so many a night! . . . No! I will not be the dupe! Immediately will I speed to support Morakanabad. By my formidable arts the clouds shall sleet hail-stones in the faces of the assailants, and shafts of red-hot iron on their heads. I will spring mines of serpents and torpedoes from beneath them. . . ."

(from *Vathek,* by William Beckford, 1784)

we find that, by contrast, Mary Shelley's narrative style reads like a scientific treatise; yet her effect is far more horrifying than any-thing in *Vathek.*

There is, also, a directness of description, a sort of eye-witness convincingness about the portrayal of her principal characters, as when Frankenstein describes his newly-created Monster:

His limbs were in proportion, and I had selected his features as beautiful. Beautiful!—Great God! His yellow skin scarcely covered the work of muscles and arteries beneath; his hair was of a lustrous black, and flowing; his teeth of a pearly whiteness; but these luxuriances only formed a more horrid contrast with his watery eyes, that seemed almost of the same colour as the dun white sockets in which they were set, his shrivelled com-plexion and straight black lips.

The minute, clinical particularisation of hair, teeth, eyes, sockets, lips, shows, of course, exactly what the man who pieced the creature together would have noticed, and this effect is achieved merely by wasting no words on "effects," as may be more fully realised when the passage is contrasted with a similar piece from a later Gothic novel which enjoyed considerable fame in its time,

> Her skin was yellow as the body of a toad; corrugated as its back. She might have been steeped in saffron from her finger tips, the nails of which were of the same hue, to such proportions of her neck as were visible, and which was puckered up like the throat of a turtle. To look at her, one might have thought the embalmer had experimented her art upon herself. So dead, so bloodless, so blackened seemed the flesh, where flesh remained, leather could scarce be tougher than her skin. She seemed like an animated mummy.
>
> (from *Rookwood,* by William Harrison Ainsworth, 1834)

This is good writing, and so far as imagery and phraseology go, it is superior to Mary's. But it fails, where Mary's account succeeds, in the effect of immediate and realistic reportage; for it commits the fault of talking round itself—the fault that an extreme romantic theme will not stand up to. Even that supreme worker-up of atmosphere, Mrs. Radcliffe, does not seem to achieve the clean stabs of ghastliness that we find in *Frankenstein.* Mary's descriptive passage, once more, may be compared with Mrs. Radcliffe's portrait of a monk:

> His figure was striking, but not so from grace; it was tall, and, though extremely thin, his limbs were large and uncouth and as he stalked along, wrapped in the black garments of his order, there was something terrible in his air; something almost superhuman. His cowl, too, as it threw a shade over the livid paleness of his face, increased its severe character, and gave an effect to his large melancholy eye which approached to horror. . . . There was something in his physiognomy extremely singular and that cannot easily be defined.
>
> (from *The Mysteries of Udolpho*, by Mrs. Radcliffe, 1794)

Those last words "cannot easily be defined" seem an irritating confession of ineptitude from one whose purpose it is to define. I have quoted a typical passage of Mrs. Radcliffe's, and that vague "something terrible in his air" or the "something almost superhuman" occur throughout her voluminous volumes and volumes. Mary Shelley, however, by bearing a definite image of her character in mind, succeeded in conveying it in a style which, if we examine it carefully, is denuded of melodramatic elaboration—the incidents, alone, are melodramatic. What is probably the most melodramatic incident in the novel will furnish an example—where Frankenstein discovers his murdered bride:

She was there, lifeless and inanimate, thrown across the bed, her head hanging down, and her pale and distorted features half covered by her hair. Everywhere I turn I see the same figure—her bloodless arms and relaxed form flung by the murderer on its bridal bier.

The point I wish to establish is, not that Mary Shelley excelled as a prose writer—I believe otherwise—but that where her comparatively utilitarian style is combined with an elaborate theme, her writing is distinctive. In the case of *Frankenstein* this combination was a strong contributive factor to its novelty and success as a fictional genre, as well as the story's continuing adaptability to theatre, film and television. The horror produced by Gothicism was dissipated in vapour, but *Frankenstein*'s sharp outlines intensified the horror element to a most sinister degree.

Frankenstein is beset by many faults—mainly those of technique. The story could have been better constructed; the chain which links important events together is weakened by improbable situations. More important is the poverty of characterisation, and by this I do not mean that the principal characters, Frankenstein and the Monster, are defectively portrayed, but that all other characters are weak. I believe the imbalance of construction to be due partly to Mary's inexperience as a writer, and partly to an over-deliberate striving to create suspense.

The calculated slyness in Frankenstein's patient and prolonged account of his early life, which closes with his remark to Walton:

But I forget that I am moralising in the most interesting part of my tale; and your looks remind me to proceed.

is too excessive a preparation for the story Frankenstein immediately plunges into, the creation of the Monster. And between the excellent and highly-charged scene in the Orkneys—

Looking up, I saw, by the light of the moon, the dæmon at the casement. A ghastly grin wrinkled his lips as he gazed on me, where I sat fulfilling the task which he had allotted to me. Yes, he had followed me in my travels; he had loitered in forests, hid himself in caves, or taken refuge in wide and desert heaths; and he now came to mark my progress, and claim the fulfilment of my promise.

As I looked on him, his countenance expressed the utmost extent of malice and treachery. I thought with a sensation of madness on my promise of creating another like to him, and trembling with passion, tore to pieces the thing on which I was engaged.

—between this and the fulfilment of the climax it is working towards (the Monster's reprisal by the murder of Elizabeth) Frankenstein wastes too long in being wrongfully arrested for the murder of his friend Clerval, and in being ineffectually released, before returning to marry Elizabeth. The real fault of construction in *Frankenstein* is in the timing of important events. Impatience is evoked where suspense was intended.

Very often, however, Mary's efforts are effectively justified. It is true that the Monster's absence from the scene of action between Chapters V and X is noticeable; but very swiftly after his reappearance the impact Mary intended him to make is made. Having recently learned that the Monster is the murderer of William and the cause of Justine's being hanged, the reader's sympathy is transported, in Chapter XI, to the Monster, as he unfolds the story of his struggles and development. Murderer and fiend as he is, it is his most casual words that seem to arouse the deepest pity; had he appeared earlier in the narrative, the reader would by now have become inured to his plight. For example, he tells how he discovered a fire left in a wood by someone, and having found the elementary advantages of it, was forced by circumstances to leave the spot:

In this emigration, I exceedingly lamented the loss of the fire which I had obtained through accident, and knew not how to reproduce it. I gave several hours to the serious consideration of this difficulty.

The last sentence "I gave several hours (. . .)" with all its primitive implications of mankind's patient attempts to grapple with nature, gives pathetic force to the Monster's narrative, which would not have been so apparent had we not till now been occupied with Frankenstein's fate, the murder of his brother and the hanging of Justine—had we not, in fact, first conceived the Monster as a villain.

This alternating play upon the sympathy of the reader is *Frankenstein*'s highest claim so far as the structural technique of the work is concerned, and compensates for the minor faults of improbable incident. I consider they are minor faults, since the story as a whole induces a basic "suspension of disbelief." It is true, the epistular convention of the first few pages has a clumsy lack of conviction (though it is skilfully handled in the last pages where the opening situation is picked up, and suspense held very nicely). And it is unlikely that the nurse Justine should be hanged on so slight evidence; that the Monster should so conveniently find a cloak beneath a tree; that he should discover a hide-out so secure as that adjacent to the cottager's dwelling; or that a foreign visitor should so obligingly receive linguistic instruction which the Monster is in a position to overhear and benefit by. But the Monster himself is so incredible, and yet, we are persuaded, so real a being, that we can accept these implausible aids to his development and history.

As I have suggested, I think that *Frankenstein*'s main failing lies not in its construction, but in general characterisation. But also I believe its greatest power to occur in the specific development and depiction of the two protagonists, Frankenstein and the Monster. These are characters, however, so essentially complementary to each other, so engrossed one with the other, and in so many ways facets of the same personality, that they defeat powerful characterisation, which demands a positive interplay of different temperaments.

But within these limitations, and concentrating intently upon her main figures, Mary Shelley performed a feat of individual portraiture which she was never again to repeat. Though the preliminary five chapters postpone the real substance of the tale, they are not wasted, for they methodically build up an interest in Frankenstein. He is established as an exceptional personality, and seems incidentally in his adolescent stage to reflect the person of Shelley—a role which he discards when the Monster is created, and which is then adopted by Frankenstein's friend, Clerval. Frankenstein's temperamental category is settled in a brief, clear passage:

> I confess that neither the structure of languages, nor the code of governments, nor the politics of various states, possessed attractions for me. It was the secrets of heaven and earth that I desired to learn; and whether it was the outward substance of things, or the inner spirit of nature and the mysterious soul of man that occupied me, still my inquiries were directed to the metaphysical, or, in its highest sense, the physical secrets of the world.

Then, with insight into adolescent behaviour, the reaction of child against parent, and its consequences, are demonstrated:

> I chanced to find a volume of the works of Cornelius Agrippa. I opened it with apathy; the theory which he attempts to demonstrate, and the wonderful facts which he relates, soon changed this feeling into enthusiasm. A new light seemed to dawn upon my mind; and, bounding with joy, I communicated my discovery to my father. My father looked carelessly at the title page of my book, and said, "Ah! Cornelius Agrippa! My dear Victor, do not waste your time upon this; it is sad trash."
>
> If, instead of this remark, my father had taken the pains to explain to me that the principles of Agrippa had been entirely exploded, and that a modern system of science had been introduced, which possessed much greater powers than the ancient, because the powers of the latter were chimerical, while those

of the former were real and practical; under such circumstances, I should certainly have thrown Agrippa aside, and have contented my imagination, warmed as it was, by returning with greater ardour to my former studies. It is even possible that the train of my ideas would never have received the fatal impulse that led to my ruin.

Mary also understood, young though she was herself, how profoundly the youthful mind is influenced by the appearance and personality rather than the intelligence and wisdom of an older person. This question of Cornelius Agrippa, moreover, seems to have formed in Frankenstein an instinctive nerve-centre. When he arrives at college, M. Krempe, the first professor whom he encounters, unwittingly strikes at this point of sensitivity, which makes Frankenstein the more acutely aware of the older man's unfavourable exterior:

He was an uncouth man, but deeply embued in the secrets of his science. He asked me several questions concerning my progress in the different branches of science appertaining to natural philosophy. I replied carelessly; and, partly in contempt, mentioned the names of my alchymists as the principal authors I had studied. The professor stared: "Have you," he said, "really spent your time in studying such nonsense?"
(. . .) M. Krempe was a little squat man, with a gruff voice and a repulsive countenance; the teacher, therefore, did not prepossess me in favour of his pursuits.

It is another teacher, M. Waldman, tolerant, benevolent and attractive, who becomes the presiding genius of Frankenstein's career. His lecture on chemistry is the turning point:

"The ancient teachers of this science," said he, "promised impossibilities, and performed nothing. The modern masters promise very little; they know that metals cannot be transmuted, and that the elixir of life is a chimera. But these philosophers, whose hands seem only made to dabble in dirt, and their eyes to pore over the microscope or crucible, have indeed performed miracles. They penetrate into the recesses of na-

[175]

ture, and show how she works in her hiding places. (. . .) They have acquired new and almost unlimited powers; they can command the thunders of heaven, mimic the earthquake, and even mock the invisible world with its own shadows."

Thus Frankenstein was seduced—not by a denunciation of his first and deepest enthusiasms, but by a transformation of them; the ancient wizards gave way to modern scientists who were wizards, nevertheless. M. Waldman's personality is, however, the vital stimulus (his voice, Frankenstein said, was the sweetest he had ever heard), but it is only in retrospect that Frankenstein recognises this fact:

Such were the professor's words—rather let me say such the words of fate, enounced to destroy me. As he went on, I felt as if my soul were grappling with a palpable enemy; one by one the various keys were touched which formed the mechanism of my being: chord after chord was sounded, and soon my mind was filled with one thought, one conception, one purpose.

After the creation of the Monster, since Frankenstein loses to him an integral portion of his being, his character is a study, and a well-executed one, in the mounting obsession of a lost soul to find itself.

But the Monster's development is a larger proposition than Frankenstein's. He does not, like Frankenstein, inherit a civilized way of thought—he inherits nothing but life itself, and the whole gamut of mankind's journey from savage to modern times is played throughout the years of his life.

It is with considerable difficulty [the Monster tells Frankenstein] that I remember the original era of my being: all the events of that period appear confused and indistinct. A strange multiplicity of sensations seized me, and I saw, felt, heard, and smelt, at the same time.

From among these elementary sensations, he distinguishes first hunger, thirst and cold. He eats, drinks, and covers himself; and his next instinct is revealed in primitive moon-worship:

No distinct ideas occupied my mind; all was confused. I felt light, and hunger, and thirst, and darkness; innumerable sounds rung in my ears, and on all sides various scents saluted me: the only object that I could distinguish was the bright moon, and I fixed my eyes on that with pleasure.

His faculties of discrimination develop, and he begins to acquire, even, an aesthetic sense:

I distinguished the insect from the herb, and, by degrees, one herb from another. I found that the sparrow uttered none but harsh notes, whilst those of the blackbird and thrush were sweet and enticing.

By imitation, trial and error, the Monster learns the rudiments of survival; the domestic manners of the cottagers, whom he observes from the peep-hole in his hut, awaken his communal instincts; while the books he (miraculously) comes by—*Plutarch's Lives, Sorrows of Werther* and *Paradise Lost*—are carefully selected by the author to stimulate the mental process which his learning of language has initiated.

Once more, Mary Shelley emphasises the influence of outward appearance on human relationships. The Monster has evolved into an intelligent though simple man. "Who was I? What was I? Whence did I come? What was my destination?" the Monster was then able to ask himself; and he has acquired a moral sense:

I felt the greatest ardour for virtue rise within me, and abhorrence for vice, as far as I understood the signification of those terms, relative as they were, as I applied them, to pleasure and pain alone.

Yet, he discovers, all human creatures with whom he meets flee before his hideous approach. A canker of resentment eats into him, and it is Frankenstein, his creator, whom he accuses for his miserable solitude. When he seizes a young child, in the desperate hope of educating him as a friend, this hope is forgotten when the Monster learns that the child is a relation of Frankenstein's. He recounts:

"He struggled violently. 'Let me go,' he cried; 'monster! ugly wretch! you wish to eat me, and tear me to pieces—You are an ogre—Let me go, or I will tell my papa.'

" 'Boy, you will never see your father again; you must come with me.'

" 'Hideous monster! Let me go. My papa is a Syndic—he is M. Frankenstein—he will punish you. You dare not keep me.'

" 'Frankenstein! you belong then to my enemy—to him towards whom I have sworn eternal revenge; you shall be my first victim.'

"The child still struggled, and loaded me with epithets which carried despair to my heart; I grasped his throat to silence him, and in a moment he lay dead at my feet."

The development of the Monster's character does not cease here, although his first murder gives it a new direction. It is only after his almost-completed female counterpart is destroyed by Frankenstein that he is depicted as an all-out perpetrator of evil. One important factor in the unfolding of his character is his lack of emotion. What passes for emotion—his need for companionship, his feelings of revenge towards Frankenstein—are really intellectual passions arrived at through rational channels. He is asexual, and demands his bride as a companion, never as a lover or even merely a mate; his emotions reside in the heart of Frankenstein, as does Frankenstein's intellect in him.

Neither of these characters, therefore, is brought to full maturity. It is impossible that they should be, for if they were, *Frankenstein* would be a different story. We cannot but admire the patient, analytical and perceptive record of the Monster's evolution, and Frankenstein's arrival at adulthood. It is not without relevance to this point, however, that the novel was the product of a girl in her teens, herself an immature character.

Mary Shelley was immature when she wrote; but she had courage, she was inspired. *Frankenstein* has entertained, delighted and harrowed generations of readers to this day.

Chapter 12

The Last Man

An undercurrent of uneasiness about the social scheme can usually be detected below the most complacent surface of nineteenth-century fiction. But as early as 1826 (the year that the first steamship crossed the Atlantic), Mary Shelley, in *The Last Man,* went further. Social progress and reform, she said in effect, will occur, and, incidentally, the reformers will be corrupted and further reforms will be necessary. But of what avail, she asked, will be the little politics of mankind if it is faced with the threat of universal devastation? It is a question that recent events have thrust upon us, and which we can only answer, as Mary did, by conjecture. Her own view was ruthlessly pessimistic. Mankind, if faced with a common danger, was her answer, will band together with an appearance of common virtue, but within this decreasing community the strong will exploit the weak, to the very end.

It is possible that *The Last Man* will hold a more pertinent appeal for present-day readers than it did even in Mary's time, when it was received as an entertaining though highly fantastic story. Not that Mary herself had a consciously-formulated message, prophecy or warning to convey. Her theme was the objectified result of personal distress of mind.

By the spring of 1824, Mary, only a few months returned from Italy, had started her third novel as a means of earning a living for herself and her son. But she was at a very low creative ebb. "Amidst all the depressing circumstances that weigh on me, none sinks deeper than the failure of my intellectual powers; nothing I write pleases me," her journal records.

"The last man!" she writes, again. "Yes I may well describe that solitary being's feelings, feeling myself as the last relic of a beloved race, my companions extinct before me." This passage is dated 14th May 1824. On the following day she received news of Byron's death at Missolonghi. "This then," states her next journal entry, "was the coming event that cast its shadow on my last night's miserable thoughts. Byron had become one of the people of the grave—that innumerable conclave to which the beings I best loved belong. I knew him in the bright days of youth, when neither care nor fear had visited me—before death had made me feel my mortality, and the earth was the scene of my hopes."

The death of Byron affected Mary profoundly; her emotions were released; the moods of introspection, from which she had been drawing no more fertile a feeling than self-pity, became objectified; her mind became more expansive and flexible and her creative power returned. By 8th June, Mary's journal entries had become almost exultant. "What a divine night it is. I have just returned from Kentish Town; a calm twilight pervades the clear sky; the lamp-like moon is hung out. . . . If such weather would continue, I should again write. . . . I feel my powers again, & this is, of itself, happiness."

Mary Shelley's was not the type of creative mind that generates its own flow of inspiration. Her talent depended very much on the fluctuating influences of external things, like the weather. When she notes in her diary the magnificence of the June evening, it was not to herald a prolonged access of delight, but merely a returning impulse to create. Apart from such rare occasions, her dejection throughout the composition of *The Last Man* was more or less constant. "Time rolls on," she wrote in October, "Time! And what does it bring? (. . .) What can I do? How change my destiny? Months change their names, years their cypher." Her outlook at this time was aggravated by a lack of warmth she detected in her friends. Jane Williams, whom Mary professed to love "better than any other human being," failed to return the affection in like measure, being already occupied with Hogg. The poet Procter, for whom Mary undoubtedly felt a considerable regard, visited her occasionally, then ceased when his business (the publication of Shelley's poems) was over; and Mary lamented sadly the loss of this acquaintance "whose gentle manners were pleasing, & who seemed to a degree pleased."

Added to this, her relations with Shelley's father were conducted on those taut lines that continued to the end of Sir Timothy Shelley's days. Mary had been forced, under threat of her small allowance being stopped, to promise never to bring Shelley's name before the public during Sir Timothy's lifetime.

From this abyss, brimming with deep waters of despondency, her imagination drew its morose sustenance and fed, in turn, the theme of her novel. In losing Shelley, she had suffered a disruption of what she now conceived to be her personal harmony; she entertained an inherent contempt for the social framework of her time which was confirmed by her present dependence on the prejudice of an unscholarly old man; and mankind, in the shape of her most cherished friendships, seemed to have deserted her. These circumstances presented her with a proposition which she successfully translated, in imaginative terms, into the three phases of her novel—the disintegration, in turn, of family, of society, and finally of universal man.

In her obsession with the appurtenances of destruction we find the paradox which is manifest in all tragic art; for this obsession was offset by her equal obsession with construction—a desire to re-create the features of disaster. Mary had, in fact, attempted to write a tragic play but was dissuaded by her father to whom she showed a draft. "It is laziness, my dear Mary," he wrote, "that makes you wish to be a dramatist. It seems in prospect a short labour to write

a play, and a long one to write a work consisting of volumes."
Mary's tragedy, then, took the form of her novel.

It is clear that the character of Lionel Verney is Mary herself; Adrian is an idealised version of Shelley; and Raymond, a more realistic portrait of Byron. As Verney's meeting with Adrian fairly early in the narrative results in the humanising of Verney, the widening of his interests, the refinement of his thought and the resolution of his personal embitterment, so, it now seemed to Mary, had Shelley become her spiritual mentor and salve, and to a large extent this was true. Yet it is noteworthy that Mary, conscious still of Shelley's otherness, that part of him which remained exclusively foreign and exceptional, portrays his fictional counterpart as unmated:

> Adrian, the matchless brother of my soul, the sensitive and excellent Adrian, loving all, and beloved by all, yet seemed destined not to find the half of himself. (. . .)
>
> He often left us, and wandered by himself in the woods, or sailed in his little skiff, his books his only companions. He was often the gayest of our party, at the same time that he was the only one visited by fits of despondency; his slender frame seemed overcharged with the weight of life, and his soul appeared rather to inhabit his body than unite with it.

And Mary's creative and intellectual awakening through Shelley is apparent where Verney says,

> For my own part, since Adrian had first withdrawn me from my selvatic wilderness to his own paradise of order and beauty, I had been wedded to literature. I felt convinced that however it might have been in former times, in the present stage of the world, no man's faculties could be developed, no man's moral principle be enlarged and liberal, without an extensive acquaintance with books. To me they stood in the place of an active career, of ambition, and those palpable excitements necessary to the multitude. The collation of philosophical opinions, the study of historical facts, the acquirement of languages,

were at once my recreation, and the serious aim of my life. I turned author myself.

Involved as Mary was in the memory of Shelley, her portrait of him cannot compare, for conviction, with the shrewd picture she draws of Byron as Lord Raymond:

> No two persons could be more opposite than Adrian and he. With all the incongruities of his character, Raymond was emphatically a man of the world. His passions were violent; as these often obtained the mastery over him, he could not always square his conduct to the obvious line of self-interest, but self-gratification at least was the paramount object with him. He looked on the structure of society as but a part of the machinery which supported the web on which his life was traced. The earth spread out as an highway for him; the heavens built up as a canopy for him.

That antipathy Mary had experienced towards Byron on her first meeting with him is apparent here; so, too, is the more engaging side of his personality:

> He soon conquered my latent distaste; I endeavoured (. . .) to keep in mind every thing I had heard to his disadvantage. But all appeared so ingenuous, and all was so fascinating, that I forgot everything except the pleasure his society afforded me.

Evidence of the physical analogy between the novel and its author occurs throughout; she depicted, in terms of enormously wide invention, the narrow and individual process which led to her own isolated situation in the years immediately following Shelley's death.

II

In many ways *The Last Man* reveals its author, but none so much as through its philosophical attitude. For, of all her novels, this most manifestly reveals her as Godwin's daughter, as Shelley's wife, and as a student of Platonic literature.

Godwin's influence on the work reveals itself indirectly. Her vision of a future British Republic, for example, is a disenchanted one. Her concept of human nature embodies no conviction in its perfectibility. Yet the mere fact that she introduced a republic as the sociological landscape of her work divulges that sphere of influence, the tendency of thought, on which she was nurtured. And though no other novelist of her time ventured to posit this political hypothesis, it was no challenge to the status quo on Mary's part, but an instinctive attitude conditioned by her birth and upbringing. And where Godwin's is an authoritative voice in this novel, his theories are interpreted with more practical conclusiveness than in anything Godwin himself produced in the imaginative way. When we consider the rancour, the unmitigated oppression of the poor by the rich, so crudely portrayed in *Caleb Williams*, for instance, it is possible to see *The Last Man* as a fulfilment of what Godwin failed to achieve in novel form, for Mary was more objective in her fiction than was that rationalist in his.

So far as Mary attempts to interpret *Political Justice*, the changes in government she represents are brought about by peaceful means in accordance with Godwin's theoretical revolution, but not altogether through the rational processes of example and education, which he advocated. It was Mary's practical sense of human relationship and her insight into the British temperament that enabled her to translate Godwinism into realistic terms. So that, when Verney and Raymond arrive at Parliament, which is meeting to elect a Protector, and find the opposing parties violently attaching "opprobrious epithets" to each other, "to my inexperience," then says Verney, "we at first appeared on the eve of a civil war." But he soon discovers that

> Even as the destructive flames were ready to break forth, I saw them shrink back; allayed by the absence of the military, by the aversion entertained by every one to any violence, save that of speech, and by the cordial politeness and even friendship of the hostile leaders when they met in private society.

Shelley's philosophy, in its metaphysical distinction from God-win's is, however, a more dominant influence, and one which is traceable from Shelley's prose writings as well as from his poetry, and which must certainly owe something to his conversations with Mary. (I should make it clear that I am discussing here those aspects of Shelley's thought which Mary adapted to her novel, and not merely those which are shown as emanating from the Shelleyan character, Adrian.) His non-absolute view of good and evil; his equation of thought with the life-force; his pacifism; his image of man as a Prometheus figure; inform and direct Mary's imagination in *The Last Man*. Thus, she shows that as the human race dimin-ishes, losing its status as "mankind" and becoming merely a number of people, so all moral concepts become meaningless: good and evil mean only pleasure and pain, life and death. As Shelley believed the individual intellect to perish with the body, so Mary relentlessly pursues his argument:

A sense of degradation came over me [Verney says]. Did God create man, merely in the end to become dead earth in the midst of healthful vegetating nature? (. . .) Were our proud dreams thus to fade? (. . .) How reconcile this sad change to our past aspirations, to our apparent powers!

Sudden an internal voice, articulate and clear, seemed to say:—Thus, from eternity, it was decreed: the steeds that bear Time onwards had this hour and this fulfilment en-chained to them, since the void brought forth its burthen. Would you read backwards the unchangeable laws of Neces-sity? (. . .)

If my human mind [Verney continues] cannot acknowledge that all that is, is right; yet since what is, must be, I will sit amidst the ruins and smile.

The attitude of ironic acceptance in the final sentence is by no means Shelley's; the passage merely demonstrates Shelley's intently interested mind operating in the teeth of the deadly ultimate issues of his enquiry. And Mary took Shelley's conclusions to a further stage; for whereas Shelley must have admitted at least a certain immorality to man, proceeding in his progeny, Mary removed even this possibility, positing his theoretical proposition in a stark, simplified form.

And again it is Shelley's sense of mankind's limited destiny, and his consequent conviction of the futility as well as the evils of war, that are echoed by Adrian's exhortation to his army:

> Sheath your weapons; these are your brothers, commit not fratricide; soon the plague will not leave one for you to glut your revenge upon; will you be more pitiless than pestilence?

Shelley's ideas of universal love, looked upon by some of his critics as rather immature, are illustrated by the narrative's hypothesis in their most rational form. Death, common to all, and magnified here in the shape of pestilence, renders the human race precious, and therefore cherishable; a candidate for preservation, as are rare species of animals. When Mary tells us:

> Man existed by twos and threes; man, the individual who might sleep, and wake, and perform the animal functions; but man, in himself weak, yet more powerful in congregated numbers than wind or ocean; man, the queller of the elements, the lord of created nature, the peer of demi-gods, existed no longer.

she is emphasising and clarifying her own apprehension of Shelleyan thought by the not very honest method of removing as many obstacles to his argument as possible; by reducing mankind "the lord of created nature" to man, the individual, who existed by two's and three's. We may detect here an implicit criticism of Shelley's ideas of society. Where those ideas are impractical, she seems to imply, is in their application to social man: take away society and observe man truly as an individual, and only then Shelley's ideas are valid. In fact, she turned the rational humanism of Shelley back upon itself.

But what she consciously desired to convey was a conception she had acquired from Shelley of mankind's pitiable plight, symbolised by the fate of individual man. The incident where Adrian succeeds in intervening between the opposing armies, by focussing attention on one man dying from wounds, is an example.

Adrian tore off his military scarf and bound it round the sufferer—it was too late. (. . .) "He is dead!" said Adrian. (. . .) The fate of the world seemed bound up in the death of this single man. On either side the bands threw down their arms.

The conclusions of this incident, the relinquishing of arms in the heat of battle, for idealistic reasons, is, of course, Shelley's romantic optimism, and serves to show how far his influence extended to Mary's naturally pessimistic and realistic view of life.

Where Mary departs from Shelley's influence, however, is through a demonstrative process of "denuding." She depopulates both the physical territory of the novel and the dialectical scene, while Shelley amasses his population, as it were, both in his work and his argument. Shelley's precise comprehension of the beginnings of things becomes more mystical and tenuous as they progress towards ultimates (the speech of Asia, beginning "There was the Heaven and Earth at first" in Act II, Scene 4 of *Prometheus Unbound* may be taken as an example in point); whereas Mary, in *The Last Man,* concerns her more prosaic and literal mind with issues which she renders more intelligible as they proceed.

Shelley's indirect influence may also be discernible throughout the work in its Platonism. But I am inclined to think that it was directly from her Greek studies, and particularly her reading of *The Republic,* that Mary grasped the notions which she delineates, of situation leading to situation; of one type of society causing another; of the sort of individuals bred from and breeding their correlative forms of government. Evidence of her study of Plato is apparent in detail and in general. Her depiction of tyrant following on the heels of democrat, and her portraiture of various aspects of the politically ambitious nature, are isolated examples of the Platonic signature on her mind. This, combined with her ability to follow ideas to their extremities, and her close observation of social man, rewards her novel with a philosophical unity very rarely achieved in a work of so comprehensive a range.

III

If *The Last Man* were to be called a Gothic novel, the qualification must be added that it exists as such only in so far as an improbable theme of horror maintains an illusion of probability. As in *Frankenstein,* this story offers nothing supernatural, and very little except plain horror that is proper to the Gothic convention. But this horror is enough to reveal its Gothic affinities. It is true that the plague does not descend from the clouds as from the wrath of a fiend; but it does ascend from the earth, evolving from microbe to monster and sinuously progressing across the whole terrestrial scene. And the Greek Princess Evadne, her exotic temperament, her high-flown actions and her final passionate prophecy are in the Gothic style. As in *Frankenstein,* however, although the effects are horrific the methods are not those of the horror-novel proper; as in *Frankenstein,* the Gothic element is chastened by the rational.

It is further chastened by realism, and still further by a domestic note. It is not, therefore, a Gothic novel entirely; nor is it realist fiction, for the whole work is a fantasy; and neither is it a domestic tale, for the work deals with society at large as well as family life; moreover, it is not a sociological novel, since the disintegration of the social scene leaves a large portion of the book to the study of individual man. *The Last Man,* in fact, defies classification in any accepted fictional genre; but that is not to question its value as such. I would describe it as a triptych of fiction—a group of three futuristic pictures, associated with, yet distinct from, each other.

The pastoral domesticity of the opening is vivified by the peremptory figure of Raymond, and with his death a self-contained tale would terminate, did he not leave a vacancy for the Protectorate, and did he not meet his death in a city already devastated by plague. These two stray factors, subsidiary to the opening theme, are taken up and developed to prominence in the next phase, where the domestic motif progresses merely as an undertone to the fanfare of political intrigue attempting to justify itself in the face of encroaching disaster; finally, political and social aspects are gradually discarded, leaving the ideological essence of the book denuded of all but a solitary protagonist endeavouring to come to terms with existence.

Mary Shelley does not set out to offer any surface continuity, but adopts the technique of utilising each phase to prepare for the next; the primary theme of each phase becomes secondary in the next. Structurally, it is a symphonic technique—a pattern composed of movements evolving one from the other.

One of the unique features of *The Last Man* is its fusion of fantasy with realism. The opening is pitched on a recognisable, rural level; and plausibility is also established by a precise fixture in time, the year 2073, to which Mary does not pay more than passing regard in the ensuing pages, since its purpose is fulfilled. These are the factors which provide the gradient for her story.

Her domestic opening has another advantage; for this early scene of action, placed in a setting of leisure, cultivation and nobility, in which the best of human behaviour is expressed, provides an artistic contrast with the ultimate havoc of the prospect. The idyllic start is soon tempered by the introduction of political complications, in which Mary Shelley shows a knowing sense of detail. The effect of realism is now conveyed in an acceptable manner, though the basic fantasy of a Republic is already present; and helps to tide the reader's credence over the ensuing Grecian battle scenes where Mary is all too lavish. The Grecian episode culminates with an explosion co-incident with Raymond's entry into Constantinople— a clumsy enough contrivance, but one which serves, once more, as a contrast to subsequent events. Against the violence of battle and of Raymond's death, the patient, insidious approach of universal disaster is the more effective. Meanwhile, the element of fantasy increases, and continues to increase to the very end; but by a method of juxtaposing the specific realism of incident and the general fantasy of the plague, the fantasy itself is not apparent, but invokes an effect of realism.

The growth of this realist-fantasy depends upon Mary Shelley's view of death, a view which was something more than pessimistic acceptance. Her attitude at this time was a positive one of loathing and abhorrence. She shows death, indiscriminate and irrefutable; and the exhaustive method by which she waylays the reader to observe, now this activity of the plague, now that consequence, reveals how deeply her imagination was engaged by the subject.

Her imagination was powerful, and it was of the type that always has relation to practical life. Before the plague reaches England its shores are besieged by refugees. A state of emergency exists, similar to the war-time conditions of twentieth-century Europe. Owners of large estates offer asylum to the homeless, their park-land is ploughed and sown with crops:

> A fashion was set. The high-born ladies of the country would have deemed themselves disgraced if they had now enjoyed, what they before called a necessary, the ease of a carriage.

Attendant upon the arrival of the plague in England, Mary describes a wave of hedonism, also forcibly reminiscent of the mass impulses that accompany modern warfare:

> The ties of public opinion were loosened; (. . .) the theatres were open and thronged; dance and midnight festival were frequented—in many of these decorum was violated, and the evils, which hitherto adhered to an advanced state of civilization, were doubled . (. . .) enjoyment might be protracted to the verge of the grave.

The horror of the general situation, of death's constant presence, gains emphasis as Mary demonstrates its effect on all aspects of civilized life. There is a peculiar aptness about her morbidity; it is not the mere depiction of horror in which she delights, but the imaginative amassing of evidence towards a tragic end. And this evidence seems to be summed up when she presents Verney at a performance of *Macbeth*, hearing the lines spoken:

> Alas, poor country;
> Almost afraid to know itself! It cannot
> Be called our mother, but our grave: where nothing,
> But who knows nothing, is once seen to smile;
> Where sighs, and groans, and shrieks that rend the air,
> Are made, not marked; where violent sorrow seems
> A modern extasy: the dead man's knell

Is there scarce asked for who; and good men's lives
Expire before the flowers in their caps,
Dying, or ere they sicken.

"Each word struck the sense," she writes, "as our life's passing bell;
we feared to look at each other. . . ."

And, as Mary's imagination was trained on incident after incident
to verify every possible manifestation of the tragedy's advance, her
psychological perception is sustained. As society is levelled, we
note its return to fundamental principles; and Mary gives close
scrutiny to individual reactions. She displays panic among the outwardly normal—in Ryland, the hard-headed politician, for example. And in her portrayal of Adrian's practical behaviour in emergency is expressed that surprising aspect of the "ineffectual" man,
in extraordinary circumstances, of which history gives many an
example.[1] We see each type of individual reacting to no effect, each
in his characteristic way: one will endure enormous deprivations
while refusing to tolerate small inconveniences; another will seize
a pitiful opportunity for power. There is scarcely a human type
escapes her notice:

In Paris there were a few, perhaps a hundred, who, resigned
to their coming fate, flitted about the streets of the capital and
assembled to converse of past times, with that vivacity and
even gaiety that seldom deserts the individuals of this nation.

The religious fanatic who gains sway over a large section of the
people Mary sees also as a political tyrant:

The preacher was as cautious and prudent, as he was cruel. His
victims lived under the strictest rules and laws, which either
entirely imprisoned them (. . .) or let them out in such
numbers, and under such leaders, as precluded the possibility
of controversy.

---

1. Shelley himself was certainly no dreamer in moments of emergency: for example, his prompt action in procuring a bucket of ice and making Mary sit in it during
her miscarriage of 1822, which saved her life.

"His power was founded on fear," Mary tells us simply; and her general deductions from this incident are noteworthy, for in them she formulates her disillusioned view of politicians:

It is a strange fact, but incontestible, that the philanthropist, who ardent in his desire to do good, who patient, reasonable and gentle, yet disdains to use other argument than truth, has less influence over men's minds, than he who, grasping and selfish, refuses not to adopt any means, nor awaken any passion, nor diffuse any falsehood, for the advancement of his cause.

IV

Adverse criticism may be directed towards *The Last Man* on the grounds of weak characterisation, want of humour, and heaviness of style. The first charge is possibly the most serious, yet the most difficult to justify since it is rather a criticism of Mary's approach to character than her handling of it. Concerning people, she did not ask the question, in what way is this person distinct from all others? but instead she asked, what is the nature of his resemblance to certain others? In fact, she was more interested in the type than in the individual, and if she did not attempt to depict the latter, her study of types of humanity is varied and sound. Adrian, for instance, is the very ideal of the idealist. Raymond is the ideal Don Juan; and Ryland, the politician of ideal corruption. For the inflexible aristocrat represented by the ex-queen; for the eccentric scholar moulded in the form of Merrival the astronomer; for the religious racketeer —for each of these there is an "original in Heaven." But these types are not caricatured; they are creatures of necessity and circumstances, and as apposite products of their society they have true and objective being. I am not sure, though, that it is desirable for fictional characters to have too objective an existence; those that are projections of their author are very often the most successful. Certainly Verney, who in his last solitary wandering symbolises Mary Shelley's own destiny, is her most interesting essay in characterisation. Here, however, there was no scope for pitting his uniqueness against that of another, which is the true test of characterisation.

To complain of Mary Shelley's prose style and her lack of humour is to complain of a root cause. Both are the consequence of a mind in which emotion is held under considerable control. The restraint of emotional expression for publication was a habit Mary had imbibed from her earliest years, and is most prominently manifest in her more emotional passages. With this is connected her apparent lack of humour, for where her prose is heavy it seems that her mood is so.

It is not really that *The Last Man* does not contain humorous situations. Her brand of humour, however, is ironic; and demands, where the irony is light, a deft turn of phraseology to be really effective; and where it is tragic, it requires a direct style that labours no point. Mary's prose was not always flexible enough to bring off these effects, and many of her ironic situations appear unnoticed even by her. But where she seems aware of such situations, she does handle them very successfully. Raymond's self-analysis when his wife has discovered his infidelity is an example of Mary's comic-irony:

> Raymond staggered forth from this scene, as a man might do, who had been just put to the torture, and looked forward to when it would be again inflicted. He had sinned against his own honour, by affirming, swearing to, a direct falsehood; true, this he had palmed on a woman, and it might therefore be deemed less base. (. . .) Truth and falsehood, love and hate lost their eternal boundaries, heaven rushed in to mingle with hell; while his sensitive mind, turned to a field for such battle, was stung to madness.

Her tragic irony, however, is more dramatic and more cogent, and occurs at its best in a passage describing the last travels of the straggling remnants of humanity through France. The despairing, near-mad company begin to sense the supernatural everywhere.

> A ghost was depicted by every blighted tree; and appalling shapes were manufactured from each shaggy bush. . . . Once, at the dusk of the evening, we saw a figure all in white, appar-

ently of more than human stature, flourishing about the road, now throwing up its arms, now leaping to an astonishing height in the air, then turning round several times successively, then raising itself to its full height and gesticulating violently. Our troop, on the alert to discover and believe in the supernatural, made a halt at some distance from this shape; and, as it became darker, there was something appalling even to the incredulous, in the lonely spectre, whose gambols, if they hardly accorded with spiritual dignity, were beyond human powers. Now it leapt right up in the air, now sheer over a high hedge, and was again the moment after in the road before us. By the time I came up, the fright experienced by the spectators of this ghostly exhibition, began to manifest itself in the flight of some, and the close huddling together of the rest. Our goblin now perceived us; he approached, and, as we drew reverentially back, made a low bow. The sight was irresistibly ludicrous even to our hapless band, and his politeness was hailed by a shout of laughter;—then, again springing up, as a last effort, it sunk to the ground, and became almost invisible through the dusky night. This circumstance again spread silence and fear through the troop; the more courageous at length advanced, and, raising the dying wretch, discovered the tragic explanation of this wild scene. It was an opera-dancer, and had been one of the troop which deserted from Villeneuve-la-Guiard: falling sick, he had been deserted by his companions; in an access of delirium he had fancied himself on the stage, and, poor fellow, his dying sense eagerly accepted the last human applause that could ever be bestowed on his grace and agility.

This is the irony of the Dance of Death. But Mary Shelley's irony is mostly in situation, seldom expressed in a word or a phrase, and less seldom in dialogue. Her style is best suited to plain narrative, and does not move well in incidental commentary or in conversational pieces.

Mary Shelley was gifted with a considerable command of language. Her diction is precise, her vocabulary large, and she is obviously selective; though sometimes it is the platitudinous phrase which she selects, and her preciseness is occasionally prim. But on the whole, she expresses herself with greater clarity and force than do many of her more renowned contemporaries. If she has no nice stylistic methods, she in no way distracts the reader by clumsy expression or irrelevant floweriness. And while the restraint of her prose style, proceeding from the purposeful logic she employs and not from expressive ineptitude, has a sorry effect on her dialogue, it has compensating advantages so far as the subjects she handles are concerned; for her style possesses a kind of mesmeric evenness that goes well with a powerful theme.

Mary was content to let the theme take its own effect; she was wary of piling on the agony. And it is notable that where her prose does become intensified, it is in those passages where the action or the theme of horror is temporarily dormant.

It is more cold within her [says Verney of Perdita in a reflective moment], than a fire left by gypsies in wintertime, the spent embers crowned by a pyramid of snow.

And during another lull in the action, where Verney contemplates a dead man, his words give the impression of heightened awareness:

Half insanely I spoke to the dead. So the plague killed you, I muttered. How came this? Was the coming painful? You look as if the enemy had tortured, before he murdered you.

His next words mark a return to the normal tempo of the narrative:

And now I leapt up precipitately, and escaped.

In this way, too, Mary succeeds in creating an atmosphere for her story; and she also employs the graphic technique of introducing the motif of storm in order to convey an atmosphere of foreboding. All the Brontë sisters did this, incidentally, and Mary is no less effectual when she prepares for an approaching disaster with the ominous sound of contending seas and winds.

The disposal of atmosphere throughout *The Last Man* is, indeed, one of its most remarkable qualities, so unobtrusively suggested is it, and varied. Many a purely informative paragraph contains a quiet sentence or a word so evocative as to immediately direct our response to some fresh or unsuspected meaning. Such an atmospheric suggestiveness occurs in a passage as unmomentous as this:

> In about a fortnight the remainder of the emigrants arrived from England, and they all repaired to Versailles; apartments were prepared for the family of the Protector in the Grand Trianon, and there, after the excitement of these events, we reposed amidst the luxuries of the departed Bourbons.

It is the last few words that yield a suffusion of nostalgia. So, too, the vast desolation experienced by the wandering fugitives is communicated, when in the last stages of the plague they reach the Swiss Alps—

> Our misery took its majestic shape and colouring from the vast ruin, that accompanied and made one with it. (. . .) This solemn harmony of event and situation regulated our feelings, and gave as it were fitting costume to our last act.

—providing an aura of ritual to the ending of a species.

The summoning of atmosphere, at its best a verbal achievement in *The Last Man,* is however, limited by Mary Shelley's inability to handle intimate emotional situations. The scene of the proud ex-queen's sentimental remorse at her daughter's tomb-side is an example. Mary usually solved this difficulty by avoiding such scenes altogether. For instance, when her story develops to the point where Verney, Adrian and the girl Clara are the sole population of the earth, Mary confronts herself with a problem of individual relationships which she complicates further by her careful study of Clara's emergence from childhood:

> Before we quitted Milan, a change had taken place in her habits and manners. She lost her gaiety, she laid aside her sports, and assumed an almost vestal plainness of attire.

[196]

But to no purpose. Clara's fate is sealed, not only by the author's incapacity to cope with the issues presented, but by the reading public of 1826 who would not consent to witness a girl selecting her mate in a world where there is no clergyman to marry them.

Vast events, general ideas, passions like ambition and universal love are what Mary manipulates with ease; and the greater merits of *The Last Man* reside in its general aspects, where a comprehensive wisdom and foresight are manifest. The points made by some biographers regarding the "prophetic" incidents in the novel—for example, where the Royal Family takes the name of Windsor—are not intended here; but that her fertile imagination is given earthly roots, is brought within the range of acute probability, by her sagacity and discernment.

The conception of *The Last Man* is eminently a product of the early nineteenth century. The subject was variously treated by numerous poets during the years 1816–26, notable among them Campbell, Byron, Hood and Beddoes. Campbell's poem *The Last Man* (1823) preceded Mary's novel.

> The Sun's eye had a sickly glare,
>   The Earth with age was wan,
> The skeletons of nations were
>   Around that lonely man!
> Some had expired in fight,—the brands
> Still rusted in their bony hands;
>   In plague and famine some!
> Earth's cities had no sound nor tread;
> And ships were drifting with the dead
>   To shores where all was dumb!

These lines of Campbell undoubtedly influenced Mary's approach to her subject. And Byron's poem *Darkness* (1816) is in a similar spirit:

> The world was void,
> The populous and the powerful was a lump,
> Seasonless, herbless, treeless, manless, lifeless,
> A lump of death—a chaos of hard clay.

Simultaneously, the theme was appearing on the canvasses of fashionable painters.[2]

As the factory gates nightly emitted their begrimed victims like smoke from their chimney stacks; as every whistle-stop on the new railroad engendered its Mechanic's Institute; so mankind lost confidence in its natural faculties. Science lined up with industry to form a force as vast and irrational as Mary's Plague; and all premises seemed to point to a Last Man.

"I neither pretend to protect nor govern an hospital," says Ryland, the Protector, "—such will England quickly become." It was a universal hospital and finally a universal morgue that Mary envisaged, before the French Symbolists had cried in their several ways, *"Cette vie est un hôpital,"* to be echoed by Rilke and T. S. Eliot; and before the possibility of the world's entire devastation was only a bomb's-throw away.

This Mary Shelley had begun to anticipate in *Frankenstein.* There science destroys his discoverer; but there the issues between the two have an equal run, and Frankenstein is in a position to challenge his Monster with a chance of success. But in *The Last Man,* the menacing force has become as impersonal and impartial as nature, by which the individual man is held in isolated subjection.

So Mary Shelley saw herself. Ultimately we must return to the fact that it is from her own experience of solitude, from the personal landscape of devastation she felt around her, that her wonderful story draws life.

2. The theme subsequently recurs in poetry down to the present time: see, for example, James Kirkup's poem *The Last Man* in his book *The Submerged Village and Other Poems* (Oxford University Press, London, 1951).

Chapter 13

Perkin Warbeck

In common with thousands of young people of her day, Mary Shelley read the Waverley Novels as fast as they appeared. In Pisa with Shelley in 1820 she began *Ivanhoe* one day and finished it the next. By December 1821 she was back at *Ivanhoe* again, and once more consumed it in the space of two days.

The subject of *Ivanhoe* had suggested itself to Scott as a means of providing a change from his former "Scottish Romances," and of showing his readers he could compose in more than one key; and it was possibly with something of this feeling that Mary decided to write her historical romance, *Perkin Warbeck*. She must have realised by now that the public was becoming inured to Gothicism, and though horror was in many ways her forte, she was beginning to take public demand into greater account. For one thing, her need for money had started to corrode her need for creative satisfaction. *The Last Man*'s reception was not commensurate with the imaginative effort she spent on it, nor indeed, with its deserts. Had Mary been able, or willing, to disregard the public, she might now have fulfilled that powerful promise which *The Last Man* held out.

This time Mary looked for a subject which would restrain the vaster impulses of her imagination, and at the same time prove her ability to handle a theme entirely different from any she had attempted before. "An historical subject of former times must be treated in a way that affords no scope for *opinions,* and I think you will have no reason to object to it on that score," she wrote to John Murray, who she hoped would commission the novel. No doubt she felt that this restraint was the safer course, and probably restrained her "opinions" the more since she was under the impression that Murrays' wanted no polemics. The book was nearly finished when Murrays' told her they could not publish it—news which disappointed Mary deeply. In her anxiety to place the book, at the end of 1829, she assured Henry Colburn, who finally published it, that the work was finished and at the copying stage, but it is worthy of note that the same day she confessed to the friend who was acting as her agent that all was not written and unless she received an immediate agreement, "I should not have spirits to proceed." This statement illuminates the fact that in the last chapters of her book, written after Murrays' rejection, she did obtrude something of her own convictions, the ban on "opinion" having assumed less urgency in her mind.

As an entity, *Perkin Warbeck* is of less value than are its component parts, which merit attention since they confirm certain stable elements in Mary's writings. They distinguish her, at her weakest, from the lady and gentleman amateurs of her time who slapped-up endless facile tales for the gilt-edged annuals then in currency; and at her best, in *Perkin Warbeck,* Mary fills a more sensitive, a more disciplined and a more convincing capacity than ever did Mrs. Radcliffe, Jane Porter and other vaguely historical romancers before Scott himself.

But as an entity, *Perkin Warbeck* has remarkably happy points, faulty as it is in many of the essentials of good fiction: the theory of Warbeck's case put forward by Mary Shelley is a highly engaging one which occupies an important place in the development of literature on the theme. And this theory is fortified by Mary's scrupulous acquirement of knowledge on the subject. In this sense she emulates Scott's example with greater fidelity than any other woman writer before George Eliot. Scott would have approved of the way in which Mary set about her task; in fact, he may have expressed approval. For in the course of her research Mary wrote to the famous novelist begging him to help her with "any document, anecdote or even ballad connected with him [Perkin Warbeck] generally unknown" on her subject. And Scott, who had already praised *Frankenstein,* was certainly courteous enough to have replied. Was it he, for instance, who put her on to the old Burgundian chronicle from which she took the following epigraph to her book?

> *J'ai veu filz d'Angleterre, Richard d'Yorc nommé,*
> *Que l'on disoit en terre, estinct et consommé,*
> *Endurer grant souffrance; et par nobles exploitz,*
> *Vivre en bonne esperance, d'estre Roy des Angloys.*

The story of Perkin Warbeck's rise and fall set Mary to digging up manuscripts and histories of the period; and as part of her tale was to have its setting in Spain, she was not content until she was thoroughly saturated in Spanish history and topography.

Her tale opens on the 22nd August 1485, the day of the Lancastrians' final victory over the Yorkists at Bosworth Field, and ends shortly after the execution in 1499 of Perkin Warbeck.

The historical Warbeck claimed to be Edward the Fourth's younger son, Richard, Duke of York, who was imprisoned in the Tower with his brother; he based his pretentions to the throne of Henry the Seventh on the claim that his brother had died in the Tower, himself having escaped to friends and a childhood of obscurity. Warbeck caused the king serious trouble by his activities in France, Ireland, Cornwall and in Scotland, where he was accepted as the rightful king of England by James the Fourth, and given James's cousin Lady Katherine Gordon in marriage. After a final attempt at insurrection in Cornwall, Warbeck was captured and kept prisoner by Henry. He escaped and was recaptured but for reasons of expediency was beguiled by King Henry into a second attempt, whereupon he was executed. At the time of his capture,

Warbeck confessed to being, after all, the son of a merchant and repeated this confession at the scaffold.

Mary Shelley's story offers the theory that Warbeck was, in fact, the younger of the princes in the Tower, who on his brother's death, had been secretly placed by his uncle under a Yorkist nobleman's charge; reports of the boy's death were then circulated and his uncle was free to name himself Richard the Third. On the latter's death at Bosworth Field, the young Richard, Duke of York, is sent for safety out of the country to live under the name of Perkin Warbeck with the family of a Spanish sea-faring adventurer. When he grows up, Richard ventures forth to claim his birthright, the throne of England occupied by Henry, and also to espouse the lost cause of the White Rose. From now on, historical fact is more or less followed in the narrative. As Bacon, whose life of Henry the Seventh Mary Shelley had studied closely, describes it, "The news hereof came blazing and thundering over into England that the Duke of York was sure alive." Richard raises some ineffectual support in Ireland, then travels to the French court where he is received royally, but is courteously asked to leave when France is threatened by England as a result of his presence. His next move takes him to the Duchess of Burgundy, a kinswoman, who supplies him with forces for his abortive attempt to land at Kent in 1495. We next find the disinherited prince in Scotland where he gains the confidence of James the Fourth, who promises to invade England in the cause of his royal guest, and who further marries Richard to Lady Katherine Gordon, a cousin of James's. The proposed subjection of England by the Scots is, however, confounded when the Scots cross the border, and to Richard's indignation begin to lay waste and pillage the very country of which he is the unacknowledged monarch. After James's ignominious retreat, Richard returns to Ireland, willingly accompanied by his bride.

Meanwhile in England, Cornish risings have been frequent, and Richard is persuaded to cross with a few followers and raise an army in this discontented area. With a force of undisciplined, rudely-armed rebels, Richard marches on Exeter, leaving Katherine in a convent sanctuary in Cornwall. An attempt to take Exeter fails, and the unkempt ranks proceed to besiege Taunton. At the end of the first day of siege, Richard receives a message which tells him that an army of trained soldiers sent by the Duchess of Burgundy is at his disposal only twenty miles away, and that the men, dispirited by news of Henry's approaching forces, threaten to return if they do not see Richard in person. Whereupon Richard departs from the camp with a small troop of followers, only to find that the message is a ruse to capture him. He reaches sanctuary in a monastery, which soon is surrounded by Henry's men, who do not dare to enter the holy place. But Richard cannot endure this means of protection and surrenders himself.

(In these last incidents and thereafter, it is noteworthy that the author departs more widely than hitherto from Bacon, who describes the pretender's flight from Taunton as a desertion, and his surrender from sanctuary as the result of Henry's offer to spare Warbeck's life if he should give himself up. Mary Shelley also makes nothing of Warbeck's confession.)

Mary Shelley's hero is taken into custody at Westminster from where he escapes; and once more he falls prey to treachery and is taken. His next prison is the Tower, where he makes friends with his fellow-prisoner, an Earl of Warwick. Together they plan an escape which miscarries, and costs them both their lives. Katherine, who was brought from Cornwall to Henry's court at the time of Richard's first capture, is treated with the courtesy befitting her rank, and after taking her grievous farewell of her husband, she continues under Henry's protection.

Threading their ways through this bare outline are the motifs of intrigue, treachery, pursuit and love. Our sympathy engaged at the outset in Richard's favour, we note, moving now from, now towards him, the figures of Monina, his childhood companion in the years of obscurity; of Frion, his brilliant, unprincipled secretary; of Sir Robert Clifford, treacherous blackguard whose fate is bound to Richard's in a curious complexity of attraction and repulsion; of James, the man of parts who is King of Scots; of Monina's father, the way-faring Moor, de Faro; and of the remarkable Lady Katherine, who becomes Richard's wife. These characters are the establishing factors of conviction in the story. Paler figures—Edmund Plantagenet; the Chamberlain, Lord Stanley; the Irish adherents to

Richard; Henry's courtiers; and the defeated Yorkist nobility—serve to fix a background of political and social scenery in the years following the Wars of the Roses.

"The principal thing that I should wish to be impressed on my reader's mind is, that whether my hero was or was not an imposter, he was believed to be the true man by his contemporaries," Mary wrote in the Preface. This had some justification. Bacon, whom Mary acknowledges as one of her main authorities, writing little more than 120 years after Warbeck's death, states that contemporary credence was given to the pretender's claim, and even hints at his own preference for Perkin Warbeck's entitlement. Bacon might have more than hinted, had he not been under a recent obligation to James the First (of England)—and that being no time to glorify a pretender. As it was, Bacon was content to remark,

> But this youth, of whom we are now to speak, was such a mercurial, as the like hath seldom been known, and could make his own part if at any time he chanced to be out. Wherefore this being one of the strangest examples of a personation that ever was in elder or later times, it deserveth to be discovered and related to the full; although the king's [that is, Henry the Seventh's] manner of showing things by pieces, and by dark lights, hath so muffled it, that it hath left it almost as a mystery to this day.

There is no doubt that Perkin Warbeck did convince James of Scotland of his bona fides, for not only did James prove his belief by giving Warbeck a royal bride, but also continued to make trouble in the north of England on behalf of his protégé, after the latter had departed for Ireland.

The account of Perkin Warbeck's career, as stated in his own confession, is now generally accepted as genuine. The fact that Warbeck, a believing Catholic, repeated this confession at the point of death might make irrelevant the question of whether it was extorted by torture or not. During Henry the Seventh's lifetime a confession, valid or otherwise, was made by a man who claimed to have participated in murdering the princes in the Tower, and at the time of Charles the Second, two skeletons approximating to the size of the princes were discovered in the Tower.

Mention is made in contemporary documents of a factor that seems to have gained fairly wide acceptance—that is, that Edward the Fourth, whom Warbeck claimed as his father, was in reality his godfather. If this was so, it seems strange that the king should be induced thus to honour an insignificant household; and if we remember that Warbeck's appearance persuaded many of the nobility that he was a Plantagenet, there may be some truth in Bacon's suggestion that Warbeck was an illegitimate son of Edward the Fourth.

But it was not Mary Shelley's purpose to examine these questions on historical grounds. Her theme was suggested to her, as she said, by "the partial pages of Bacon." John Ford's play *Perkin Warbeck* was also a considerable influence, which, as it was not properly an historical source, Mary does not mention in her Preface, although she makes an implicit acknowledgement by quoting passages from Ford as epigraphs to several chapters. Ford's drama, based, too, on Bacon's *Henry the Seventh,* excited Mary to some efforts of characterisation in which she rarely excelled elsewhere. For her handling of fictional background and the spirit informing it, she relied on Scott's *Ivanhoe.*

The latter influence, Mary failed properly to co-ordinate with the other two. Scott's was a mediaeval romance. So, too, in essence, was Mary's although situated some centuries later. And her attempt to fuse this spirit with the Renaissance sensibility of Bacon and Ford resulted only in an unequal distribution throughout the work of the separate influences of these writers. Consequently, although Mary cannot be accused of literal anachronisms, there is a confusion of attitudes in the novel, which are brought to unfortunate focus on her main character, Richard, Duke of York. This lack of integration is the more apparent since some of her subsidiary characters are well handled, and throw Richard into contrast.

Richard is a mixture of Ivanhoe, Shelley, and Ford's Perkin Warbeck; and he is further embarrassed by his equivocal role in the story, that of a rebel fighting a reactionary cause. If we may say for convenience that Bosworth Field marked the end of the Middle Ages, and suggest that the surrender of baronial potency under Henry the Seventh was the occasion of a new order, we must see in Richard's representation of the Yorkist cause, in his nostalgic yearning to revive the Wars of the Roses, a reversion to the old order. But in his attempt to claim the throne from the reigning power, he perforce plays the insurrectionary. This confusion of motives renders his personality impotent; and his continual vacillation and susceptibility to betrayal confirm him in his credulous and weak singularity.

The author's too close adherence to the spirit of Scott is exemplified by her emphasis on what remained of the unofficial "Roses" faction after Bosworth Field. Though in reality the principle of the Roses was indeed the weapon Warbeck employed, in fiction Warbeck will not stand a chance unless either the mutineer or the traditionalist in him predominates. As an instance, we may see how Ford overcomes the difficulty Warbeck's character presents by ignoring the Yorkist issue and showing his hero as the most noble of rebels. Ford, more decisively than Bacon, implies his own leaning towards Warbeck's claim, and Mary Shelley would have done well enough to clinch these implications by her open assertion of them, without introducing the Yorkist motif as a predominant one. She might even, with success, rather have presented a black-hearted villain than place her hero thus in a no-man's land of purpose.

Something of Mary Shelley's own interests may be detected in Richard's situation. She was, herself, at the time of composition approaching a state of compromise which evoked some resistance within her. The conflict she experienced between nostalgia for her rarified existence with Shelley and her new life of social observance has its counterpart in Richard's dual role. His reluctance to accept the compromise which had entwined the Red Rose with the White was Mary's, too, and she might well call her hero "Prince Lackland."

The character of Frion, Richard's Iago-like secretary who betrays his master and wins his way back into favour more often than we can credit, is one who helps to redeem the mischief done to the story by Richard. Derived, in more or less unadulterated form, from Ford's drama, this international spy fulfils with conviction the role Ford assigns him:

> Pestilent adder, he will hiss-out poison
> As dangerous as infectious . . .

Mary Shelley describes him,

He was an adept in intrigue; an oily flatterer; a man of unwearied activity, both of mind and body. It was his care to prevent York from suffering any of the humiliations incident to his position. He obtained supplies of money for him—he suffered none to approach who were not already full of zeal—when he met with any failure, he proved logically that it was a success, and magnified an escape into victory—he worked day and night to insure that nothing came near the Prince, except through his medium, which was one sugared and drugged to please.

The influence of Ford on the characterisation of the novel is its highest claim, and where Ford predominates, Mary's sober pages are animated by an exotic quality elsewhere infrequent. Scott, surprisingly, does not prove a successful influence on the characters here, possibly because he curdles so badly with Ford. There is one exception, however, in the figure of Sir Robert Clifford, who is a successful combination of Ford's version of him and *Ivanhoe*'s Bois Guilbert. Clifford is a promising youth who rapidly gives over to corruption; and his complex love-hatred emotion for Richard, his robust dedication to sin and his high-flown career of treachery until his death by Richard's hand is the more effective since he is permitted to proceed in his own being, unhampered by sentimental observations from the author.

One of Clifford's intended victims, Monina de Faro, should be mentioned, since she illustrates the contrast between those characters derived purely from Scott and those who bear Ford's touch. Monina, Richard's childhood playmate, follows the prince's fortunes in England, acting as a self-appointed agent for the White Rose. Her unnecessary presence throughout the tale can only be explained by Mary Shelley's admiration for Rebecca in *Ivanhoe*, of whom the Moorish girl, Monina, is but a dusky shadow. Like Rebecca's love for Ivanhoe, Monina's for Richard is such that she would willingly lay down her life for him and her love endures forever, though Richard marries another.

But irrelevant characters and situations in a novel cannot always be spared as easily as, we feel, could Monina and her doings. The liveliest passage in *Perkin Warbeck* is adorned by two ladies who appear momentarily. These are Lady Jane Kennedy and Mary Boyd, rival mistresses of James the Fourth of Scotland; and the account of the manner in which the two beauties "fight it out" offers one of the rarest moments in all Mary Shelley's writings; it is one of those passages from fiction that we remember though the tale itself is forgotten:

> There was a hawking party assembled in the neighbourhood of Stirling, which [King James] graced by his presence. All was, apparently, light-heartedness and joy, till a dispute arose between two damsels upon the merits of their respective falcons. (. . .)
>
> The contention between these ladies made many smile. The King betted a diamond against a Scottish pebble on Lady Jane's bird. (. . .) A heron rose from the river banks. The birds were unhooded, and up soared Lady Jane's in one equal flight through the blue air, cleaving the atmosphere with noiseless wing. Mary's followed slower; but, when Lady Jane's pounced on the quarry, and brought it screaming and flapping to the ground, the rival bird darted on the conqueror, and a sharp struggle ensued. It was unequal; for the Lady Jane's hawk would not quit its prey.
>
> "Let them fight it out," said Mary, "and the survivor is surely the victor."
>
> But the spectators cried shame—while Lady Jane, with a scream, hastened to save her favourite. The other, fiery as a borderer, attacked even her; and, in spite of her gloves, drops of blood from her fair hand, stained her silken robe. James came to her rescue, and with one blow put an end to the offender's life. Jane caressed her "tassle gentle," while Mary

looked on her "false carrion's" extinction with unrepressed indignation.

Could the savage side of women's passion be more aptly symbolised than in this shindy between two birds of elegant rearing? "Fiery as a borderer," the author observes of Mary Boyd's bird, when it draws blood from the nobler-born of the rival ladies, "in spite of her gloves." Lady Jane's falcon wins its prey, and Lady Jane her king, for Mary Boyd, we learn, is a falling star.

Though incidental relief of this sort is not introduced again with such style, and though some incidents and encounters are rather obviously contrived, there remain certain scenes which, like the one just quoted, disclose the genuine sensitivity of the artist. Such a one ensues when Richard, exhausted by protracted pursuit and betrayal, rests outside an inn just before his capture, tempting his sick horse to eat; while the three rough-hewn companions that remain to him, partake inside.

> Heron, who was warm-hearted with all his bluster, brought the prince out a flagon of excellent wine. (. . .) Richard was too ill to drink; but, as he stood, his arm on his poor steed's neck, the creature looked wistfully up in his face, averting his mouth from the proffered grain; half-playfully his master held out to him the wide-mouthed flagon, and he drank with such eagerness, that Richard vowed he should have another bottle, and, buying the host's consent with gold, filled a large can from the wine-cask; the beast drank, and, had he been a Christian man, could not have appeared more refreshed.

It is while Richard is "amusing himself thus" that the king's army descends upon them.

I have indicated this piece as an artistically successful one, not only because it is skilfully placed in the narrative, but because here Mary Shelley miraculously escapes sentimentality by a hair-breadth, and this is a thing we can nearly always discover the genuine artist doing. Had she solemnised the note in the slightest degree, did Richard give the horse his dinner instead of his wine, did the beast drink not only with thirst but with relish, the scene would have been ruined. And above all, the distinction, made by comparison, between the animal and "a Christian man" serves both to lighten the passage with a suggestion of incongruity and to decree that the horse shall remain a horse and not a sentimentalised, humanised "dumb friend."

For students of Mary Shelley's life, the figure of Richard's bride, Lady Katherine Gordon, is an interesting one, for with her Mary as good as admitted identity. The final chapter of *Perkin Warbeck* is devoted to this lady, who, having made one with Richard's cause up to the time of his death, thereafter becomes an honoured member of the court of her husband's enemy, Henry the Seventh.

In a footnote, Mary Shelley wrote:

> I do not know how far these concluding pages may be deemed superfluous: the character of Lady Katherine Gordon is a favourite of mine, and yet many will be inclined to censure her abode in Henry the Seventh's court, and other acts of her after-life. I desired therefore that she should speak for herself, and show how her conduct, subsequent to her husband's death, was in accordance with the devotions and fidelity with which she attended his fortunes during his life.

Thus Mary discloses the attempt she was making to reconcile her past life with Shelley, with the new way of life she was inclined towards—an "abode," as it were, "in Henry the Seventh's court." So, in Katherine's name, she makes her own apologia:

> There was no consolation for Katherine, which could make her for a moment forget that her present existence was but the lees of life, the spiritless remnants of a nectareous draught.

Katherine takes an active part in court life, none the less, and when a friend of Richard's accuses her of communing with her husband's murderer, she remarks, "We are all . . . impelled by our nature to make ourselves the central point of the universe," and on this solipsistic premise she takes her stand. Valid or not as her defence might be, Katherine reminds her accuser that she is a woman, guided not by reason, but by "the voice of my own soul which speaks within me."

"I try to forget; you force me back on myself. You attack, and you beseech me to defend myself. So to do, I must dwell upon the sentiments of a heart, which is human, and therefore faulty, but which has neither guile nor malice in it."

She speaks of her life with Richard, and her complete idolization of him, continuing:

"He was lost to me, my glory and my good! Little could I avail him now. (. . .) I was forced to feel that I was alone: and as to me, to love is to exist; so in that dark hour, in the gaspings of my agony, I felt that I must die, if for ever divided from him who possessed my affections.

"Years have passed since then. If grief kills us not, we kill it. Not that I cease to grieve; for each hour, revealing to me how excelling and matchless the being was who once was mine, but renews the pang with which I deplore my alien state upon earth. But such is God's will; I am doomed to a divided existence, and I submit. Meanwhile I am human; and human affections are the native, luxuriant growth of a heart whose weakness it is, too eagerly and too fondly, to seek objects on whom to expand its yearnings."

"I am doomed to a divided existence." In placing these words on Katherine's lips, Mary struck deep at her own root conflict. Over a hundred and fifty years later it is easy to see that the conflict was unnecessary. But Mary Shelley breathed the air of her times, as we breathe ours.

I have not touched on the prose style of *Perkin Warbeck* since it had developed little since *The Last Man,* but I should remark—and I think the various passages I have quoted will support me—that here her style fluctuates more noticeably between the heavy and the light, between the platitudinous and the original, than in her other writings; and the fact that she expresses herself somewhat rigidly in the opening chapters, only relaxing when her narrative gains headway, must have lost *Perkin Warbeck* many readers.

Throughout, Mary Shelley's realistic understanding of what a society looks like *en masse,* and her practical grasp of large-scale activities—her disposal, for instance, of military encampments and her ordering of battles—invite confidence in the story. And, as I hope to have shown, the reader is recompensed for some implausible situations by some memorable ones.

Chapter 14

Mary Shelley as Critic

Mary Shelley's editing of Shelley's poems was one of her most important works. Her stated object was in "giving the productions of a sublime genius to the world, with all the correctness possible, and of, at the same time, detailing the history of those productions, as they sprang, living and warm, from his heart and brain." Her Notes to the poems were intended as footnotes to Shelley's Notes, and here she recorded all the circumstances in which the poems were written—the poet's thoughts, words, moods and health at the time of composition, the places and events that disturbed and those that excited his imagination. "As a poet," she tells us, "his intellect and compositions were powerfully influenced by exterior circumstances, and especially by his place of abode." Mary was in a position to record not only things exterior to the poet but much of his inner life; she did so faithfully and well, with a consequent inestimable value to students of Shelley, for she is his first and most trustworthy exponent. Many of her own remarks on specific poems may be called to account; but they can never be merely disregarded, and, in fact, a large amount of subsequent writings on Shelley have their source in Mary's Notes.

Even those who remembered the acrimony that had once gathered round his name and work did at least realise to how great an extent her Notes had dispersed public prejudice. Browning was one of those who made an oblique acknowledgement to the effectuality of "those early authentic notices of Shelley's career."

That Mary's Notes are included in the Oxford definitive edition of Shelley's poetry is possibly the highest recognition she has received for them in this century. But as recent and as liberal-minded a critic as Herbert Read[1] took Mary severely to task for her efforts. Lamenting the "beautiful and ineffectual angel" myth of Shelley, patented by Matthew Arnold, Read declares, "Inept as Arnold was, the real villain of the piece is Mary Shelley, who, however difficult she may have found her husband in life, did nothing but sentimentalize him in death. It was she who, in the notes she affixed to the posthumous edition of his Poems, created the image of a whimsy Ariel which has ever since been so dear to superficial critics and romantic biographers. The decidedly scientific even if Platonic poet-philosopher . . . will not be such a popular figure, but he is demonstrably nearer the truth."

I have suggested elsewhere that Mary did indeed sentimentalize Shelley after his death. Evidence of this, however, occurs in her journals, which were intended for no eyes but her own, and which she used to release her private feelings.

Read's first faulty statement, however, occurs when he says that Mary "did nothing" but sentimentalize; for Mary did a great many things after Shelley's death besides bringing up a son and educating him well. But his serious mistake is in attributing the "ineffectual angel" concept to Mary's Notes. Exactly where in these Notes Mary created "the image of a whimsy Ariel" Herbert Read did not say. And in affirming that Mary's remarks on Shelley created a substantial first-hand portrait of him as a poet and thinker, I would

1. "Shelley," in Herbert Read, *Coat of Many Colours* (Routledge and Kegan Paul, London, 1945).

support my opinion with the following representative excerpts from her Notes:

The qualities that struck any one newly introduced to Shelley were,—First, a gentle and cordial goodness that animated his intercourse with warm affection and helpful sympathy. The other, the eagerness and ardour with which he was attached to the cause of human happiness and improvement; and the fervent eloquence with which he discussed such subjects. His conversation was marked by its happy abundance, and the beautiful language in which he clothed his poetic ideas and philosophical notions. To defecate life of its misery and its evil was the ruling passion of his soul; he dedicated to it every power of his mind, every pulsation of his heart. He looked on political freedom as the direct agent to effect the happiness of mankind; and thus any new-sprung hope of liberty inspired a joy and an exultation more intense and wild than he could have felt for any personal advantage.

(from *Preface to First Collected Edition,* 1839)

Shelley possessed two remarkable qualities of intellect—a brilliant imagination, and a logical exactness of reason. His inclinations led him (he fancied) almost alike to poetry and metaphysical discussions. I say "he fancied," because I believe the former to have been paramount, and that it would have gained the mastery even had he struggled against it.

(from *Note on the Revolt of Islam*)

. . . Shelley believed that mankind had only to will that there should be no evil, and there would be none. It is not my part in these Notes to notice the arguments that have been urged against this opinion, but to mention the fact that he entertained it, and was indeed attached to it with fervent enthusiasm. That man could be so perfectionized as to be able to expel evil from his own nature, and from the greater part of the creation, was the cardinal point of his system. And the subject he loved best

[215]

to dwell on was the image of One warring with the Evil Principle, oppressed not only by it, but by all—even the good, who were deluded into considering evil a necessary portion of humanity; a victim full of fortitude and hope and the spirit of triumph emanating from a reliance in the ultimate omnipotence of Good. Such he had depicted in his last poem, when he made Laon the enemy and the victim of tyrants. He now took a more idealized image of the same subject.

(from *Note on Prometheus Unbound*)

. . . He never spent a season more tranquilly than the summer of 1815. He had just recovered from a severe pulmonary attack; the weather was warm and pleasant. He lived near Windsor Forest; and his life was spent under its shades or on the water, meditating subjects for verse. Hitherto, he had chiefly aimed at extending his political doctrines, and attempted so to do by appeals in prose essays to the people, exhorting them to claim their rights; but he had now begun to feel that the time for action was not ripe in England, and that the pen was the only instrument wherewith to prepare the way for better things.

(from *Note on the Early Poems*)

His life was now spent more in thought than action—he had lost the eager spirit which believed it could achieve what it projected for the benefit of mankind. And yet in the converse of daily life Shelley was far from being a melancholy man. He was eloquent when philosophy or politics or taste were the subjects of conversation. He was playful; and indulged in the wild spirit that mocked itself and others—not in bitterness, but in sport. The author of *Nightmare Abbey* seized on some points of his character and some habits of his life when he painted Scythrop. He was not addicted to "port or madeira," but in youth he had read of "Illuminati and Eleutherarchs," and believed that he possessed the power of operating an immediate change in the minds of men and the state of society. These wild dreams had faded; sorrow and adversity had struck home; but he struggled with despondency as he did with physical pain. There are few who remember him sailing paper boats, and watching the navigation of his tiny craft with eagerness—or repeating with wild energy *The Ancient Mariner,* and Southey's *Old Woman of Berkeley;* but those who do will recollect that it was in such, and in the creations of his own fancy when that was most daring and ideal, that he sheltered himself from the storms and disappointments, the pain and sorrow, that beset his life.

(from *Note on Poems of 1817*)

His excellence is now acknowledged; but, even while admitted, not duly appreciated. For who, except those who were acquainted with him, can imagine his unwearied benevolence, his generosity, his systematic forbearance? And still less is his vast superiority in intellectual attainments sufficiently understood—his sagacity, his clear understanding, his learning, his prodigious memory. All these, as displayed in conversation, were known to few while he lived, and are now silent in the tomb.

(from *Note on Poems of 1818*)

I believe there is nothing here, nor elsewhere in Mary's Notes, to support the "ineffectual angel" myth. The aerial sprite, it is true, peeps out in such episodic passages as that where the sailing of paper boats is mentioned. But these are factual statements, not opinions of Mary's. The image was primarily a creation of Shelley's, for was it not he who claimed to have walked forty miles as though on air with no sense of fatigue? Was it not he who beheld visions, drank sherbet fizz instead of eating a square meal, and fostered impossible stories about himself, authentic though they may have appeared to him? Was it not he who sailed paper boats? This was an aspect of himself which Shelley loved to put across. Mary understood that this self-image was not the whole Shelley, but that it was important to him. He sheltered behind it, she said.

[217]

But Mary does succeed in presenting the other side of Shelley—the highly imaginative metaphysical poet, the humanist philosopher, the serious thinker.

And it was no fault of Mary's that the Ariel of Shelley's invention, not the poet-philosopher of her exposition, had adhered to his name by the time Matthew Arnold set to work on him. Arnold was impressed by Mary's Notes, and in them he claimed to find the essential Shelley. But when he comes to specify the source of his "ineffectual angel" concept, it is significant that he does not quote her, but speaks of "the Shelley with 'flushed, feminine artless face,' the Shelley 'blushing like a girl' of Trelawny." But the image had already been confirmed by the efforts, not only of Trelawny, but of Hunt, Edward Williams and others, including well-meaning Lady Shelley (Percy's wife) who, never having known the poet, made no less than a saint of him, turned a room of her house into a shrine in his honour and decreed that all who approached should remove hats and bonnets. Jane Williams, too, was not without blame; in her dotage she sat "proudly under Shelley's portrait, rising to bow to it when the great name was uttered," and declared, "He wasn't a man, he was a spirit."[2]

A great deal of all this had been put about before Arnold expressed his famous regrets about the Shelley of Professor Dowden's conception. Nor was Arnold the first critic to invest Shelley with wings, luminous or otherwise. "Can we imagine the case of an angel touched by lunacy?" had been one of de Quincey's smart queries, more than thirty years earlier. "Such an angel," he gloated, "such a man—if ever such there were—such a lunatic angel, such a ruined man, was Shelley whilst yet standing on the earliest threshold of life."

Mary, however, had neither of these angelic orders in mind when she wrote of Shelley. Nor did she pretend that he was other than the exceptional man he obviously was. During Shelley's lifetime she had written of him to Mrs. Hoppner, in refutation of slanderous reports: "You knew Shelley, you saw his face, and could you believe them?" and again, "Shelley is as incapable of cruelty as the

2. Sylva Norman, ed., *After Shelley: The Letters of Thomas Jefferson Hogg to Jane Williams* (Oxford University Press, London, 1934), p. xiv.

softest woman." She would not have written these things in such circumstances had they sounded far-fetched. Her observations in the Notes are not more excessive than these, and in many respects less so than some of Read's[3] on Shelley, which rather seem to have rejected Arnold's ineffectual angel, only to substitute de Quincey's lunatic one.

I have dwelt at length on the sort of misrepresentation Mary Shelley has been subject to, since it still crops up from time to time when new theoretical views of Shelley are being offered. Mary has seemed a convenient repository for discarded theories, and consequently her very material service to readers of Shelley could be underrated.

As a critic, Mary had gained some experience from her writings in the 1830s, on Italian, Spanish and French authors in Lardner's *Cyclopædia,* and occasional articles in such papers as *The Westminster Review.* She had edited an edition of Shelley's posthumous poems, published in 1824. And when she dealt with the first Collected Edition of Shelley's poems (1839), she did not attempt to present herself in the light of a detached commentator; her Notes are appreciative essays; but where she departs from biographical exposition, we may see both the limitations and the range of her poetic sensitivity.

The first principle she assumes is the "difficult" yet major quality of Shelley's poetry. "More popular poets," she writes in her Note which follows *Prometheus Unbound,* "clothe the ideal with familiar and sensible imagery. Shelley loved to idealize the real. (. . .)" In her Preface to the 1839 Collected Edition she had said, "He loved to idealize reality; and this is a taste shared by few. We are willing to have our passing whims exalted into passions, for this gratifies our vanity; but few of us understand or sympathize with the endeavour to ally the love of abstract beauty (. . .) with our sympathies with our kind. In this, Shelley resembled Plato; both taking more delight in the abstract and the ideal than in the special and tangible."

Mary's distinctions in these passages are really between two dif-

3. Herbert Read, *In Defence of Shelley and Other Essays* (Heinemann, London, 1936).

ferent romantic outlooks of her time. It is the Platonic element in Shelley, she suggests, that makes him unique and "difficult," and she probably refers to Wordsworth and his imitators when she speaks of those who "clothe the ideal with familiar and sensible imagery."

Yet it was "the special and tangible" that Mary most admired in Shelley's poetry. In her Preface to the book she had noted, "The luxury of imagination, which sought nothing beyond itself (as a child burdens itself with spring flowers, thinking of no use beyond the enjoyment of gathering them), often showed itself in his verses: they will be only appreciated by minds which have resemblance to his own. (. . .)" But her own mind was not of such a cast to appreciate the self-generative and self-sufficient elements in Shelley's poetry. It is on these grounds that she objected to *The Witch of Atlas,* provoking Shelley's reply which begins:

> How, my dear Mary,—are you critic-bitten
>   (For vipers kill, though dead) by some review,
> That you condemn these verses I have written,
>   Because they tell no story, false or true?
> What, though no mice are caught by a young kitten,
>   May it not leap and play as grown cats do,
> Till its claws come? Prithee, for this one time,
> Content thee with a visionary rhyme.

It has not been of the vision that Mary complained, but of the lack of its application to reality. *The Witch of Atlas* is the demonstrable point at which Mary's sensitivity departs from Shelley's poetry. "Even now," she wrote, "I believe that I was in the right." She could not accept a poem which was merely about itself; she could not come to terms of recognition with its evanescent imagery. Mary's taste inclined towards the highly imaginative in poetry (*The Ancient Mariner* had haunted her from childhood), but the imaginative always translated into concrete and feasible proportions. She preferred a message. It was the lack of allegory in *The Witch of Atlas* that disturbed her. But she perceives that the poem represents the technical framework of his major poems: "This poem," she says, "is peculiarly characteristic of his tastes—wildly fanciful, full of brilliant imagery, and discarding human interest and passion, to revel in the fantastic ideas that his imagination suggested." And she not immoderately sums up the poem as "a brilliant congregation of ideas such as his senses gathered, and his fancy coloured. (. . .)"

In her Note on *The Witch of Atlas* and elsewhere in her Notes, Mary emphasises a point which we have no reason to doubt, since she was Shelley's most constant observer. In Shelley she sees the essential and "pure" lyricist subject to fluctuating repulsion against, and attraction towards, the metaphysical philosopher. Mary speaks of his frequent unhappiness, which she considered was caused by the unfavourable reception of his work; and she looks upon his "pure" imaginative poetry as a kind of escapism and light relief. He "wrote because his mind overflowed," she says in her Note to *The Witch of Atlas.* The forces from which Shelley escaped were consequent upon his intrepid enquiry into origins and ultimates; but Mary has also something more specific in mind when she writes, in her Note to the same poem, "Shelley shrunk instinctively from portraying human passion, with its mixture of good and evil, of disappointment and disquiet. Such opened again the wounds of his own heart; and he loved to shelter himself rather in the airiest flights of fancy, forgetting love and hate, and regret and lost hope, in such imaginations as borrowed their hues from sunrise or sunset. (. . .)" The human passions Mary refers to are those of his drama *The Cenci*—a work which Mary valued highly, which for personal reasons she perhaps over-estimated, but which has been more recently under-estimated.

The Cenci was a point of pride in Mary since, as she says, "This tragedy is the only one of his works that he communicated to me during its progress. We talked over the arrangement of the scenes together." Mary felt that she had discovered a new aspect of Shelley's genius when she had urged him to the composition of this work. Shelley had protested that he lacked dramatic talent—"He asserted that he was too metaphysical and abstract, too fond of the theoretical and the ideal, to succeed as a tragedian. . . ." And on the evidence of *The Cenci* Mary triumphantly declared him to have been mistaken. There are many who would say that it was Mary who was mistaken, that Shelley's only completed realistic verse-drama was an aberration. I believe her to have been right, and that *The Cenci* shows most powerfully what Shelley could do with his eye on realistic narrative. Where she was mistaken was in her juxtaposition of *The Witch of Atlas* and *The Cenci,* with the implication that these represented two classifications of Shelley's poetry. *Prometheus Unbound* might have been her more appropriate alternative.

Though Mary obviously entertained a profound respect for *Prometheus Unbound,* taking exceptional care with her Note on the poem, she must be understood to have rated *The Cenci* higher. The Fifth Act of *The Cenci* particularly delighted her. "It is the finest thing he ever wrote," she asserted, "and may claim proud comparison not only with any contemporary, but preceding, poet." As a critic of poetry, then, we must see Mary's tastes inclining towards the "special and tangible," which she has attributed in her Preface, to more popular poets than Shelley—though perceptive enough within those limits (Act V of *The Cenci* may not be the finest thing Shelley wrote, but it is the finest Act in the drama). It is very much a novelist's way of thinking. Yet T. L. Beddoes, whose interest was poetic drama, also spoke of the supremacy of *The Cenci.*

Mary's opinions, however, do not obtrude themselves; nor does she attempt to analyse the text of Shelley's work, for this was not her purpose. But that she was capable of close critical analysis is apparent in an incidental remark of hers in *The Last Man.* She quotes Wordsworth's lines,

> A violet by a mossy stone
>   Half hidden from the eye,
> Fair as a star when only one
>   Is shining in the sky.[4]

where, she says, "Wordsworth has compared a beloved female to two fair objects in nature; but his lines always appeared to me rather a contrast than a similitude." The lady of the violet, Mary suggests, "trembling to entrust herself to the very air," is not one and the same with the lady of the star, who is "set in single splendour" and therefore exceedingly prominent. This is the kind of observation

4. Mary Shelley's text (from *She Dwelt Among the Untrodden Ways*).

we have become used to in our century but Mary did not make sufficient of them for us to say whether or not she liked to examine literature textually. And her Notes on Shelley were not the place for such line-by-line examination.

It was on the authenticity of her work on the Shelley poems that Mary based her claim to assist readers of Shelley, for she was aware of her critical shortcomings. This she confirms in her Preface to the *Collected Poems.*

In the notes appended to the poems I have endeavoured to narrate the origin and history of each. The loss of nearly all letters and papers which refer to his early life renders the execution more imperfect than it would otherwise have been. I have, however, the liveliest recollection of all that was done and said during the period of my knowing him. Every impression is as clear as if stamped yesterday, and I have no apprehension of any mistake in my statements as far as they go. In other respects I am indeed incompetent: but I feel the importance of the task, and regard it as my most sacred duty. I endeavour to fulfil it in a manner he would himself approve; and hope, in this publication, to lay the first stone of a monument due to Shelley's genius, his sufferings, and his virtues.

The very large task she had before her, and which she fulfilled with commendable unobtrusiveness, was one of illustration rather than interpretation, and as such it should be judged.

Chapter 15

A Note on
Mary Shelley as a
Practitioner of Verse

Throughout her life, Mary Shelley expressed herself in verse on several occasions. She had no view of herself as a poet, to speak of, and when her friend Mrs. Gisborne wrote in praise of her poems, she replied, insisting, "One swallow does not make a summer."

There are two which deserve attention since they illustrate both a considerable sense of form and a latent part of Mary's talent—though a deeply latent one—a lyricism which very rarely makes itself apparent in her other writings. When it does, it stands out with particular grace (as when she wrote to Shelley on hearing of the death of an old friend, "Poor Curran! So he is dead and a sod is on his breast as four years ago I heard him prophesy would be the case within that year"). This lyrical faculty emanates possibly from the Wollstonecraft, Irish strain in her, which had been largely overwhelmed by Godwin's prosaic influence.

"I can never write verses," Mary told Mrs. Gisborne, "except under the influence of a strong sentiment & seldom even then." It was only under intense emotional pressure that this dormant lyricism could force its way through her extremely unyielding consciousness.

Mary correctly rated the following poem as the best thing she ever wrote in verse. It was written, she said, for music.

A DIRGE

This morn thy gallant bark, Love,
    Sailed on a sunny sea;
'Tis noon, and tempests dark, Love,
    Have wrecked it on the lee.

Ah Woe—ah woe—ah woe,
    By spirits of the deep,
He's cradled on the billow,
    To his unwaking sleep!

Thou liest upon the shore, Love,
    Beside the knelling surge,
But sea-nymphs ever more, Love,
    Shall sadly chaunt thy dirge.

O come, O come—O come!
    Ye spirits of the deep!
While near his sea-weed pillow,
    My lonely watch I keep.

From far across the sea, Love,
    I hear a wild lament,
By Echo's voice for thee, Love,
    From Ocean's caverns sent.

O list! O list! O list!
    The Spirits of the deep—
Loud sounds their wail of sorrow—
    While I for ever weep!

This poem was published in 1831. Its most immediate association is with Edgar Allan Poe's *To One in Paradise,* published some years later. I quote the stanzas from Poe in which the most remarkable resemblances in form and atmosphere occur:

> Thou wast that all to me, love,
>   For which my soul did pine—
> A green isle in the sea, love,
>   A fountain and a shrine,
> All wreathed with fairy fruits and flowers,
>   And all the flowers were mine.
>
> ....
>
> For alas! alas! with me
>   The light of Life is o'er!
> "No more—no more—no more"—
> (Such language holds the solemn sea
>   To the sands upon the shore)
> Shall bloom the thunder-blasted tree,
>   Or the stricken eagle soar!

Poe's language and imagery are, of course, less banal than Mary's. But there is a striking similarity in the rhythm and form of the two elegies; the lilting position of the word "love," the double rhyming at the end of lines 1 and 3 in both poems, and the reiteration of phrases ("Ah woe—ah woe—ah woe" in Mary's lines, and "No more—no more—no more" in Poe's). Even more noticeable does the resemblance become when we find that Poe's original (1835) version of the poem contained an additional stanza:

> Alas! for that accursed time
>   They bore thee o'er the billow,
> From love to titled age and crime
>   And an unholy pillow—
> From me, and from our misty clime
>   Where weeps the silver willow.

which is reminiscent of Mary's sea image and her "billow" and "pillow" line endings.

The alikeness of these poems may have two possible explanations. First, that Mary Shelley's imaginative "wave-length" was in many ways concurrent with Poe's. Her preoccupation with the macabre and sinister is one manifestation of this, and her melancholy disposition, another. It is possible, then, that Mary's poem is a product of a poetic sensibility—on the few occasions when this was released—similar to Poe's. But Mary's other poems do not bear out this hypothesis; and I think the greater possibility is that Poe came across Mary's poem (which was published first in *The Keepsake* album), absorbed its atmosphere, and was directly influenced by it. Poe must have read and admired *Frankenstein,* and would naturally, if he found a poem by Mary, pay particular attention to it. If this is so, it was a most salutary, if unwitting, service on Mary's part.

Another curious point arises, when we find that when Mary came to reprint her poem in one of her Notes to the 1839 edition of Shelley's poems, she altered her 1831 text to read,

> This morn thy gallant bark
> Sailed on a sunny sea:
> 'Tis noon, and tempests dark
> Have wrecked it on the lee.
> Ah woe! ah woe!
> By Spirits of the deep
> Thou'rt cradled on the billow
> To thy eternal sleep.

with similar abbreviations in the subsequent lines.

It is my own view that, between 1835, when Poe's dirge was first published, and 1839, when Mary reprinted hers, she had read the poem by Poe, and becoming self-conscious about their affinities, attempted to avoid making them conspicuous by altering her lines. For it is precisely at the points of resemblance that she made these alterations—the word "love" at the end of lines 1, 3, 9, 11, etc. is omitted; and her thrice-repeated phrases in lines 5, 13 and 21 are now but twice-repeated. I cannot think of any other solution which would explain why Mary should mutilate her lyric to so sorry an extent.

If we accept the original, 1831, version of Mary's poem as the authoritative and superior one, two factors become apparent: first, a lack of originality in diction and image—the only noteworthy phrase being "the knelling surge"; and second, a skilfully balanced

[227]

framework. It is the constructive attributes of the poem which succeed in confirming the theme and in creating its very pure elegiac mood. The mood is pure rather because of the limp diction than despite it; for where originality of language and image occur in a lyric (and especially in a nineteenth-century lyric) the issues implied in the poem are apt to become complicated. Poe's lyric *To One in Paradise,* having begged comparison, seems a convenient case in point: it is a superior poem to Mary's; it is superior in diction, though as we have seen, resembles hers in form; yet it is not so pure a lyric, since Poe contrives, by various accesses of fancy, to invite sympathy on several scores at once. We are posited with the image of the dead girl, that of the bereft poet, of lost hope and of life losing one meaning to gain another ("And all my days are trances" . . . etc.). While in Mary's lyric, all is focussed on the drowned youth—the "spirits of the deep," the "sea-nymphs" and "Echo's voice," combine towards the pure and single end of lament, which her somewhat bathetic final line occurs too late to arrest.

I do not believe that Mary's poem is an important one outside the scope of this book, but one of the reasons why I find it interesting is that this quality which I have called "lyrical purity" is not prominent in nineteenth-century lyricism, which tends to introduce a metaphysical argument, a moral or a message.

The choruses in *Prometheus Unbound* were probably Mary's influence here, but these are not entirely self-contained, and less so, indeed, than the choruses in George Darley's later *Nepenthe,* which are nearer Mary's tone:

> In the caves of the deep—lost Youth! lost Youth
> O'er and o'er, fleeting billows! fleeting billows
> By the heavy death-bells of the deep,
> Under the slimy drooping sea-green willows,
>   Poor Youth! Lost Youth!

But this is to move away from the formality of Mary Shelley's lines where they are more akin to the eighteenth century. The real source of their "purity," their closeness to poetry for the lyre, may be due to their having been composed for music. The poem is rescued from mere sentimentality because a melodious rather than a poetical usage of language predominates, and because the quite intricate, though apparently simple, construction is addressed for song rather than speech.

She wrote an autobiographical poem, *The Choice*—a piece of one hundred and fifty odd lines—while staying with the Hunts in Italy after Shelley's death. It is not a satisfying work, being mainly autobiographical reflection, with an over-riding sentiment of regret for the loss of Shelley which is dampened by self-pity. There is also a statement of that remorse influenced by Hunt's inquisitorial prods at Mary's conscience, and which extorted their penalty in the confessional terms of:

> . . . cold neglect, averted eyes,
> That blindly crushed thy soul's fond sacrifice:—
> My heart was all thine own—but yet a shell
> Closed in its core, which seemed impenetrable,
> Till sharp-toothed misery tore the husk in twain,
> Which gaping lies nor may unite again.
> Forgive me! let thy love descend in dew
> Of soft repentance and regret most true.

But these lines, in all their bad Augustanism, are the most dismally unsuccessful in the poem, and it is hardly fair to quote them as entirely representative. The Augustan—and not always the bad Augustan—influence is a presiding factor in this early poem; it is much of a monotone and contrasts strangely with her few later lyrics. Here is the voice of pre-Romantic sentiment, while yet in its "happy" and lucid accents:

> 'Tis thus the Past—on which my spirit leans,
> Makes dearest to my soul Italian scenes.
> In Tuscan fields the winds in odours steeped
> From flowers and cypresses, when skies have wept,
> Shall, like the notes of music once most dear,
> Which brings the unstrung voice upon my ear
> Of one beloved, to memory display
> Past scenes, past hopes, past joys, in long array.

Pugnano's trees, beneath whose shade he stood,
The pools reflecting Pisa's old pine wood,
The fireflies' beams, the aziola's cry
All breathe his spirit which can never die.
Such memories have linked these hills and caves,
These woodland paths, and streams, and knelling waves
Fast to each sad pulsation of my breast
And made their melancholy arms the haven of my rest.

The merits of the poem are mainly descriptive ones, which, if we can drain off the sentimentality, are pleasurable enough, the more especially where as in the above passage, the generalisation of "Past scenes, past hopes, past joys, in long array" turns immediately to the particularised "Pugnano's trees (. . .)," etc., reflecting a point of virtuosity from eighteenth-century descriptive poetry.

There is, however, one passage which I think snatches a more considerable portion of the virtues of late eighteenth-century verse, accompanied as it is with an intensified degree of personal feeling and conviction:

And thou, strange star! ascendant at my birth,
Which rained, they said, kind influence on the earth,
So from great parents sprung, I dared to boast
Fortune my friend, till set, thy beams were lost!
And thou, Inscrutable, by whose decree
Has burst this hideous storm of misery!
Here let me cling, here to the solitudes,
These myrtle-shaded streams and chestnut woods.

But this strengthened tone is not sustained. Written during the rawest period of grief, a long poem on the subject by a writer unused to expressing herself in verse can hardly have been a satisfactory one throughout. What the poem best serves to illustrate is the eighteenth-century colouring of Mary's mentality. It would be a temptation to assume that between the composition of this descriptive elegy in 1823 and her elegiac lyric in 1831 her fundamentally traditional mind absorbed the new Romantic spirit. But I do not believe this to be the case, nor that Mary ever did become wholly at one with the currents of the Romantic revival. This fact, I think, is what makes her lyric difficult to place in its historical background; and more significantly, it was what helped to set her out of gear with the world. To a great extent Mary Shelley inherited an environment fifty years or more behind her time, and occupied one fifty years ahead of her.

Chapter 16

Conclusion

The word "conflict" can be used too freely to interpret inconsistencies in a subject of literary criticism or biography. All people contain within them the elements of conflict. In some, however, the battle wages more vigorously, more unequally and longer than in others, and such people eventually reveal a salient inconsistency to the world; Mary Shelley was one of these.

Those who met her casually noticed her most apparent antithetical features. The woman, they said, contradicted the writer. It is very easy to separate Mary Shelley the woman from the writer. Those of her contemporaries who had known her from Shelley's lifetime usually judged her as a woman only; and their judgments were accordingly one-sided, as has been the verdict of anyone who has looked upon her only as Shelley's wife. But those other, casual friends—the people who had become aware of her as the author who was Shelley's widow—reacted very differently. For one thing, their attitude towards her was noticeably more tolerant and more respectful.

There was Thomas Lovell Beddoes, for example, who had met Mary when arranging for the publication of Shelley's poems, and who obviously held her in regard both as a woman ("Why did you not, when last in town, pay your respects to Mrs. Shelley at Kentish town?" he enquired of Thomas Kelsall) and as a writer ("Have Darley, C. Lamb, Mrs. Shelley etc. printed? In a word have you anything worth reading?" he asked on another occasion).

But Mary embodied a paradox for these post-Shelleyan acquaintances. It was Beddoes, once more, who located an incongruity between the woman and the writer in Mary, when he wrote to Kelsall: "Now you must tell me all about the Last Man; I am very glad that Mrs. S[helley] has taken it from the New Monthly Fellow —and am sure that in almost every respect she will do better than either of us: indeed she has no business to be a woman by her books." And another literary acquaintance, Lord Dillon, was expressly fascinated by the contrasting elements in Mary: "I own you look more sly than I think you are," he told her in 1829, "and therefore I never was so candid with you as I think I ought to be. Have not people who did not know you taken you for a cunning person? You have puzzled me very much. Women always feel flattered when they are told they have puzzled people. I will tell you what has puzzled me. Your writings and your manner are not in accordance. I should have thought of you—if I had only read you —that you were a sort of my Sybil, outpouringly enthusiastic, rather indiscreet, and even extravagant; but you are cool, quiet and feminine to the last degree—I mean in delicacy of manner and expression. Explain this to me."

"Explain this to me"—Mary could not explain it to herself. And it would be falsifying an assessment of Mary Shelley to attempt to align these two most obvious antitheses of her nature, when stronger, concealed elements in her remain incommensurable. For she was one in whom contrast, and therefore conflict, was perpetual, and in this respect she is not unique within the artistic species. If we are to see the whole woman, we must witness the conflict.

Throughout this book, I have tried to define the sources of

conflict as they transmit themselves from Mary's life and work. I have suggested that *Frankenstein* reflected a state of strife between Mary's emotional and her intellectual lives; that her basically classical temperament (I do not mean this in a categorical literary sense) was not nurtured on its appropriate classical serenity but was fostered upon a setting of romantic turmoil. Her quiet, feminine delicacy of manner, which Lord Dillon remarked, and which contradicted the tone of her written word, noted by Beddoes, was merely a sign of her fundamental allergy to conflict.

From these causes, I believe the full play of instinct on her imagination to have been foredoomed. The passions she portrays most successfully in her novels are passions of the intellect. Where affairs of love are intended we find affairs of sentiment, and the closer we look at her individuals the further do they recede imperturbably into prototypes.

But it required a more active source of agitation to strike up the major issue that ravaged the creative potency of *Frankenstein* and *The Last Man*, and finally razed her independence of thought. I have already put forward the proposition that after Shelley's death Mary was increasingly subject to the opposing forces of the ideal, personified by her life with Shelley, and the reality which necessity thrust before her.

Knowing Shelley seemed to go to everyone's head who knew him; and Mary had experienced eight years' contact with that most heady of geniuses. Speaking of Shelley, T. S. Eliot said that "the weight of Mrs. Shelley must have been pretty heavy." I am sure that, ultimately, it was the other way round. For Shelley created an illusion about himself which he left as legacy to Mary. It was an illusion that fostered in her the memory of their life together in a form that never was on land or sea, and which set her perpetually at odds with existence.

When Shelley composed *The Revolt of Islam* in 1817, he believed himself to be a dying man. It was a fair and suggestive enough prophecy for Mary that he placed on feminine lips:

> These were forebodings of my fate—before
> A woman's heart beat in my virgin breast,

It had been nurtured in divinest lore:
    A dying poet gave me books, and blessed
    With wild but holy talk the sweet unrest
In which I watched him as he died away—
    A youth with hoary hair—a fleeting guest
Of our lone mountains: and this lore did sway
My spirit like a storm, contending there alway.

Selected Bibliography

Works by Mary Shelley

FICTION

Frankenstein; or, The Modern Prometheus (originally published 1818; reprinted by Oxford University Press [edited by M. K. Joseph], London, 1969, and in various other editions).

Valperga; or, The Life and Adventures of Castruccio, Prince of Lucca (G. & W. B. Whittaker, London, 1823).

The Last Man (Henry Colburn, London, 1826; reprinted by University of Nebraska Press [edited by Hugh L. Luke, Jr.], Lincoln, 1965; and by The Hogarth Press [edited by Brian Aldiss], London, 1985).

The Fortunes of Perkin Warbeck (Henry Colburn and Richard Bentley, London, 1830; reprinted in 3 volumes with an introduction by Betty T. Bennett by Folcroft Library Editions, Folcroft, Pennsylvania, 1975).

Lodore (Richard Bentley, London, 1835).

Falkner (Saunders and Otley, London, 1837).

Mathilda [sic] (University of North Carolina Press [edited by Elizabeth Nichie], Chapel Hill, 1959).

Mary Shelley: Collected Tales and Stories (The Johns Hopkins University Press [edited by Charles E. Robinson], Baltimore and London, 1976).

History of a Six Weeks' Tour, with P. B. Shelley (T. Hookham and C. & J. Ollies, London, 1817).

Lives of the Most Eminent Literary and Scientific Men of Italy, Spain, and Portugal, in Lardner's *Cabinet Cyclopædia* (Longman, Orme, Brown, Green, & Longmans; and John Taylor, London, 1835–37).

Lives of the Most Eminent Literary and Scientific Men of France, in Lardner's *Cabinet Cyclopædia* (Longman, Orme, Brown, Green; Longman & John Taylor, London, 1838–39).

Preface and Notes to *The Poetical Works of Percy Bysshe Shelley* (Edward Moxon, London, 1839, and subsequent editions).

The Letters of Mary Wollstonecraft Shelley, edited by Betty T. Bennett, 2 vols. (The Johns Hopkins University Press, Baltimore and London, 1980 and 1983 [vol. 3 forthcoming]).

The Journals of Mary Shelley, edited by Paula R. Feldman and Diana Scott-Kilvert, 2 vols. (Oxford at the Clarendon Press, 1987).

Selected Works of Reference

Mary Shelley, Author of Frankenstein, by Elizabeth Nichie (Rutgers University Press, New Brunswick, 1953).

Shelley and His Circle, 6 vols. to date (10 planned), vols. 1–4 edited by Kenneth Neill Cameron, subsequent volumes edited by Donald H. Reiman (The Carl H. Pforzheimer Library, New York, 1961–73).

Shelley: The Pursuit by Richard Holmes (Weidenfeld & Nicolson, London, 1974).

Mary Shelley: An Annotated Bibliography, by W. H. Lyles (Garland Publishing, New York and London, 1975).

Moon in Eclipse: A Life of Mary Shelley, by Jane Dunn (Weidenfeld & Nicolson, London, 1978).

Index

relation with Shelley, 8–9, 18–19, 23, 31–32, 57
Shelley's financial support of, 48, 52, 57, 70–71, 83
unpublished works of, 128–29, 130
view of mankind, 161
views on marriage, 10, 12–13, 23n2, 66
Godwin, William (half-brother of MS), 13
Godwinism, 42, 46, 184
Gothic novel, 153–54, 156, 159–60, 169, 171, 188
Gothicism, 199
Grylls, Glynn, 41–42, 86n2
Guiccioli, Teresa, 79, 80, 87, 88, 93

Hate (MS), 30–31
Hazlitt, William, 8, 18, 105
Historical fiction, 200–212
History of a Six Weeks' Tour (MS), 134, 152
History of the Inconstant Lover, 155
Hobhouse, John Cam, 86n2
Hogg, Thomas Jefferson, 55, 62, 102–103, 105, 167
legacy, 138
and publication of Shelley's works, 130, 131
relation with MS, 38, 39, 40–46, 50
relation with Shelley, 39–40
resentment of MS, 138, 139
and Shelley: correspondence, 19–20, 21–22, 33
and J. Williams, 107–108, 110, 115, 181
Hood, Thomas, 197
Hookham, Thomas, 35, 38, 39, 140–41, 142
Hoppner, Belgrave, 63, 64, 65, 79–80, 85, 86, 87n2
Hoppner, Mrs. Belgrave, 63, 64, 65, 66, 85, 218–19
Horror-novel, 154, 159, 171, 188, 199
Hunt, John, 105, 106
Hunt, Leigh, 46n9, 54, 58, 60, 62, 88, 89, 90, 98–99, 100, 103, 104, 105, 115, 130, 218

on *Frankenstein,* 167
legacy, 139
and publication of Shelley's works, 130, 132
relation with MS, 101, 113, 114, 229
Shelley's correspondence with, 70–71, 72, 75, 76–77
Hunt, Marianne, 58, 60, 67, 88, 89, 90, 98–99, 100, 104, 113

Ideology, controversial:
Godwin, 128–29, 130
Shelley, 130
Imagination:
in MS, 17–18, 146, 157, 190, 191, 197, 200, 234
in Shelley, 20–21, 58–59, 215, 220–21, 235
Imlay, Fanny, *see* Godwin, Fanny Imlay
Imlay, Gilbert, 6, 7, 10, 11, 43, 59
Irving, Washington, 109, 111–13
Ivanhoe (Scott), 199, 205, 207–208

Jones, F. L., 41, 123
Journals (MS and Shelley), 24, 25, 152
entries quoted, 24, 26, 35, 38, 39, 51, 52, 58, 59, 63, 67, 71, 83, 88, 89–92, 101–102, 114, 115, 117, 131, 133, 134, 145–46, 150, 180
mentioned, 41, 65, 128, 134
MS sentimentalization of Shelley in, 214
Journals of Mary Shelley, The (Feldman and Scott-Kilvert), *xi*

Keats, John, 58, 78–79, 80–81, 141
Keepsake, The (annual), 115, 227
Kelsall, Thomas Forbes, 105, 233
Kirkup, James:
Last Man, The, 198n2
Knox, Alexander Andrew, 136, 139–40

Lamb, Charles, 18, 51, 105
Tales from Shakespeare, 13
Lamb, Mary:
Tales from Shakespeare, 13

[245]

Shelley, Mary, works *(cont'd)*
  Last Man, The, ix, x, 65, 106,
    108, 109, 149, 179–98,
    199–200, 222, 233, 234
  Letter to Edmund Burke, 5
  Lodore, 38, 124, 126, 150–51
  lyricism in, 224–25, 228–29
  Matilda, 71, 150
  Notes to Shelley's poems, 48,
    58, 130, 131, 149, 151,
    213–23, 227
  personal distress reflected in,
    180–81
  philosophical attitude revealed
    in, 183–87
  poetry:
  —*The Choice,* 229–30
  —*A Dirge,* 225–29
  Preface to First Collected Edition,
    215
  Rambles in Germany and Italy,
    134–35, 137, 151–52
  restraint of emotional expression
    in, 193, 196
  Romanticism and, 230–31
  stable elements in, 200
  suspense in, 151
  Valperga, 72, 83, 88, 149–50
  writing, 38, 60
  see also Shelley, Percy Bysshe, and
    Mary Shelley
Shelley, Percy Bysshe, 17, 100, 146
  accusation that he disposed of
    illegitimate child (with C.
    Clairmont) in Naples, 34, 60,
    73, 84–86
  admiration for Godwin, 9, 18–19,
    28, 31
  "beautiful and ineffectual angel"
    myth, 214, 217–18, 219
  children by Harriet, 31
    see also Shelley, Percy Bysshe,
    custody battle
  controversial ideology in, 130
  conversation, 215, 216
  correspondence:
    C. Clairmont, 77
    forged, 140–42
    L. Hunt, 70–71, 72
  custody battle, 54–55, 57–59, 142
  death of, 99, 100

emotional states, 23, 216–17, 221
expulsion from Oxford, 18, 40
failure of marriage to Harriet,
  20–21, 23, 113–14
feeling of responsibility for
  humankind, 32n2
financial difficulties, 9, 18
financial support of Godwin, 48,
  52, 57, 70–71, 83
friendships, 32, 39–40, 92, 131,
  150
grief at death of son, 70
health, illness, 46, 48, 61, 62, 66,
  72
imagination, 20–21, 58–59, 215,
  220–21, 235
infatuation with E. Viviani, 75–78,
  96
influence on MS, 145, 184,
  185–87
influence on MS works, 162, 187
intellect of, 235
interest in the weird, supernatural,
  50, 153
love for, delight in MS, 33
MS's understanding and acceptance
  of, 92–93
personal characteristics, 23, 215,
  217, 218–19
philosophical attitude towards love,
  40–41, 42, 45–46, 186
philosophy of, 166, 185–87
playfulness, 216, 217
as poet-philosopher, 214–15,
  216–17, 218, 221
political views of, 32
practicality of, 97, 191n1
prone to dreams and hallucinations,
  97–98
reading, study, 39, 59, 65, 67, 72
relation with Bryon, 82–83, 84–86,
  87–88, 95
relation with Godwin, 9, 18–19,
  23, 31–32, 57
restlessness, 74, 92–93
self-image, 217–18, 234
suffered at completion of major
  work, 72n1
will, 137, 138, 139
and J. Williams, 90, 96–97,
  115–16